JOB

This very readable commentary combines scholarly insight with pastoral compassion as it addresses the question of how we should respond to God when suffering comes into our lives. Both Pastors and laymen will benefit from the way Dr Belcher clearly lays out flow of the book of Job and addresses the tough exegetical and practical questions. His summary statements are golden. Throughout the commentary, he shows how the message of the book of Job points to Christ the righteous sufferer. I personally benefitted from reading this book which also equipped me as seek to care for God's people when they suffer.

Jim Newheiser
Director of the Christian Counseling Program,
Associate Professor of Counseling and Practical Theology,
Reformed Theological Seminary, Charlotte, North Carolina

Belcher takes a new direction amongst Job commentaries. He is no ivory tower academic, theorising about suffering, or playing with the book's theology. Weaving in the story of little baby Pierce, this is scholarly and reliable commentary with a real human touch.

Jared Hood
Old Testament Lecturer,
Presbyterian Theological College, Melbourne

JOB

The Mystery of Suffering and God's Sovereignty

Richard P. Belcher, Jr.

CHRISTIAN
FOCUS

Richard P. Belcher, Jr. is the John D. and Frances M. Gwin Professor of Old Testament and the Academic Dean at Reformed Theological Seminary Charlotte. He is also an ordained minister in the PCA and pastored an urban nondenominational church in Rochester, New York for ten years. Richard P. Belcher, Jr. is the John D. and Frances M. Gwin Professor of Old Testament and the Academic Dean at Reformed Theological Seminary Charlotte. He is also an ordained minister in the PCA and pastored an urban non-denominational church in Rochester, New York for ten years.

Copyright © 2017 Richard P. Belcher, Jr.

ISBN 978-1-5271-0002-2

10 9 8 7 6 5 4 3 2 1

Printed in 2017
by
Christian Focus Publications Ltd.,
Geanies House, Fearn, Ross-shire,
IV20 1TW, Scotland, U.K.

www.christianfocus.com

Cover design by Daniel van Straaten

Printed and bound by
Bell & Bain, Glasgow

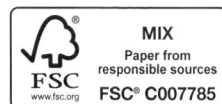

MIX
Paper from
responsible sources
FSC
www.fsc.org   FSC® C007785

Contents

Dedication

This commentary is dedicated to Pierce Franks
a delight to God
a warrior in suffering
a joy to his parents
a blessing to Christ Ridge Church

and to his parents Nik and Lindsay Franks
joyfully persevering
faithful to God
committed to the truth of Scripture
a great encouragement to God's people

Preface

Writing a commentary on Job is not easy. John Calvin has written that the goal of a commentator should be lucid brevity in unfolding the mind of the author.[1] Although I am no John Calvin, I have tried to follow his advice. My approach has been to try to explain the text simply and clearly. This is important for the book of Job because it is not always clear what is being argued in different sections of the book, especially in the speeches of the friends and Job's responses. The goal has been to make clear the argument of each passage of the book. I would encourage those who read this commentary to keep the Bible close at hand and to read the Biblical text before reading the comments on the text. My prayer is that this commentary will help God's people understand the book of Job, how it relates to life, and how it fits into the broader view of redemptive history. I also pray that the succinct explanations of the text will aid those who seek to teach and preach this book. There are Study Questions at the end of each chapter so that the book can be used as a text for a Bible study on Job.

Many along the way have helped me to write this commentary. John Hartley's commentary on Job has been a faithful companion. I would like to thank Christian Focus for this opportunity to contribute to the Focus on the Bible Commentary series. I would also like to thank my teaching assistant, Zack Keuthan, for searching down references, reading through the commentary, and a doing a host of other projects. His wife, Elly, works in the library and she

---

1. John Calvin, 'The Epistle Dedicatory' in the 'The Epistle of Paul the Apostle to the Romans' in *Calvin's Commentaries* (Grand Rapids: Baker, 1996 reprint), 19:xxiii.

has been a tremendous help in finding sources. Zack and Elly, you will be missed! I would like to thank the board of Reformed Theological Seminary (RTS), the Chancellor of RTS, Dr. Ligon Duncan, and the President of RTS Charlotte, Dr. Michael Kruger, for enabling and encouraging the faculty to write and publish. I would also like to thank my family of three daughters, two sons-in-law who are pastors, and five grandchildren, who make life so enjoyable. Many thanks to my wife, Lu, for her willingness to endure this journey so faithfully and joyfully.

This commentary is dedicated to Nik and Lindsay Franks, and their son Pierce, whose story is told in the pages of this commentary. Thank you for your honesty through the struggle, your faithful perseverance, and your commitment to Christ and the word of God. At the end of each chapter there will be reflections from them taken from their blog (www.littlebabypierce.blogspot.com) as they shared their journey with family and friends. Their story will add a personal touch to the commentary and it will be an encouragement to those who are suffering (see the end of the Introduction to this commentary for a summary of their story).

RICHARD P. BELCHER, Jr.

May 2016

Introduction

The message of the book of Job deals with suffering, which is a common problem that all human beings experience to one degree or another. However, there are complex questions arising from the problem of suffering that are not easy to answer. The book of Job does not answer all those questions. For example, the reason behind suffering is not answered in the book. Job does not learn why suffering came into his life. God does not tell him about the divine council and his conversations with Satan in chapters 1–2. The book also does not explain how the sovereignty of God and human suffering can be reconciled. It will become clear that the issue at the heart of the book is how people should respond to suffering. More specifically, it will become clear that the question is whether God is worthy of our worship even if He brings unimaginable suffering into our lives. The book is ultimately about the character of God and how human beings should respond to God when life becomes very difficult. Everybody experiences at least some measure of suffering, which makes the questions with which this book wrestles universal in nature. The message of the book of Job remains relevant for God's people who live in a fallen world and continue to hope and wait for the renewal of all things.

The Setting of the Story
The book of Job is a difficult book to comprehend. It is easy to get lost in the dialogue between Job and his friends and lose sight of the issues that are central to the book. The reader will better understand the book when certain things about it are made clear. Job is not an Israelite and he does not live in the land of Canaan. He lives in the land of Uz (Job 1:1),

which probably refers to the area of Edom. There is a clear association of Edom with Uz in Lamentations 4:21. Job is also called 'the greatest of all the people of the east' (1:3), which refers to the areas of Edom, Moab, and Ammon.

Job and his friends were not Israelites but they believed in the God of Israel. The covenant name of Yahweh (LORD) is used primarily at the beginning and the end of the book. It is used to refer to God in His discussions with Satan (Job 1:6-9, 12 and 2:1-3, 6-7) and in Job's response to his suffering (Job 1:21). It is also used to refer to God when He speaks to Job (Job 38:1; 40:1), when He confronts the friends (Job 42:7, 9), and when He restores Job's life (Job 42:11, 12).[1] During the speeches the names for God that are used are *ʾēl*, *ʾĕlôah*, and *šadday*. The first two names are ancient names commonly used by Semitic-speaking people for the deity, but are also used of the true God of Israel.[2] The third name, Shaddai, is commonly used with the patriarchs in the context of the covenant (Gen. 17:1; 28:3; 35:11; 43:14; 48:3).[3] It is clear that the God in view in the book of Job is the same God as in the rest of the Old Testament.

It is difficult to know how Job and his friends had such knowledge of the true God because they are not Israelites. There are not very many examples from Scripture of people who are outside the main covenant community who clearly worship the true God. Melchizedek lived during the time of Abraham and is identified as king of Salem and priest of the Most High God (Gen. 14:18). How he came to worship the same God that Abraham worshipped is cloaked in mystery. Other non-Israelites had contact with Israel in some way. Jethro was Moses' father-in-law (Exod. 18), Rahab had contact with the spies of Israel (Josh. 2), and Ruth had contact with Naomi and her family (Ruth 1). Jeremiah 49:7 confirms that there was a wisdom tradition in Edom in which Job and his friends participated. Bildad asks Job to consider bygone ages and to consider what the fathers have searched out (Job 8:8). It is unclear how this wisdom tradition relates to Israel's

---

1. The name Yahweh is used by Job in 12:9.

2. Jack B. Scott, 'אלה', *TWOT*, 1:42–43.

3. Victor P. Hamilton, 'שַׁדַּי', *TWOT* 2:907.

teaching, but the Edomites are descendants of Esau who would have been taught the true knowledge of God from Isaac and Rebekah. Perhaps some among the descendants of Esau carried on knowledge of the true God. The story of Job is set during the patriarchal period (roughly 2000–1700 b.c.). The evidence for this is that the wealth of Job is measured in the abundance of animals he possessed (Job 1:3). Job also acted as a priest for his family by offering sacrifices on their behalf (1:5), which fits the picture of the patriarchs offering sacrifices at altars throughout the land of Canaan (Gen. 12:7-8). The summary of Job's life and the description of his death are similar to the summary of Abraham's life and the description of his death. Job lived 140 years, Abraham lived 175 years, Isaac lived 180 years, and Joseph lived 110 years. Abraham is described at his death as 'an old man and full of years' (Gen. 25:8) and Job is described as 'an old man, and full of days' (Job 42:17).

Authorship and Date

The book of Job does not make any claim concerning authorship and it has been dated to every period of Israel's history. The fact that the book fits into the patriarchal period has led to the conclusion that Moses is the author.[4] However, others place the book in the Solomonic era because wisdom literature flourished under Solomon[5] or in the time of Isaiah because of possible affinities with Isaiah.[6] Certainly, by the time of Ezekiel the story of Job was known because Ezekiel mentions Job in 14:14.[7]

---

4. Gleason Archer, *A Survey of Old Testament Introduction* (Chicago: Moody Press, 1974), 456.

5. Edward J. Young, *An Introduction to the Old Testament* (Grand Rapids: Eerdmans, 1952), 309.

6. John E. Hartley, *The Book of Job* (Grand Rapids: Eerdmans, 1988), 13-15, 19.

7. There is debate concerning whether Job was an actual historical individual. The evidence that supports the view that Job is a real historical person includes the fact that the first verse of the book is very similar to the first verse of Judges 17 and 1 Samuel 1, two passages that relate historical events. Also, Job is mentioned outside of the book of Job. His name occurs alongside two other historical individuals in Ezekiel 14:14, 20 (Noah and Daniel), and in James 5:11 he is set forth as an example of steadfastness. Finally, if God did not actually subject a righteous person to this trial, the essential tension of the book is significantly diminished.

A variety of arguments are used to try to confirm the date of the book. It is interesting that the Hebrew text of Job at Qumran is written in the paleo-Hebrew script, like the Pentateuch, which is used to support Mosaic authorship of the work. Parallels between Job and the other books of the Bible are used to support a date during the period of the monarchy. Job 28 is similar to Proverbs 8, and Job 7:17 may be a negative allusion to Psalm 8.[8] Some argue that the message of the book would fit well into the exilic or post-exilic period to encourage Israel to endure faithfully in the face of extreme loss and suffering.[9] The emphasis, however, on the innocence of Job's suffering does not fit well with the fact that Israel is in exile because of her sin. Also, any connections to Edom and its wisdom would be difficult to make after the fall of Jerusalem because of the actions of Edom against 'her brother Jacob' (Obad. 10) when Jerusalem fell.[10] An earlier date of the book seems more likely than a later date. It is easy to see why some would leave the date of the book open.[11] It makes sense that the book of Job would become prominent during the flourishing of the wisdom literature under Solomon and it is likely that the book goes back to an earlier historical period.

Type of Literature (Genre) and Structure
There are questions concerning the genre and the structure of the book. Both issues affect its interpretation and meaning. Genre discussions involve the comparison of Job with literature from other nations that deal with the problem of theodicy (the defense of God's justice in the face of evil) and the suffering of the righteous. Such comparisons clarify the similarities and the differences between the literature. The

---

8. Will Kynes, *My Psalm Has Turned into Weeping: Job's Dialogue with the Psalms* [Berlin: Walter De Gruyter, 2012]) presents the best argument that Job does refer to several psalms in the debate with his friends. Raymond C. Van Leeuwen ('Psalm 8:5 and Job 7:17-18: A Mistaken Scholarly Commonplace?' in *The World of the Aramaeans I: Biblical Studies in Honour of Paul-Eugene Dion*, eds. P. M. Michelle Daviau, John W. Wevers, and Michael Weigl [Sheffield: Sheffield Academic Press, 2001], 205-15) argues against Job's use of Psalm 8.

9. Gerald H. Wilson, *Job* (Peabody, MA: Hendriksen, 2007), 2.

10. Hartley, *Job*, 19.

11. Tremper Longman III and Raymond Dillard, *An Introduction to the Old Testament* (Grand Rapids: Zondervan, 2006), 225.

most likely comparisons with Job come from Egypt, Babylon, and Ugaritic.[12] A comparison of Job with these works shows its uniqueness. This uniqueness is expressed well by Andersen:

> Job stands far above its nearest competitors, in the coherence of its sustained treatment of the theme of human misery, in the scope of its many-sided examination of the problem, in the strength and clarity of its defiant moral monotheism, in the characterization of the protagonists, in the heights of its lyrical poetry, in its dramatic impact, and in the intellectual integrity with which it faces the 'unintelligible burden' of human existence. In all this Job stands alone. Nothing we know before it provided a model, and nothing since, including its numerous imitations, has risen to the same heights. Comparison only serves to enhance the solitary greatness of the book of Job.[13]

The book of Job is not hard to outline, but how the different parts of the book fit together is a debated topic. An analysis of the structure of Job helps to explain the genre and message of the book.[14] The following outline identifies the major sections of the book:

I.   Prologue (1–2)
II.   Job's Lament (3)
III. The Cycle of Speeches (4–27)
IV.   The Wisdom Poem (28)
V.   Job's Last Speech (29–31)
VI.   Elihu's Speeches (32–37)
VII. God's Speeches and Job's Responses (38–42:6)
VIII. Epilogue (42:7-17)

The Prologue and Epilogue are narrative and the rest of the book, which is composed of speeches, is poetry. Some argue that the original story only contained the Prologue and

---

12. For comparisons between Job and other literature of the ancient Near East see Richard P. Belcher, Jr., 'Job,' in *A Biblical–Theological Introduction to the Old Testament*, ed. Miles Van Pelt (Wheaton, IL: Crossway, 2016), 357-72; see also Ernest C. Lucas, *A Guide to the Psalms and Wisdom Literature* (Downers Grove, IL: InterVarsity Press, 2003), 132-33.

13. Francis I. Andersen, *Job: An Introduction and Commentary* (Downers Grove, IL: Inter-Varsity Press, 1974), 32.

14. Longman and Dillard, *Introduction*, 227.

Epilogue, which told the story of a man who was tested by God through suffering, but he remained faithful to God and was then rewarded for his faithfulness with material blessings.[15] But it is questionable whether the prologue and the epilogue by themselves make a complete story. The dialogues are necessary for the argument of the book.[16] The Prologue gives the reader important information about Job that will affect how the reader evaluates the arguments between Job and the friends. Job is clearly proclaimed innocent in relationship to his suffering, so that when the friends argue that Job is suffering because of his sin, the reader knows the friends are wrong. The sovereignty of God is also clearly established in the Prologue.

Job's response to his suffering in chapters 1–2 is a model response of praise to God and submission to God's will. However, in chapter 3 Job's response changes from compliance to complaint as he questions God and wishes that he had never been born. Chapter 3 also begins the cycle of speeches that are written in poetry. Poetry is not the normal way people speak to each other, but it may function to give the book more universal appeal and application. One can accept a certain amount of artistic license in the poetic speeches while at the same time accepting them as being accurately presented.[17] There are questions related to the cycle of speeches. There is not a complete third cycle and there is some doubt as to who is speaking toward the end of the cycle. The best approach is that there is not a complete third cycle because the discussion between Job and the friends breaks down and accomplishes nothing.

There is also debate concerning the function of the Wisdom Poem in chapter 28 and the purpose of the Elihu speeches in chapters 32–27. Does Elihu say anything different from the friends of Job? Does he move the argument forward? What is the purpose of his speeches? The specific message of Elihu in relationship to the friends is difficult to comprehend, but he

---

15. Norman C. Habel, *The Book of Job* (Philadelphia, PA: Westminster Press, 1985), 25 mentions this view.

16. Andersen, *Job*, 43.

17. Longman and Dillard, *Introduction*, 233.

does approach Job differently and he does emphasize certain things that the friends did not. Elihu's speeches will fall short of fully answering the questions related to the suffering of Job but he will prepare the reader for the speeches by God.

God responds to Job in two speeches which explore the wonders of God in creation and His ability to rule the world He has created. God does not tell Job about the events that took place in chapters 1–2, nor does He explain to Job why he is suffering. God does confront Job concerning certain things he has said about God's justice. The response of Job to God's speeches is also debated, but an argument can be made that Job repents of calling into question God's justice. Then God addresses the friends and tells them that they have not spoken concerning God what is right as Job has (42:7). This sounds confusing, because if Job spoke what was right about God, then why did he need to repent? Several distinctions will help answer these questions.

Job is not suffering because of any sin that he has committed (situation A). The friends try to argue that Job is suffering because of his sin. This argument is a misunderstanding of the deed-consequence relationship presented in the book of Proverbs (called retribution theology or divine retribution).[18] In making this argument the friends say some things about Job and God that are not accurate. However, Job is correct concerning the basic argument. He is not suffering because of his sin even though he is not able to rectify in his mind his suffering and the sovereignty of God. But Job is more willing than the friends to explore the mystery of God's sovereign ways. So when God tells the friends that Job has spoken correctly, God is affirming Job's side of the debate with the friends. However, in his suffering and in debate with the friends, Job does say some things that question God's justice (situation B). For these things he needs to repent and change his views. In other words, Job is not suffering because of his sin (situation A), but once he is suffering, he says some things about God that are not correct for which he must repent (situation B). It helps if the reader can distinguish between these two situations. The first situation concerns the basic

18. Longman and Dillard, *Introduction*, 229.

argument between Job and the friends. The second situation concerns statements which Job makes about God in the middle of his suffering. Job is correct about the first situation (A). He questions God's justice in the second situation (B) for which he must repent.

One can tell from the structure of the book that a lot of talking takes place in it. The book revolves around dialogue and the presentation of arguments. The suffering of Job is what sparks the debate, but other emphases include the character of Job, the character of God, and how people should respond to suffering. How one responds to the various situations of life is part of what it means to be a wise person. How to understand the events of life is part of what wisdom is all about. So where is wisdom to be found in the debate that rages in the book? The issue of wisdom is a key issue of the book because wisdom is the ability to apply the truth to situations. Where is wisdom to be found in this debate between Job and his friends? This question ultimately is answered in the wisdom poem in chapter 28 and God's response to Job's suffering in chapters 38–42. Thus 'wisdom debate' is a descriptive term to describe the book because it focuses both on Job's response to his suffering and on the question of where is true wisdom to be found.[19]

About Pierce

The two issues of response to suffering and the source of true wisdom will also be explored in this commentary through the story of Nik, Lindsay, and Pierce Franks. The following comments, written by Lindsay Franks, set the stage for their story:

> Pierce Nikolas Franks was born on April 12, 2011 at twenty-three weeks, five days gestation. At almost seventeen weeks premature, his prognosis was bleak. In fact, we were given the option and encouraged to refrain from medical intervention and merely let nature take its course. Words such as 'non-viable' were used to describe our son in the minutes before his birth. We were told that there was a slim (5 per cent) chance that our son would survive and that if he did, he would be faced with numerous complications. Cerebral palsy, blindness, deafness – those were

---

19. The term 'wisdom debate' is used by Longman and Dillard, *Introduction*, 232.

all things that were very real and possible complications of his extreme premature birth.

However, against all odds, Pierce survived. At birth, he weighed a whopping 1lb., 8oz. (670 grams) and was twelve inches long. He endured a grueling 118-day stay in the NICU, four surgeries (PDA ligation,[20] VAD placement,[21] ROP laser surgery [eye surgery] and VP Shunt placement),[22] and numerous ailments (including Chronic Lung Disease, ROP [Retinopathy of Prematurity], Bilateral Grade III/IV brain bleeds, hydrocephalus[23] and sepsis[24]).

Today, Pierce is a healthy baby, thriving at home! And while he still has some obstacles to overcome, he has come so far. He is not deaf. He is not blind. He is meeting new milestones every day. There is no doubt that Pierce is a miracle and that God is at work in his life.

For more on Pierce's life, including pictures, go to www. littlebabypierce.blogspot.com.

Study Questions

1) Who was Job, where did he live, and when did he live? Is it surprising that Job is not an Israelite?

2) Does the book of Job seek to explain why we suffer? If not, why should we study it?

3) How does the structure of the book help the reader understand the argument of the book?

---

20. PDA stands for Patent Ductus Arteriosus, a heart problem that occurs in some babies soon after birth where abnormal blood flow occurs between the two major arteries connected to the heart. Ligation refers to tying a blood vessel with a ligature.

21. VAD stands for Ventricular Access Device. It is a temporary shunt that allows doctors to drain excess cerebrospinal fluid manually by tapping it and drawing off fluid with a needle.

22. A ventriculoperitoneal (VP) shunt is a medical device that relieves pressure on the brain caused by fluid accumulation.

23. Hydrocephalus is excessive accumulation of fluid in the brain.

24. Sepsis is a serious condition that occurs when a child's body overreacts to an infection. This leads to uncontrolled and widespread inflammation and clotting in small blood vessels. Blood flow to different body parts decreases and may lead to organ failure.

4) What is the basic argument of the friends in their discussion with Job? Do you hear that view promoted today?

5) How could God declare that Job has spoken right in relationship to the friends (Job 42:7)? How is it helpful to distinguish two situations in evaluating Job's words?

6) Is it wrong to question God's ways?

1

The Prologue: Suffering and the Worship of God

(Job 1–2)

The prologue sets the stage for what will transpire in the rest of the book, including the poetic speeches that follow. Most of the major participants in the story are identified. It gives important information to the reader that Job and the other participants in the story do not possess. It will also raise a major question that the book will address: is God worthy of worship only because He blesses us? How should we respond to God when suffering comes into our lives?

The character of Job (Job 1:1-5)

The book begins with a description of where Job lives, his character, and his wealth. The land of Uz and the 'people of the east' are associated with the general area of Edom (see the Introduction). Job is not an Israelite but his character is described as one who worships the God of Israel. He is described as blameless (1:1), a word that signifies wholeness. It is used to describe sacrificial animals that are without blemish. The word 'blameless' does not describe someone who is sinless but someone who is not a hypocrite, and the term 'upright' (1:1) emphasizes faithful adherence to what is right, including a just treatment of others. Job is a person of integrity who feared God and turned away from evil. The fear of God emphasizes that a person has an awe and reverence for God that is willing to put God first in life. It expresses trust in God and a faithful obedience of Him inspired by love.[1] This expression is common in the wisdom literature of the Old Testament and will be a key theme in a later chapter in the book (Job 28).[2] Job is presented as a man who is righteous and wise.

Job is also a person who is greatly blessed by God. He is very wealthy. Job 1:3 describes a large estate. The large number of camels suggests great status and participation in caravan trade. Five hundred oxen could till a sizeable acreage. Female donkeys give milk and bear offspring. Large number of servants are needed to work such an estate. Job also has many children (seven sons and three daughters). He demonstrates concern for their spiritual welfare by functioning as a priest for his family. He offers burnt offerings for his children in case they have sinned by cursing God in their hearts. The issue of cursing God will be a key theme in the first several chapters of Job.[3]

Heavenly Drama, Round 1: Job's Possessions (Job 1:6-22)

This section opens with a heavenly council composed of the Lord (Yahweh) and the sons of God, a term for angels or heavenly messengers. They present themselves to give an accounting to God of their activities and to receive further instructions. Another figure appears at this council who is identified as *haśśāṭān* (the noun *śāṭān* with the definite article). This noun can refer to an accuser or an adversary

---

1. Hartley, *Job*, 67.

2. Tremper Longman III, *Job* (Grand Rapids: Baker, 2012), 79. He points out that the terms used to describe Job's character are commonly used of the wise in Proverbs.

3. The word translated 'curse' is really the Hebrew word for 'bless' (*brk*). This is a regular occurrence in the book of Job and it is clear that the meaning is 'curse'. Perhaps the author does not want to use the word 'curse' so close to the word 'God' (Longman, *Job*, 81). However, there are passages where the words 'curse God' appear (Lev. 24:15), so the use of 'bless' for 'curse' in Job may be a stylistic preference for the author or even a part of the artistry of the story (Carol A. Newsom, 'The Book of Job' in *The New Interpreter's Bible* [Nashville, TN: Abingdon Press, 1996], 4:346). Avoiding the word 'curse' means that it has no place in the world view of chapters 1–2 (Carol A. Newsom, *The Book of Job: A Contest of Moral Imaginations* [Oxford: Oxford University Press, 2003], 55).

(Num. 22:22; 1 Sam. 29:4; Ps. 109:6), a meaning which fits very well in Job 1 because this figure is going to bring accusations against Job. Normally this noun is not used with the article, but in Job 1–2 and in Zechariah 3:1-2 it is used with the article ('the satan').[4] Some are hesitant to identify this being with Satan because there is not much said in the Old Testament about him. However, passages refer to beings or spirits who are working against God's purposes (Gen. 3:1; 1 Sam. 16:14). In light of the role of this being in Job 1–2 and Zechariah 3 it makes sense to think of a heavenly angel who is trying to hinder the purposes of God. It is clear from the New Testament that there is a being called Satan, the devil, who is actively seeking to make trouble for God's people (Rev. 12:15-17).

This heavenly being is presented as an outsider to the heavenly council. The word 'also' in 1:6 gives the idea that he is an addition to the group. His name means 'adversary' or 'accuser' and here he attacks the integrity of Job's faith. When God asks him from where he has come, he answers in a way that emphasizes a restless roaming about: 'going to and fro on the earth and from walking up and down on it' (1:7). His role seems to be to stir up trouble, whereas God's servants would be sent out to accomplish His purposes.[5]

God is the one who initiates the discussion about Job and affirms his blameless and righteous character (1:8). Not only does God use the same terminology from 1:1 to describe Job, He also calls him 'my servant'. This phrase signifies a faithful, obedient follower of God and is used of Abraham, Moses, and Joshua. Satan, however, argues that Job only fears God because God has blessed his work and his possessions have increased. In fact, God has protected Job by putting a hedge around him to keep away all problems (1:10). In other words, Job fears God because of the blessings God has given him.

---

4. There is debate about the use of the definite article with the noun śāṭān. Some argue that the article makes the term a title rather than a personal name (Hartley, Job, 71) and that it should be translated as 'the adversary' or 'the accuser'. However, there is a grammatical category where the noun plus the article becomes equivalent to a proper name (Bruce K. Waltke and M. O'Connor, An Introduction to Biblical Hebrew Syntax [Winona Lake, IN: Eisenbrauns, 1990], 249, who use haśśāṭān as one of the examples of this grammatical category).

5. Andersen, Job, 83. He calls Satan 'a restless, ubiquitous being, a vagabond among the angels'.

Satan argues that if God would 'touch all that he has', then Job would curse God (1:11). Yahweh puts all that Job has in Satan's hands except for his health.

In verses 12-19 a series of tragedies strike Job like waves pounding the shore. An Arabian tribe called the Sabeans took the oxen and the donkeys and killed the servants.[6] While the lone survivor is telling Job of this tragedy, another servant arrived to report that lightning fell from heaven and consumed the sheep and the servants watching them. Then another servant came to report that the Chaldeans (the Babylonians) took the camels and struck down the servants. And then, finally, a servant reports that while his sons and daughters were feasting in their oldest brother's house a great wind knocked down the house and killed them all. In one day Job loses everything of value except his wife and his life. He literally goes from riches to rags. Just one of these events would have been difficult to take, but put them all together and Job must have been devastated; especially difficult must have been the loss of his children.

Job's response is remarkable (1:20-22). His actions express grief and mourning but he also falls on the ground to worship Yahweh. He prostrates himself before the Lord in submission. The first statement Job makes recognizes the reality of the human condition: 'Naked I came from my mother's womb and naked I shall return.' Human beings come into this world with nothing and they leave it with nothing. There is no removal van behind the hearse because we cannot take anything with us in death. If we come into this world with nothing, then everything we receive is a gift from God. Job acknowledges God's sovereignty when he states, 'The Lord gave, and the Lord has taken away.' Satan is wrong about Job because even though Job has lost all his possessions and his children, he does not curse God. Rather, he blesses the name of Yahweh. The comment at the end of the chapter emphasizes that the suffering Job experienced was not because of sin and that even in this suffering he did not sin or charge God with wrong (1:22). Job passed the first test.

---

6. It is thought that the lightning may have caused a fire that consumed the sheep and the servants (Robert L. Alden, *Job* [Broadman & Holman, 1993], 59).

Heavenly Drama, Round 2: Job's Health (2:1-8)

Chapter 2 begins with another divine council where the sons of God present themselves before the LORD and Satan also appears. The LORD initiates the conversation with Satan about Job. Just like the first session Job is identified as a blameless and upright man who fears God and turns away from evil. However, the added comment by God is that Job continues to hold fast his integrity even though Satan had incited God against him to destroy him without reason (2:3). It is clear that Job is not suffering because of his sin. In other words, the bad things that have come into his life are not a result of any wickedness he committed. Also, Job has continued to respond in a way that holds fast his integrity, which means that his response in 1:20-22 was honorable and honoring to God.[7]

Satan responds by saying that God has not really touched Job where it hurts.[8] If God would only take away Job's health, then he would curse God to His face. Satan's response to God in 1:9-11 and 2:4-5 is an attack on both God and Job. Satan questions Job's faith in God as merely self-interest. Job only worships God because of all the good things with which God has blessed him. If those blessings are taken away, then Job would no longer worship God. But this is also an attack on God's character because it implies that He is not worthy of being worshipped for who He is but only for the good things He gives people. This raises the questions of whether God is worthy of worship in and of Himself or do people love Him only because of what He does for them?

God responds to Satan with the words, 'Behold, he is in your hand; only spare his life' (2:6). Satan is limited by God regarding what he can do to Job. God is sovereign over the affairs of angels and human beings. His sovereignty is seen in that He is the one to whom the sons of God come to present themselves, including Satan. God is the one who initiates the discussion with Satan about Job. God is the one who takes full

---

7. Job's response at this point of the book can be characterized as patient submission.

8. This seems to be the meaning of 'skin for skin!' (2:4). Another possible meaning might be that a person would give anything in exchange for his life (August Konkel, 'Job,' in *The Cornerstone Biblical Commentary*, ed. Philip W. Comfort [Carol Stream, IL: Tyndale House Publishers, 2006], 6:40).

responsibility for Job's plight when He concedes that Satan had persuaded Him to act against Job (Job 2:3).[9] God limits how far Satan can go in hurting Job. Job's complaint will be against God even though Satan is the immediate cause of the pain Job experiences. God's sovereignty is mysterious because there is much we do not understand concerning it, but we do know that God is not the author of sin (James 1:13, 17; 1 John 1:5) and that He uses secondary causes to accomplish His purposes (WCF 3.1).[10]

It is clear that Satan is the immediate cause of Job's illness because he left the presence of God and struck Job with 'loathsome sores from the sole of his foot to the crown of his head' (2:7). Many identify these sores with boils that are accompanied by the continual discharge of pus and the blackening and peeling of the skin. Job scrapes himself with a broken piece of pottery that may indicate that these sores needed scratching because of itching. There are periodic descriptions of Job's condition throughout the book. The symptoms of Job's illness include fever with chills (21:6; 30:30), darkening and shriveling of the skin (30:30), red eyes swollen from weeping (16:16), diarrhea (30:27), sleeplessness and delirium (7:4, 13-14), bad breath (19:17), emaciation (19:20), and excruciating pain throughout the body (30:17).[11] Job is sitting at the garbage dump, an ash heap, where the outcasts and the destitute dwell. His normal way of life is over – his children, goods, and business are gone. Moreover, his health is now gone. He has lost everything. God has allowed Job's faith to be tested. Is God worthy of worship only because of the good things He gives us?

Different Responses to Suffering (Job 2:9-13)

It is not always easy to know how to respond to a person who is suffering. This section highlights different responses

---

9. Hartley, *Job*, 79–80.

10. See Westminster Confession of Faith 3.1: 'God from all eternity, did, by the most wise and holy counsel of His own will, freely, and unchangeably ordain whatsoever comes to pass; yet so, as thereby neither is God the author of sin, nor is violence offered to the will of the creatures; nor is the liberty or contingency of second causes taken away, but rather established.'

11. Ibid., 82.

to Job's suffering. His wife responds with the words, 'Do you still hold fast your integrity? Curse God and die' (2:9). There are different ways of understanding her response. The early church fathers were very negative toward her, calling her the assistant of Satan and claiming that one of the trials of Job was that his wife did not die.[12] It is understandable why some would be negative toward her because her words, 'curse God and die,' reflect the words of Satan. If Job would respond in that way Satan would be correct in his assessment of Job. However, the first words she utters about Job's integrity are a reflection of the words of God (2:3). She raises the crux of the issue which will be debated in the rest of the book in a pointed way.[13] One must remember that she too has lost her wealth, her position, and her children. When people lose their security it is easy to respond out of panic because life is no longer sure and the future is uncertain. She also expresses pity toward Job.[14] She sees that he is suffering greatly and offers a statement that would at least enable him to bring his suffering to an end. She responds out of desperation to Job's situation[15] and says some things that she might not normally say.

Job responds, 'You speak as one of the foolish women would speak' (2:10). He does not call his wife foolish but compares her words to the words of a foolish woman. He recognizes her frailty and allows her to speak out of her desperation while still calling her to a better perspective. If Job's friends in the pursuing dialogue would have treated him in the same way, much of the book of Job would not have been written!

Job responds to his suffering by saying, 'Shall we receive good from God, and shall we not receive evil?' The word translated 'evil' is the word *ra'*. It combines into one word what English expresses in two words. One meaning refers to what is morally evil, which is the meaning when Job is

---

12. Konkel, 'Job,' 6:42. Augustine stated the first and Chrysostom stated the second.

13. G. Wilson, *Job*, 31.

14. Konkel, 'Job,' 6:42. The response of Job's wife can be characterized as panicked pity.

15. Elmer Smick, 'Job,' in *The Expositor's Bible Commentary*, ed. Tremper Longman III and David Garland (Grand Rapids: Zondervan, 2010), 4:720.

described as a man who turns away from evil (1:1; 1:8; 2:3). This word can also be used to accentuate the grievousness of something that is intrinsically harmful to one's physical well-being, even though no moral judgment has been made.[16] In Job 2:7 this word is used to describe the sores that afflict Job as 'loathsome'. The best way to understand this word in 2:10 is in the sense of calamity or misfortune. Job is asserting that we should not expect to receive from God only good because He may send misfortune our way, as Job himself is experiencing. For a second time the integrity of Job's response is asserted: 'In all this Job did not sin with his lips' (2:10). Job patiently submits to what he has received from the hand of God.

The response of Job's three friends is given in 2:11-13. Each of the friends is identified by name and place: Eliphaz the Temanite, Bildad the Shuhite, and Zophar the Naamathite. Their initial response to Job's suffering is very helpful. They come to show him sympathy and comfort that are demonstrated by their actions. They see how bad the situation has become because they are not able to recognize Job. They mourn with Job by weeping aloud, tearing their robes, and putting dust on their heads. They are willing to be with Job at the ash heap and they sit with him for seven days. The remarkable thing is that no one said a word to him during this time because they saw that his suffering was very great. The friends need to be commended for their presence with Job, their identification with Job, and their sympathetic silence toward Job in his suffering. There is a great temptation at times to offer shallow platitudes of hope, or even to speak principles of truth before a person is ready to hear them. People need time to process periods of heartache in their life. We should not be too quick to try to defend God. A silent, sympathetic presence is many times the best initial response to suffering.

The Sovereignty of God
The sovereignty of God and human response to suffering are related to each other because sometimes the way people respond to suffering is dependent upon their view of God.

---

16. David W. Baker, רַע (rʿʿ I), in *NIDOTTE*, 3:1154.

Some people have trouble with the way God is portrayed in Job 1–2. Is this a God who uses Job to make a point, and the suffering of Job does not really matter? Is this a God who is fickle and unstable, who can be manipulated by Satan (2:3: 'you incited me against him without cause')? Is this a God who plays with Job, uses him as a pawn to seek to win a bet with Satan? Does God really care about Job, or does He just want to win a wager against Satan? God is not really making a bet with Satan. In a wager a person does not know the outcome. However, God knows the outcome because He has ordained it. But does this make it any easier to worship this God?

The sovereignty of God is a great mystery but it is also a tremendous comfort. If God is not in charge of the events of this universe, and the events of our lives, who or what is? If Satan is in charge, then we are all doomed to destruction because he will do everything that he can to destroy us. If chance is what rules the universe and the events of my life, then it does not matter what any of us do. There is no rhyme or reason to life, so it does not matter if I bless you or if I put poison in your drink. The sovereignty of God gives us hope because even in the horrible hardships and suffering of life, God is able to bring unimaginable good out of horrible suffering. God has ordained every aspect of our lives in order to work out His purposes for our good and the good of His people. We struggle with this because we are limited in our human understanding so that many times all that we can see is the horrible bad things that result from suffering. We do not see how God can use it for good. We do not see the invisible and innumerable impact that certain events have on others. We do not always see that the suffering of our lives will resound to His glory and to our sanctification, and ultimately to our glorification.

The God that we worship is not a capricious, fickle, unstable tyrant in the sky. He is the God who took the time to form Adam from the dust of the ground and who forms each of us in the womb. He knows every fingerprint, every mole, every quirk, and even the number of our hairs. He provided for our salvation through the death of His Son who took upon Himself all our suffering and pain through the horrible death of the cross. He pours forth the abundance of the riches of His grace even in suffering. By grace we have been saved through faith and have been seated with Christ in the heavenly places (Eph. 2:6). We have the promise that in the coming ages He might show the immeasurable riches of his grace in kindness toward us in Christ Jesus. Even now in the suffering and heartache of life God is demonstrating in us the immeasurable riches of His grace. There is such an abundance of grace that we have received in Christ that His grace should be pouring forth from our lives no matter what we are experiencing. This abundant grace will be manifest in us on that last day when Christ comes in victory and we will shine forth as trophies of His grace. All the pain, heartache, questions, and suffering are being used in our lives to show forth the power of the gospel of Jesus Christ. He is worthy of our worship even in suffering.

Welcome Baby Pierce

'Be still and know that I am God.' Those were the last words I recited as I closed my eyes in what was the scariest moment of my life. Yesterday, I started experiencing some mild contractions in the morning. By two o'clock in the afternoon, what had been mild turned into intense, consistent contractions. I knew something was terribly wrong so we packed into the car and headed straight for the hospital. At the hospital, I was told that I was already 2cm dilated, but the fast and furious contractions were making my labor speed right along. Within minutes of walking through the emergency room door, there were swarms of people buzzing around me. I was flipped on my head, given pills/shots/IVs, and hooked to all kinds of monitors – all in an attempt to stop labor. From that point, it seems like such a blur. When my contractions intensified and didn't break in between, we were told that I was fully dilated and that an emergency C-section was necessary. I was rushed to the operating room, and before I knew it I was being placed under general anesthesia. Up until this point, almost every comment from the hospital staff (aside from our wonderful midwife), had been preparing us for what seemed like a pretty bleak situation for Pierce.

Words such as 'non-viable' were used to suggest our unborn child's condition. So needless to say, as I lay there alone (Nik wasn't allowed back in the operating room because of the conditions), on that cold operating table, pain surging through my body, I felt completely hopeless. And then I remembered the phrase my midwife told me when I first came in: 'Be still and know that I am God.' Immediately I was reminded of God's presence. A sense of comfort flooded over me. I knew God was there. I was reminded of His sovereignty. And most importantly, I knew that He and He alone could save our tiny baby.

I awoke in the recovery room, and was told that our 1 lb. 8 oz. son was in 'stable' and 'good' condition. Their main concern was to get him transferred to Levine Children's Hospital. It took them about two hours to get Pierce transferred and I followed shortly after. We were only allowed to see him for about a minute as they wheeled him to the ambulance.

Yesterday was, and still is, the scariest day of my life. I was lying there helpless. The desire to hold my baby was so strong, but yet I couldn't even touch him. But God is gracious. He grants us the strength that we need. And last night, He met us and comforted our broken hearts.

But the biggest praise is that Pierce was and still remains stable. Thanks be to our gracious God. He is slowly being weaned off the ventilator and is doing a great deal of breathing on his own. This is a HUGE victory for our little champ. He has proved to be a fighter. And all day today God has used Scripture as well as other people to offer us hope and encouragement.

Many of you have asked how we are doing and to be quite honest, it has/will be a rollercoaster of emotions. We have been overwhelmed and humbled by the outpouring of prayers and support from our friends and family. And we have been reminded of our hope during this difficult time – Jesus Christ. Our Lord has been so gracious to us and we feel confident that He is at work in little Pierce's life. While we have great physicians here, we are reminded that He is the only one that we can call upon to save Pierce. We ask that you intercede on our behalf and continue to pray

for Pierce. Pray that he will remain free from infection, that
his lungs will be mature and that he will not experience any
brain bleeds.

Christ is All,
Lindsay Franks (4/13/11)

Study Questions

1) How is the character of Job described in Job 1? Is Job a sinless man? What does the word 'blameless' mean?

2) What does the noun 'satan' mean? How is this character presented in Job 1? How does he question Job's faith and God's character?

3) How does God affirm the character of Job? Is Job suffering because of sin he has committed?

4) What are the various responses to suffering in Job 1–2? How does Job respond to his suffering? Does that surprise you?

5) What does it mean to fear God as one is experiencing suffering?

6) Is God only worthy of worship because of the good things He gives people? What does this say about God Himself?

7) How is the sovereignty of God presented in these chapters? Why is it such a comfort in the midst of suffering?

2

Job's Lament: I Wish I Had Never Been Born

(Job 3)

A major issue of Job 1–2 is whether Job will curse God. Satan believed that Job would curse God if all his possessions were taken away, but instead Job worshiped God. Satan also believed that if Job would lose his health, he would curse God, but Job submitted to God's sovereignty. Even when Job's wife in desperation encouraged him to curse God and die, Job called her to a better perspective. The emphasis of Job 1–2 is that Job did not sin or charge God with wrong. Thus the reader is shocked when chapter 3 begins, 'After this Job opened his mouth and cursed.' The Job of chapter 3 hardly seems the same person as the Job of chapters 1–2.

There are other changes that take place in Job 3. The prose narrative of chapters 1 and 2 ends and the poetic speeches begin. The divine perspective of chapters 1 and 2 is gone and the reader is left with a limited, human perspective. And of course, Job's attitude changes in relationship to his suffering. How can this be explained? Does Job curse God?

Job's Curse (Job 3:1-10)

Job 3 contains a curse (3:1-10) and a lament (3:11-26). The focus of the curse is the day Job was born. In a variety of ways Job pleads that the day of his birth would be obliterated so that the events on that day would not have occurred. The accumulation of phrases is stunning:

> Let the day perish on which I was born (v. 3)
> Let that day be darkness (v. 4)
> Let gloom and deep darkness claim it (v. 5)
> Let thick darkness seize it (v. 6)
> Let that night be barren (v. 7)
> Let those who curse it curse the day (v. 8)
> Let the stars of its dawn be dark (v. 9)

Job is calling for a reversal of creation in reference to his birthday. Instead of God's command in Genesis 1:3, 'let there be light' ($y^eh\hat{\imath}$ '$\hat{o}r$), Job pleads 'let there be darkness' ($y^eh\hat{\imath}$ $h\bar{o}\check{s}e\underline{k}$). Job calls on God not to seek the day, which is a call for God to remove His providential care so that the day would not exist.[1] The stars give the night its character from dusk to dawn and their becoming dark could destroy that night (v. 9) so that Job would not have been born.[2] The darkness that Job longs for is the darkness of death, a darkness associated with the realm of the dead. The 'deep darkness' of 3:5 is the word that occurs in Psalm 23:4 ($\underline{s}alm\bar{a}we\underline{t}$), translated as the 'shadow of death' (ESV, NAS, KJV). There is an emotional aspect of fear, sorrow, and danger that accompanies this word.[3] When Job calls for 'deep darkness' to claim the day of his birth he is calling for the powers of death to overtake the day. In verse 8 Job calls on skilled sorcerers to rouse the powers of evil to curse the day of his birth. Leviathan is a mythological sea monster who represents the forces of chaos associated with the evil of this world.[4] If such forces were unleashed against the night of his birth, that night would be barren. There would be no joy and no hope for light. The culminating reason for Job's curse is that if he had not been born he would not be experiencing trouble in his life (v. 10). Job does not curse God. He curses a day in

---

1. Hartley (Job, 93) shows that whatever God attends to or seeks realizes its full potential (Isa. 62:12).

2. Robert S. Fyall, Now My Eyes Have Seen You: Images of Creation and Evil in the Book of Job (Downers Grove, IL: Inter-Varsity Press, 2002), 59.

3. James D. Price, צלל, NIDOTTE, 3:809.

4. Fyall, Creation and Evil in the Book of Job, 142-43.

the past that cannot really be changed, which is a parody of a curse.

Job's Lament (Job 3:11-26)

Job's lament is not like the typical laments found in the Psalms. The lament psalms ask a lot of questions but they also plead with God to deliver them. They also express confidence that God has heard the prayer of the psalmist or that He will answer his plea. Job's lament is different. He does not call on God to deliver him. The 'why questions' in Job's lament continue the curse of 3:1-10 and focus on why Job did not die at birth:

(1) Why did I not die at birth (v. 11)?

(2) Why did the knees receive me (v. 12)?

(3) Why was I not as a hidden stillborn child (v. 16)?

(4) Why is light given to him who is in misery and life to the bitter of soul (v. 20)?

(5) Why is light given to a man whose way is hidden (v. 23)?

These questions are followed by comments that explain the questions. The first three questions and the comments that follow (3:11-19) ask why death did not take place at birth. The benefit of death at birth is that Job could avoid his suffering. Job reflects on what it would be like in the place of the dead. He first describes people who were notable and successful in life, such as kings and counselors who rebuilt ruins and princes who were wealthy (vv. 14-15). Job could be 'sleeping' with the mighty instead of sitting at the ash heap. The point is not that death is so wonderful, but that life has become so intolerable.[5] The comments following the third question describe a different class of people, including the weary, the wicked, the prisoners, and the slaves. The wicked are known for stirring up trouble but they too are free from the difficulties of life. Death has freed the slave from his master and so they are at rest. Job longs to experience such rest and to be free from his suffering.

---

5. Wilson, *Job*, 40.

The fourth and fifth questions use the word 'light', which stands in opposition to the darkness expressed in Job's curse. If darkness represents death, then light represents life. The 'bitter in soul' long for death. The word 'longing' (ḥāḵāh) occurs in the psalms as waiting on God (Pss. 33:20; 106:13), but Job waits on death. Normally there is joy when the psalmist has confidence in God to deliver, but Job would rejoice in finding the grave. The desire is so strong that it is sought after like hidden treasure.

Job also describes a man whose way is hidden because he has lost the meaning or purpose of life. In chapter 1 Satan had complained that God had protected Job and all his possessions by putting a hedge around him. Job, however, does not feel protected by God. He uses the same concept to express his feeling that God has trapped him in his suffering so that he cannot escape.[6]

Job ends the lament with a focus on himself. There are nine uses of the pronouns I, my, or me in verses 24-26. He expresses the constant nature of his suffering. Job's sighing is as common as bread and his groaning pours forth like water. Job's anguish has become as common as food and drink. He expresses the impact of suffering on his life with the use of three words that stress restlessness when they are negated (not at ease, not quiet, no rest). Peace evades Job because of his suffering. He gives an insight into the psychological nature of his suffering when he states 'the thing that I fear comes upon me, and what I dread befalls me' (v. 25). It is natural for people to fear what the future may bring and Job has become consumed with angst concerning his situation. This statement, however, does not mean that Job believes he is getting what he really deserves. Such a view would subvert the purpose of the whole book. These words show that Job had thought about these matters enough to know that he could not consider himself exempt from the possibility of disastrous loss.[7]

---

6. The verb in 1:10 is *šwḵ* and the verb in 3:23 is *śkḵ*. Meanings associated with the former are 'hedge in' or 'shut in' and meanings associated with the latter are 'block off' or 'cover'.

7. D. A. Carson, *How Long, O Lord? Reflections on Evil and Suffering* (Grand Rapids: Baker, 1990), 159. He also states that because Job had thought about this issue, he was prepared for it (as best as one can prepare for such a devastating loss). This may explain why his initial response is so noble.

Job's words in chapter 3 should not be interpreted to mean that he is suffering because he had sinned. His innocence is clearly established in chapters 1–2. However, Job does say things from his experience of suffering that question God's actions. It is helpful to distinguish between these two situations. From standpoint A (chapters 1–2) Job's suffering is not related to anything wicked that he has done. He is blameless and righteous. But from standpoint B (chapters 3–27) Job speaks words that wrestle with God and his situation, and he will at times call God's justice into question. The friends do not recognize the difference between these two standpoints and will argue that Job is suffering because of his wickedness. Later in the book, when God tells the friends that they have not spoken of him what is right as Job has (Job 42:7), the reference is to the main argument of the debate. The friends have been wrong in arguing that Job is suffering because of his sin. God is not declaring that everything that Job has said in the wisdom debate (chapters 3–27) has been correct. God does accuse Job of speaking of things he does not understand (Job 38:2) and of calling into question God's justice (Job 40:8), for which Job has to repent (Job 42:1–6).

Suffering can change a person's perception of life and God. The patient, submissive Job of chapters 1 and 2 highlights the intellectual dilemma faced by the people of God: God is sovereign over the events of this life and yet suffering can overtake a person who fears God. The protesting Job of chapter 3 shows that believers may wrestle with this dilemma by venting their anguish and anger.[8] Grief over suffering is not expressed in rational ways. And yet Job does not go so far in his anguish to change his basic conception of God. A rabbi named Harold Kushner was so distraught over his son's illness and death that it changed his idea of God. He wondered how God could be both all-powerful and good if He allowed bad things to happen in this world. He felt like he had to choose between a God who was all-powerful but not good, or a God who was good but not all-powerful. He came to the conclusion that God was a good God but that He was limited in what He could accomplish. If God was both

---

8. Konkle, 'Job,' 6:48.

all-powerful and good, then his son would not have become sick and died.[9] Job will also wrestle with the character of God but he does not completely change his view of God. Neither does he seek the solution of suicide to end his suffering which would be a failure of faith by taking the power to grant life into his own hands. Even in his protesting, it is an argument with God because God is the only one who will be able to respond to his suffering in a satisfying way. Little did Job know that God would one day become a human being and endure the suffering of the cross for our sin in order to secure our salvation. Followers of Christ have even more reason to persevere in the midst of suffering because we see clearly His victory over suffering, sin, and death.

Hope in Christ's Presence

Tonight it appears that, after about twenty-four hours, Pierce has come out of what is referred to as the 'honeymoon period'. Our doctors warned us not to get our hopes up. He had done exceedingly well all day today. We had several friends stop by and he was doing remarkably well. His oxygen levels were good, his heart rate was good and, in fact, they had planned on extubating him in the morning (removing his tubes). We were warned, however that his chances for survival (25-30 per cent) had not changed.

We were warned about this so-called 'honeymoon phase'. We were warned. But yet, we were not prepared for the devastating emotions that unfolded in a course of a few moments as we watched our son's vitals drop drastically. It became apparent that his immature lungs just weren't able to tolerate this weaning off process and the doctors switched him back to the oscillator (a higher powered ventilator). Right now the doctors are saying he is definitely sicker than he has ever been. This is a turn for the worse. But yet in all of this, in the darkest of times, God has been gracious.

---

9. Harold S. Kushner, *When Bad Things Happen to Good People* (New York: Avon Books, 1981).

We ask you to pray that Pierce's lungs will clear up and that he will be able to be weaned off total ventilation. Please pray that his vitals stabilize. It appears that he is what is referred to as a 'touch-me-not'. Our nurse put it this way, 'He just doesn't want anyone messing with him!' This means that the slightest touch irritates our little guy and this can throw his vitals off. We know that our God is faithful and loving. We know that He can mature our guy's lungs. Please, please be fervent in prayer. Please lift Nik and I up as watching our son in pain without the option of holding/touching him has been the most emotionally trying thing either of us have ever had to deal with.

And lastly, we want to remind everyone of the hope that resides in us. We know that Christ is with Pierce. That Christ is with us. And that as Scripture teaches us, Christ holds everything together. He is our hope, our anchor, and our strength. Our deepest desire is that He will use Pierce's life in order to glorify Himself and radiate the truth of the Gospel. We know He will be faithful to do that – and faithful to heal our son.

Nik and Lindsay Franks (4/14/11)

Study Questions

1) What does Job curse in chapter 3? Does he curse God?

2) How is Job's lament different from the laments in the Psalms? What does he express with his laments?

3) How does Job feel God is treating him?

4) Can suffering change a person's view of God and life? How?

3

Eliphaz: A Counselor Who Misses the Mark

(Job 4–5)

After Job's lament, there are three cycles of speeches in Job 4–27:

First Cycle	Second Cycle	Third Cycle
Eliphaz (4–5)	Eliphaz (15)	Eliphaz (22)
Job (6–7)	Job (16–17)	Job (23–24)
Bildad (8)	Bildad (18)	Bildad (25)
Job (9–10)	Job (19)	Job (26–27)
Zophar (11)	Zophar (20)	
Job (12–14)	Job (21)	

Eliphaz and Bildad make three speeches but Zophar only makes two speeches. Job responds to each of the speeches. Without Zophar's third speech the third cycle is incomplete, which demonstrates that the debate has collapsed. The problem with this wisdom debate is not the general theology of the friends but the application of their theology to Job's situation. In other words, the issue concerns wisdom and where wisdom is to be found.

Eliphaz is the most prominent of the friends and the most eloquent spokesman. In each cycle his speeches are longer than the other two friends. He is also the most articulate in terms of rhetoric.[1] He may be the oldest of the friends because he speaks first. His basic argument is stated in 4:7-8: the innocent do not perish, but those who sow trouble are the ones who reap it. Of course the implication is that if Job is experiencing trouble then he must have done something to cause it.

In 4:1-6 Eliphaz cautiously approaches Job to speak with him. He feels compelled to speak (4:2) because of Job's reaction to his suffering.[2] In the past his words have been a source of instruction[3] and strength to those who were weak and in danger of stumbling (4:3-4). But now Job finds himself in a position of weakness and it seems he is about to stumble because he is dismayed by his suffering. In fact, twice Eliphaz raises the question whether Job is impatient. Job has lost his calm confidence and is rattled by the events of his life. He has failed to live up to the standards he has raised for others.[4]

Eliphaz sets forth his major arguments in the form of questions and in these questions he also seeks to give advice to Job. Many of the questions expect a 'no' answer, but the first set of questions has the purpose of calling Job back to the foundation of his life. His confidence should be found in his response of the fear of God and his hope should be found in the integrity of his actions (4:6). In other words, if Job has been upright and if he responds in the right way, he should not have anything to worry about.

The basic principle of the argument is stated in verse 8: those who sow trouble also reap trouble. Eliphaz may be responding to Job's words that if he had not been born then he would not be experiencing trouble (3:10).[5] The word 'remember' in verse 7 is reminding Job of the truth they would both affirm.[6] Two rhetorical questions in verse 7 introduce

---

1. Hartley, *Job*, 103.

2. The verb *nāsāh* in verse 2 means to put someone to the test. Eliphaz is going to challenge Job's words (Longman, *Job*, 115).

3. The verb *yāsar* can mean 'correction' or education of a moral nature. Job had been effective in counseling others in times of distress by giving insight into God's disciplinary use of affliction (Konkel, 'Job', 6:51 and Hartley, *Job*, 105).

4. Hartley, *Job*, 106.

5. The word 'trouble' (*'āmāl*) is used in both passages.

6. Clines, *Job 1–20*, 124.

the principle. Has the innocent ever perished?[7] Where has the upright ever been cut off? This set of questions does not deny that the righteous suffer, but when they do suffer their suffering will not lead to death. The righteous will not experience a premature death.[8] The innocent and the upright do not perish because they avoid the negative consequences of those who sow trouble. Job is not dead yet, so he is able to have confidence in his piety (v. 6).

Eliphaz has confidence in this principle because he has seen it at work in the world (v. 8) and God is behind the principle (v. 9). These two ideas are not opposed to each other. The wicked suffer because of the consequences of their own actions. The principle that people reap what they sow is built into the way the world works. The wicked, however, may also find themselves the direct object of God's wrath (v. 9). [9] The roar of the lion is fierce and strikes fear into people, but they may also at any time perish for lack of prey or for broken teeth (vv. 10-11).[10] In other words, some unforeseeable calamity may strike at any moment to bring the wicked down.[11]

The third set of questions addressed to Job occurs in verse 17. They come from a vision of God in the night described in verses 12-16. Eliphaz is overwhelmed by fear and trembling because the vision comes from a spirit whose form and appearance were not clearly seen even though a voice was heard. The voice asks the two questions that Eliphaz puts before Job. The purpose of introducing the questions in this way is to impress upon Job that the source of the questions is God. The questions, therefore, must be important.

The questions are stated in verse 17 with an explanation of the meaning of the questions in verses 18-21. Eliphaz heard these questions, 'Can mortal man be in the right before God?

7. This question may also be a response to Job's statement, 'Let the day perish on which I was born' (3:3). Both statements use the verb 'ābad for 'perish'.

8. Clines, *Job 1–20*, 124.

9. Konkel, 'Job,' 6:52.

10. Hartley (*Job*, 108) comments that we are not told how the teeth of the lion are broken, but Psalm 58:6 suggests that God is responsible for their broken teeth.

11. Clines, *Job 1–20*, 128.

Can a man be pure before his Maker?'[12] After the build-up of a direct revelation from God these questions seem mundane. The point is that the righteous can never be perfectly righteous so that they should expect to suffer in this life based on their failures. But this suffering will never cause the righteous to perish or to be cut off in their prime.[13] This view supports the principle that people reap what they sow and that Job deserves the suffering he is experiencing. The explanation in verses 18-21 argues from the greater to the lesser. If the angels, who are heavenly beings, can be charged with error, how much more can those who are frail and weak creatures of dust be charged with error. It is impossible to avoid error. The horrible end of those who suffer because of their error is described in verses 20–21. They die quickly and suddenly without understanding the reason for their downfall.[14] This description may be a warning to Job not to reject the wisdom being offered to him, lest he end up like them. It is impossible for human beings to completely avoid sin, which means that human beings cannot completely avoid suffering. But Job does not have to worry because he has lived a life of piety (4:6). The implication is that if Job would confess what he has done wrong the suffering would end.

The fourth set of rhetorical questions occurs in 5:1. These questions and the explanation that follows also allude to Job's situation. Eliphaz leaves Job with little hope that anyone, including the angels, would answer his questions. Eliphaz seems to be removing any other option of help so that Job will appeal to God (5:8).[15] In 5:2-7 Eliphaz paints a picture of a fool, who is destroyed by the strong emotions of anger

---

12. Some English translations, such as the NIV [1984], translate Job 4:17 as a comparative (based on the preposition *min*): 'Can a mortal be more righteous than God?' The meaning would be that Job is implicitly claiming that he is more righteous than God through his attitudes and actions that show his refusal to repent (see Richard Whitekettle, 'When More Leads to Less: Overstatement, *Incrementum*, and the Question in Job 4:17a,' *JBL* 129 (2010): 445-48). Clines (*Job 1–20*, 132) argues from the general context that the comparative view is not the right view.

13. Clines, *Job 1–20*, 128.

14. Hartley, *Job*, 114-15.

15. Konkel, 'Job,' 6:56. Longman (*Job*, 122) acknowledges that this view fits what Eliphaz tells Job to do in 5:8, but he also suggests that the point might be that no one will answer Job.

and jealousy (v. 2).[16] Even though the fool seems to be secure he is always in danger of losing what is dear to him. His children and his harvest can easily be lost. The explanation for this loss is due to the human condition. Affliction and trouble do not just spring up from the ground for no reason. Trouble accompanies human beings as naturally as sparks fly upward. Of course, the vexation and jealousy of the fool add to the possibility that the fool will experience trouble. Eliphaz paints this picture of a fool with the hope that it will act as a warning to Job.[17] He does not directly call Job a fool nor does he say that Job has lost his children and his crops because he is a fool. The implication, however, seems clear that Job should consider whether this picture of a fool fits his own situation. Maybe he has done something foolish to bring on his suffering.

Eliphaz moves from asking Job rhetorical questions to giving advice as to what he would do if he were in Job's situation. The first word of advice is given in 5:8 and is followed with reasons why Job should accept the advice (5:9-16). Job should seek God and commit his cause to God.[18] Instead of cursing the day of his birth and wishing he had never been born, Job should seek help from God. The main reason for this advice is that God regularly does great and marvelous things. More specifically, the great things that God accomplishes lead to great reversals. He makes sure the devices of the crafty[19] do not succeed and the schemes of the cunning are quickly brought to an end. Their plans end in darkness. The lowly, however, are set on high and those who mourn are lifted to safety. He delivers the needy so that the poor have hope and injustice is stopped. Eliphaz may

---

16. Hartley, *Job*, 117.

17. Longman, *Job*, 123.

18. There is debate about what the second half of verse 8 means. Part of the discussion concerns the meaning of the word *dibrāh*, translated by many English translations as 'cause' (ESV, KJV, NAS). Clines (*Job 1–20*, 116) argues that Eliphaz would be unlikely to concede that Job had a legal case, so he opts for the meaning 'utterance' or 'speech' and translates the phrase, 'to God I address my speech.'

19. The term 'crafty' ('*ārûm*) can have the positive meaning 'incisive perceptions' (1 Sam. 23:22) or the negative meaning of cunning activity (Ps. 83:3), depending on whether a person is acting in wisdom or folly (Hartley, *Job*, 121, n. 16). The negative meaning is used here.

fear that Job has placed himself in the category of the crafty because he had called on darkness to overtake the day of his birth (Job 3). Job is lowly, he is mourning, and he is in need of being delivered. God is able to lift him up if he would turn to God.

The second word of advice to Job puts his suffering in the context of God's discipline (5:17). In fact, people who are disciplined by God are blessed because God is treating them like a faithful father.[20] The blessing connected to discipline is laid out in 5:18-27. God uses suffering to restore people. He may wound and shatter, but the ultimate purpose is to heal (v. 18). Restoration brings one into a position where the blessing of God can be poured out again. God's deliverance brings protection from disasters, from death in famine, and from the power of the sword (vv. 19-20). The numerical saying of verse 19 shows that even though there may be many difficulties in life (six troubles), the final blow of death will not be struck ('in seven no evil shall touch you').[21] Fear of destruction will be taken away (vv. 21-22) because there will be harmony with creation (v. 23). Peace will reign once again so that one's possessions and children will be many and a person will live to a ripe old age. In light of these blessings, Eliphaz encourages Job not to despise the discipline of God. His suffering is for his good and will lead to blessing.

Eliphaz can be characterized as a counselor who misses the mark. He asserts a lot of general things that are true. People do reap what they sow. Human beings are not always right or pure before God. People should seek God. God does discipline His people. The question is whether these are good explanations for Job's suffering. Job 1–2 has established the blameless character of Job and that his suffering is ultimately from the hand of God. The problem with Eliphaz is not his theology; rather, the problem is the application of that theology

---

20. Suffering as God's discipline is not emphasized again in the debate, but it is raised again in the argument of Elihu. Part of the reason for this is that the friends are going to focus on Job's wickedness as a cause of his suffering (E. W. Nicholson, 'The Limits of Theodicy as a Theme of the Book of Job' in *Wisdom in Ancient Israel: Essays in Honour of J. A. Emerton*, ed. John Day, Robert P. Gordon, and H. G. M. Williamson [Cambridge: Cambridge University Press, 1995], 78).

21. Hartley, *Job*, 126.

to Job's situation. He misuses proverbs by misapplying them. Although he does not attack Job directly, he makes enough allusions to Job's situation to make his point. Twice children are mentioned. The first mention is in the description of the fool whose children are far from safety. The second mention is in the restoration of children as a result of God's discipline. It would be hard for Job not to make the connection because he has just lost his children. Is that evidence that he is a fool? Will children be restored if he does not despise the discipline of God?

Eliphaz also misses the mark by emphasizing theology apart from compassion. He does not take the time to find out about Job's situation. The silence of the friends should have been followed by concern for Job instead of dissecting what he said. There is very little sympathy expressed for Job. The heart of Eliphaz is not touched by Job's suffering. Job's speech in chapter 3 must have been heart-rending, but Eliphaz shows little emotion and is only interested in theological reflection.[22] Job's words spoken in pain are words of desperation, not words of theological precision. Wisdom includes understanding the situation and responding appropriately. Above all else Job needs compassionate understanding, not theological analyses. There will come a time for theological reflection but it must come in the context of compassion.

Hour 41

We just got back from seeing the little guy. God has shown His grace throughout this ordeal but it is going to take more and more grace to get through this. He began regressing in his lungs yesterday, so they had to revert back to an oscillating machine. He is doing fine on that. However, recent blood tests show high levels of potassium which likely means that he is bleeding internally somewhere. Last night was rough and he got bruised a lot while they were working on him, but the doctors do not think that it was enough to give off the high levels

---

22. Derek Thomas, *The Storm Breaks: Job Simply Explained* (Darlington: Evangelical Press, 1995), 81.

of potassium. So they are going to go ahead and do an ultrasound on his brain because they believe that is where he could be bleeding. Please pray for him. Blood in the brain or not, God is sovereign over Pierce's body and life. We are pressing forward in faith. God is a God 'who gives life to the dead and calls into existence the things that do not exist' (Rom. 4:17). He can heal Pierce's lungs, brain, liver, intestines, and any part of his body with one word. God is in control of all things and has purposes in this moment that we cannot see at this time or may never see in this life. Lindsay and I have been pressed harder in this more than any other time in our life, still we are not crushed or in despair. We have been greatly humbled by all the prayer. Please, please don't stop praying.

'The Lord is at hand; do not be anxious about anything, but in everything by prayer and supplication with thanksgiving let your requests be made known to God. And the peace of God, which surpasses all understanding, will guard your hearts and your minds in Christ Jesus' (Phil. 4:5-7).

Grace and peace,
Nik and Lindsay Franks (4/14/11)

Study Questions

1) What is the basic argument of Eliphaz?

2) What are some general things that Eliphaz says to Job that are true?

3) How does Eliphaz confront Job in an indirect way rather than a direct way?

4) How else does Eliphaz miss the mark? Why is it important to have more than just good theology when helping people? How can you show compassion when you counsel people?

4

Job: Betrayed by Both Man and God

(Job 6–7)

Job's response to Eliphaz can be divided into two parts. In chapter 6 he defends his curse-lament (Job 3) and he accuses Eliphaz of failing to bring him comfort in his suffering. In chapter 7 Job addresses God directly by lamenting the difficulty of his situation and by accusing God of harassment.

Betrayed by Friends: Where is Loyalty?
Job defends his curse-lament by demonstrating the reality of his suffering (6:1-7). He recognizes that his words have been rash but that is due to the gravity of his situation. With an outburst of emotion, he wishes he could demonstrate the enormity of his suffering.[1] If one were to weigh his anguish, it would be heavier than all the sand of the sea. Job's grief is unbearable, which explains his rash reaction.

By a series of rhetorical questions in verses 5–6 Job further explains his outburst of chapter 3. The questions of verse 5 mean that as long as an animal has food it does not make noise. Job would not be expressing his anguish if he was not suffering. As Andersen puts it, 'Job also has a right to bray

---

1. Hartley, *Job*, 131.

like a hungry wild ass and to bellow like a starving bull.'[2] The questions of verse 6 state that tasteless food is not eaten unless one adds salt to it. Job applies this picture to his own situation in verse 7. The food mentioned could be literal food that is not edible and makes him sick. Or, this 'food' could refer to the tasteless and repulsive things that Job is experiencing in his life.[3] It is also possible that tasteless food might refer to the advice given to him by Eliphaz. It is of no help and he will not have anything to do with it.[4] If only Job's friends had understood the depth of his suffering, they might have responded in a different way.

The reality of Job's suffering cannot be separated from God's actions against him (v. 4). Job does not perceive God as a father who is disciplining him (5:17) but as a hunter who is pursuing him. God is seen as an enemy who has attacked him with poisoned arrows that go deep into his spirit. Job is struggling spiritually because he is terrified by God.

Job continues to speak about God in verses 8–13. In this section Job longs for death even as he asserts that he has not denied the words of the Holy One. Job has a strong hope that God will put him out of his misery by crushing him. Job refers back to his curse in Job 3 and wishes that God would activate it against him.[5] Even if being cut off by God brought great pain, it would be worth it to be free from his excruciating suffering. By the use of the word 'hope' (*tiqwāh*) he mocks Eliphaz' use of the word (4:6; 5:16). Eliphaz believed that Job had hope for the future but Job's only hope was a quick death.[6] In verses 11-13 Job confesses that he has no strength to continue patiently waiting for God to act on his behalf. His own inner resources are depleted, so it is better to face death because he knows his integrity has not been compromised.

---

2. Andersen, *Job*, 128.

3. Hartley, *Job*, 133.

4. Longman, *Job*, 138.

5. Hartley, *Job*, 134.

6. Newsom, 'Job,' 4:387.

Job next argues that his friends have dishonored him and they have forsaken God (vv. 14-23). By not showing him kindness they have abandoned the fear of the Almighty. Their mistreatment of Job is evidence that they no longer have reverence for God. Someone who fears God would show kindness to someone who is suffering (v. 14). Instead, the friends are like an empty stream bed that gives the hope of water but then disappoints with a dry bed. Many a caravan has been disappointed and has even perished for lack of water (vv. 15-19). Job's friends, called brothers, are just as disappointing to Job. They have no refreshing water to offer him.[7] Their hope of help has ended with betrayal. Job asks a series of questions that emphasizes that he has not asked the friends to do anything extraordinary (vv. 22-23). But they have been afraid of his situation and so have not known how to respond. Job uses an important word to describe what he desires from the friends. The word 'kindness' is the Hebrew *ḥeseḏ*, which describes a response that comes from loyalty. Job feels betrayed because the friends have not shown any love that would help and protect him.[8]

Job exhorts the friends to show him where he has gone astray (vv. 24-30). He is willing to receive teaching from the friends because upright words are very forceful. Their words of reproof, however, miss the mark. They do not understand that his words have the character of wind because they are the speech of a despairing man. They are acting treacherously against Job and are like those who cast lots over the fatherless. Job wants them to look at his face and he pleads that they would treat him with justice. They should show him where he has gone wrong, for his vindication is at stake. It is interesting that Job characterizes his words as rash and as wind, but he can also assert that he has not denied the words of the Holy One. Perhaps one who expresses grief should be given some latitude in what they say because their words are not always logical. It is also hard to know if the statement in verse 10 refers to words before his suffering struck him, or refers to his words in the midst of suffering. If the latter, Job's perception may not be quite accurate.

7. Hartley, *Job*, 138.

8. Longman, *Job*, 140.

Betrayed by God: Quit Harassing Me

Job turns his thoughts to God in chapter 7. It is unclear at
the beginning of the chapter who Job is addressing, but it
becomes clear that he is speaking to God when he uses the
imperative 'Remember' (v. 7).[9] Job laments his hard lot in life
in verses 1-10 and complains to God of harassment in verses
11-21.

Job begins with a question concerning the lot of human
beings on the earth (v. 1). Man's existence is 'hard service'
and his days are like the days of a hired hand. Job expounds
on this question by showing how his life has become a life
of hard service. At least the slave enjoys the shade and the
worker enjoys his wages,[10] but Job's life is full of empty
months with long nights of misery and a lack of sleep. His
days are swift and end without hope. His flesh is clothed with
worms and dirt and his skin pusses and hardens (vv. 2-6). Job
asks that God would remember that his life is fleeting as a
breath with little hope of seeing any good again. As quickly
as the clouds fade and vanish, so Job will quickly go down to
Sheol with no hope of return. Not even God will behold him
anymore.[11] Soon he will be gone forever (vv. 7-10).[12]

Because Job's life is short he will not restrain his speech
but will complain in the bitterness of his soul. His basic
complaint is that God is tormenting and harassing him. Job
wonders if he is such a threat that he should be put under
guard as the sea monster.[13] He has no comfort in bed because
God terrifies him with dreams. Job just wants to be left alone
for a few days. Job seems to allude to Psalm 8:4 in 7:17. In
Psalm 8 the psalmist expresses wonder at the attention God
pays to human beings and the high place God has given
to them within creation. In chapter 7 Job expresses concern

---

9. Hartley, *Job*, 142. The rest of Job 7 makes sense only if it is addressed to God.

10. Hartley, *Job*, 145.

11. Longman, *Job*, 145.

12. One minute, Job complains about the endless months of misery, and the
next minute he complains about the swiftness of life. Andersen (*Job*, 134) points
out that such conflicting thoughts are bound to rage in the mind of one who is 'full
of tossing' (7:4).

13. G. Wilson, *Job*, 70. Some biblical texts reflect the idea of conflict between
God and the sea serpent, Leviathan (Isa. 27:1). Later in Job 41:1-10 Leviathan will
be a symbol of evil in the world.

that God gives so much attention to human beings that He never leaves them alone. Both passages use a verb that means 'visit' (*pāqad*). Psalm 8:4 uses the verb positively and it is translated 'care for'. In Job 7:18 the verb is used negatively to express God's overbearing oversight. Why does God pay so much attention to a human being, constantly visiting him and testing him? If God would look away for just a few moments, long enough for Job to swallow his spit, he would experience relief. Even a few seconds of relief would be welcome. Job then sets forth a hypothetical situation that if he has committed sin surely his sin is not grievous enough for the amount of suffering he is experiencing.[14] Job feels that God has marked him out and that he has become a burden to God. Why put Job through this suffering if He can just pardon his iniquity? God can restore the relationship if He so desired.[15]

Job believes that he has been betrayed by both his friends and God. He feels that both have let him down by the way they have responded to his suffering. The friends have betrayed his trust by attacking what he has said and by accusing him of sin. God has betrayed his trust by His silence even though there had been a good relationship between them.

The Righteous Sufferer

There is a pattern in Scripture of a person feeling betrayed by God and/or friends. Such patterns in Scripture fall under the category of typology, which can be defined as the interpretation of earlier events, persons, or institutions in biblical history which anticipate later events, persons, or institutions. The way God has acted in the past becomes a pattern for the way God will act in the future. The fulfillment of the type, called the anti-type, must be greater than the type.

---

14. Longman, *Job*, 148. He comments that Job does not admit to sin but states that even if he had sinned there would not be justification for the depths of his suffering. Such a statement assumes that there is an equal relationship between sin and suffering and righteousness and blessing. This view of the friends will be questioned by Job as the debate continues.

15. Hartley, *Job*, 142. He argues that Job is speaking more realistically here about his situation and his relationship with God in contrast with the curse-lament in Job 3. He sees this as evidence that Job is beginning to cope with the reality of his situation.

It is worth exploring whether there is in Scripture a type of a righteous sufferer.

The first one to suffer unjustly in Scripture is Abel who is murdered by his brother Cain because God accepted Abel's sacrifice but did not accept Cain's sacrifice (Gen. 4:1-16). Abel is the first in a long line of those who have been put to death for being in the right. Comparisons are also made in the New Testament between Abel and others who suffered unjustly. In this way he might stand as a paradigm of a righteous sufferer. His blood is called 'righteous blood' (Matt. 23:35) and its shedding demands a just response (Gen. 4:11-16). Jesus mentions all the righteous blood shed on earth from Abel to Zechariah. Those in Jesus' day who were responsible for shedding righteous blood will also suffer the consequences of their actions. The book of Hebrews commends the faith of Abel (Heb. 11:4) and even compares the shed blood of Abel with the shed blood of Jesus. The blood of Jesus speaks a better word than the blood of Abel (Heb. 12:24). Genesis 4:10 states, 'The voice of your brother's blood is crying to me from the ground.' Most likely Abel's blood cries out for justice. Jesus is the mediator of a new covenant and His sprinkled blood speaks a better word than the blood of Abel (the antitype). Abel was a son of Adam who brought right sacrifices because of his faith. Jesus was a son of Adam who lived a completely righteous life and offered Himself as a sacrifice on behalf of others. Abel was struck down by his own brother Cain and Jesus was lifted up on the cross by His own people. The blood of Abel called out for justice and the blood of Jesus called out for justice, but Jesus' blood was also the instrument through which the wrath of God was satisfied. Jesus' blood satisfied the justice of God so that it also pleads for sinners. It secures eternal redemption (Heb. 9:12) instead of condemnation and curse. Jesus' blood accomplishes what Abel's blood could never accomplish.

Comparisons between Abel and Jesus include the concepts of unjust suffering, suffering for being righteous, the role of blood, and death. Not every person who suffers unjustly experiences death. When death does not occur the one suffering has an opportunity to respond to their suffering. If suffering is prolonged or is very intense it is easy for the sufferer to become disillusioned with their acquaintances or with God. Jeremiah's suffering is caused by the reaction of the people to the message of judgment that he preached. His own people plotted against him. He felt abandoned by God (Jer. 20:7, 14-18). Job was suffering because of Satan's attacks against him, but it was ultimately due to the mystery of God's sovereignty. He was not suffering because of his sin. He felt betrayed by the friends because they believed that he was suffering because of his sin. Job felt abandoned by God because there was only silence on God's part. In a similar but greater way Jesus suffered according to the Father's plan to redeem sinful human beings. He also did not suffer because of His own sin. He was rejected by His own people and felt abandoned by God (Matt. 27:46). Jesus suffering, and then death, accomplished what no other person's suffering and death could accomplish: salvation through faith in Him.

The type of a righteous sufferer exists in the Old Testament. Such a person teaches us that the righteous do at times suffer without cause that friends may betray such sufferers, that the sufferer may feel abandoned by God, and that some who suffer unjustly may even be put to death. And yet, such suffering is not meaningless because we see how God accomplished His purposes for our salvation through the greater suffering of Christ. We can commit ourselves to God even in suffering because we are confident that God can accomplish His purposes through our suffering. Our suffering is not in vain in the Lord.

Brain Ultrasound: Only God Can Sustain Pierce

To the doctor's surprise, Pierce's brain ultrasound came back better than expected. With the potassium levels as high as they were, the doctor was expecting some serious bleeding. There is bleeding, but the bleeding is at a grade 2 level. Basically, he is bleeding into his spinal fluid. It can clean itself out, but it could also clot and cause the ventricles to be unable to drain the spinal fluid. That problem and the health of his lungs are what we need to pray for right now. Pray that this bleeding will pass and that Pierce will not have to have his ventricles drained and a stint put in. At his size, he is likely too small to have the surgery. We are sensing God's presence and your prayers and the defying of medical opinion has already begun to take place. Please continue to pray that his lungs will develop quickly and that his organs will follow suit.

As the Lord sustains Pierce, it is going to be a roller-coaster for us. For the last two days Lindsay and I have been sustained only by the grace of God, which I am sure was fueled by your prayers. We need to return many of your calls and emails but I don't know exactly when that will happen. Most of the time all we can do is pray, cry, and doze off from exhaustion. Let me say, God has taken very good care of us. We have found favor in the eyes of the staff. Yesterday, one of the day-nurses requested to have Pierce in her care permanently; please pray for her.

Please do not get the idea that things are going well. Twelve years ago they would not even have given you the option to try and sustain a twenty-three-week old preemie. Today, twenty-three weeks is the cut off. Again, there is only a 25-30 per cent chance of his surviving. But God takes no account of odds or percentages. 'He is in the heavens and He does what He pleases.' He has allotted to each of us the number of days that we have on this earth, and we pray that He has given Pierce an abundance of days. In many ways, all of our lives are just as fragile as Pierce's. We are all sustained by our Creator. My lungs go up and down because God allowed me to take another breath. And it is the same with Pierce. God's love, though, is amazing. You and I don't deserve it but He gives it freely. God gave His Son for me so that I might know for sure that He loves me and that He loves Pierce more than me. Pierce is in his Creator's hands. The Lord is able to pull Him through. Keep praying. God is not some psychological false hope, He is the True and Living God.

'Now to Him who is able to do far more abundantly than all that we ask or think, according to the power at work within us, to Him be glory in the church and in Christ Jesus throughout all generations, forever and ever. Amen' (Eph. 3:20–21)

                              Grace and Peace,
                              Nik and Lindsay Franks (4/14/11)

Study Questions

1) What reason does Job give for his rash words? If the friends understood this aspect of his speech, how might they have responded differently?

2) How does Job perceive God differently than the friends have presented God? What does he long for God to do?

3) On what basis does Job argue that God is harassing him? Does Job cross the line here in the way he speaks about God?

4) Have you ever felt abandoned by friends and God in suffering?

5) Is there such a thing as a righteous sufferer? Does this comfort or concern you?

5

Bildad: The Defender of
God's Justice
(Job 8)

Bildad aggressively jumps into the debate by reprimanding Job with a rhetorical question: 'How long will you say these things, and the words of your mouth be a great wind?' Perhaps he is responding to Job's complaint that the friends have not spoken the right words (6:24-25).[1] Bildad characterizes Job's words as a great wind. Job had acknowledged that his words were wind (6:26), but the reason behind his words were his desperate situation. His point was that it is useless to reprove someone when that person speaks out of despair. Bildad calls Job's words 'wind' because he thinks that Job speaks many words and says nothing of substance.[2] He believes Job has questioned the justice of God in his wordy, windy speech.

The basic thesis is stated in verse 3 in two rhetorical questions: 'Does God pervert justice? Or does the Almighty pervert the right?' The answers to these questions are an obvious 'no'. God is a God of justice who does not bend or make crooked what is right.[3] The justice of God can be

---

1. Hartley, *Job*, 155.

2. Longman, *Job*, 155.

3. Hartley, *Job*, 155. The concept of justice used by Bildad is the judicial concept that rewards the innocent and punishes the guilty, not the executive concept of the authority of a sovereign to govern his people (see Sylvia H. Scholnick, 'The Meaning

demonstrated in the events of life. God punishes the wicked and rewards the righteous. Bildad applies this principle to Job's situation, but not in a direct way. Bildad argues that if his children have sinned then God has delivered them into the hand of their transgression (v. 4). The use of the word 'if' softens the argument, and yet there is really no doubt what has happened because the children are dead. If there is calamity in someone's life, then that person must have done something to bring on that calamity. If Job's children have been destroyed, then they must have done something wrong to bring on their own destruction.

Bildad then applies this principle to Job in verses 5-7. The use of the word 'if' in reference to Job may be a 'sign of delicacy'.[4] Job is still alive and has the opportunity to respond. Job must seek God and plead with the Almighty for mercy. This assumes that Job is suffering because of his sin, just like his children. Bildad may allude here to Job's words where Job wonders why God does not just pardon him; otherwise, God will seek him and he shall be gone (7:21). According to Bildad, Job should not wait around as if God is going to seek him. Rather, Job must seek God and plead for mercy. Furthermore, if Job is pure and upright, as he claims he is, then God will act on his behalf to restore him and give him a great future.

The evidence for God's justice is set forth in verses 8-20. The first evidence is taken from the teaching of the fathers (vv. 8-10). Job is encouraged to inquire of the past and to consider what the fathers have taught. The reason the past is so important is because Job and the friends have not lived very long and so they do not have the same depth of knowledge as the ancients. One single life is too short to give perspective on how life is supposed to operate. There is not enough time to gain such knowledge. Job should listen to the past instead of calling the wisdom of the past into question.[5]

Evidence of God's justice is also given from nature. Two rhetorical questions are offered concerning whether plants

---

of *mišpaṭ* in the Book of Job,' *JBL* 101.4 [1982]: 521-29). This distinction will be important later in the book.

4. Clines, *Job 1–20*, 204.

5. Hartley, *Job*, 158.

can grow where there is no water. Of course, the obvious answer is that they cannot grow without water because they would wither (vv. 11-12). The analogy is made with the paths of those who forget God. Just as without water a plant will perish, so without God a person's life will perish. The hope of the godless will perish because his confidence and trust is no firmer than a spider's web. There is no foundation to his hope. No matter how sturdy their dwelling it cannot provide the security they seek (vv. 13-15).[6] The final example also uses a plant to illustrate the point that the success of the wicked is fleeting (vv. 16-19). A plant might look like it is flourishing with roots spread over the garden, but if those roots are among a pile of rocks and not deep into the soil, then that plant will be easily destroyed with nothing left in its place.[7] The godless may appear to be successful but that success will not last.[8]

In conclusion, Bildad restates the basic principle of retribution (vv. 20-22). There are two groups of people and God acts toward each group according to their character. On the one side, God will not reject a blameless (*tăm*) man. On the other side, God will not take the hand of evildoers to lead them (Gen. 19:16) or to support them (Isa. 41:13; 42:6).[9] If Job is righteous then God will restore the joy of his life (v. 21) and those who hate Him will be ashamed (v. 20a). If Job has sinned and is part of the wicked, then there is no hope for him because the wicked will come to an end (v. 20b). The righteous are rewarded and the wicked are destroyed. There is no category in Bildad's thinking for someone who is blameless and is suffering.

---

6. Konkel, 'Job,' 6:74.

7. Longman, *Job*, 158.

8. The meaning of verse 19 is debated. The ESV, and many other English translations, translate it 'Behold, this is the joy of his way, and out of the soil others will spring.' Hartley (*Job*, 162) understands verses 16-19 as describing the righteous. In this view, verse 19 describes the joy of the plant because it has survived the threat to its life. Others take verses 16-19 as a description of the wicked whose lives are easily destroyed. Instead of the noun *māśôś*, which means 'joy', it has been suggested that the noun is *māsôs*, from the verb *māsas*, which means 'dissolution' (the *ś* and the *s* both have the 's' sound). The 'dissolution of his way' would refer to the end of his life (Clines, *Job 1–20*, 200).

9. Clines, *Job 1–20*, 210.

The readers know from the prologue that Job is blameless (1:1) and that he is not suffering because of his sin (1:8, 22; 2:3, 10). In Bildad's theology suffering must lead back to sin. If Job is suffering and he is blameless, then the justice of God must be questioned. There was a similar dilemma surrounding the crucifixion of Jesus. Those at the cross derided Jesus as they called on Him to save Himself if He was the Son of God (Matt. 27:40). The chief priests and the elders mocked Jesus by saying if He was the King of Israel He should come down from the cross and then they would believe Him. They also mocked His trust in God because God was not delivering Him from the cross (Matt. 27:41-43). In their thinking if Jesus was the Son of God, then He would not be hanging on the cross. How could God let such a righteous person suffer? The suffering of Jesus is evidence that He is not who He claims to be. The cross, then, became a stumbling block to many Jewish people (1 Cor. 1:18-25). God, however, was accomplishing His purposes of salvation for His people in the cross of Christ. God in His infinite wisdom can use suffering to accomplish purposes that are hidden from the human perspective. A simplistic view of the deed-consequence relationship distorts the justice of God and how He works in the world. It is dangerous for human beings to defend the justice of God because the world is more complex than the theology of Bildad will allow.

Why Do Bad Things Happen to Good People?

Many around me have posed a question similar to the title of this blog. Nurses have sympathized with me by saying things such as, 'We just don't understand how some good mothers like you, those who try do everything right by the book, can have such sick babies, and yet bad mothers, those who have done nothing to ensure a healthy pregnancy, can walk out of the hospital with a healthy, full-term baby.' Others have said, 'I just don't know why God allows this to happen to such good people.' I can't say that I haven't ever selfishly asked God, 'Why us? Why did this have to happen to us?' But, I'd like to share with you an answer to that question. Hopefully it will bring you as much comfort as it does for me and Nik.

There is a book entitled *When Bad Things Happen To Good People* that is often used in grief counseling. It's written by a Jewish rabbi who struggled after his son died at a young age. While I think the author, Kushner, makes several good points, this book is terribly flawed in its line of thinking. You see, even the title suggests something that is fundamentally wrong – none of us are 'good' people in God's eyes. The Bible teaches us that, 'None is righteous, no, not one; no one understands; no one seeks for God' (Rom. 3). We are all sinners. We all choose things over God. And it is only by God's grace that, as believers, we have been covered by Christ's righteousness.

Therefore, to suggest that God owes us 'good' people 'good' things goes against the reality of this fallen world. This may sound cold, or cruel, but the question we should be asking God is, 'Why do good things happen to bad people?' You see, the fact that God allows any of us pleasures in this life is grace. And when you understand that God owes us nothing but death, His grace abounds all the more! I know this concept is hard to swallow when the plague of entitlement has ravaged through America. We expect God to be a genie in a bottle that gives us whatever we want, when we want it, and then if He doesn't, we get mad at Him. But when you realize that the God of the Universe, the God whom you and I rebel against every day, cares enough to bless us, and bless us frequently, how amazing that truly is!

Secondly, to understand God's hand in this situation, we must understand God's character. Everything that God allows and ordains is for His glory. He uses everything for good. Since Nik and I moved to Charlotte, there have been about 20 people for whom we've fervently prayed to come to an understanding of the Gospel. We've prayed numerous times for opportunities to share our faith with them. And now, we have many of them as a captive audience. So I'd like to propose a question to those of you who are reading this. Have you ever thought that God might be allowing this to happen so that you might be drawn closer to Him? In other words, perhaps God, being rich in mercy, is using Pierce and his life to bring you to an understanding of how much He loves you. We pray that this is the case. We pray that God is using this to advance His kingdom. And already, we have received numerous emails of how God is working in your lives. And for that, we are thankful. If God is allowing our suffering to bring glory to His name, we humbly rejoice. Daily we trust God to grant us hearts that are full of faith (because our hearts can, and do quickly turn astray), that can proclaim, 'Christ is enough. He is more than enough for me. He will sustain us. And He will glorify Himself through Pierce's life.' And friends, Christ is truly more than enough. He is the only thing that will ever bring you satisfaction in this life. And He is pursuing you. He will do whatever it takes to bring you to faith in Him. Cling to Him tonight.

Much love,
Lindsay Franks (4/23/11)

Study Questions

1) Compare and contrast the different views of Job's words as wind.

2) How does Bildad use the concept of children in his speech?

3) What evidence does Bildad give for God's justice? How does Bildad apply the principle of retribution?

4) How does the death of Christ challenge Bildad's basic argument against Job? How should this inform attempts to defend God's justice in this world?

5) What is the problem with the question, 'Why do bad things happen to good people?'?

6

Job Wrestles with His
Perception of God
(Job 9–10)

Job's response to Bildad covers two chapters. The first part of Job's speech is Job's reflections on whether he can resolve his suffering by presenting his case to God (9:1-35). Job ponders the possibility of entering into a debate with God to uncover the causes of God's hostility toward him. This section is full of legal language. God is spoken of in the third person.[1] Job addresses the friends about God in chapter 9 and then he will address God Himself in chapter 10.[2] Job also changes moods and positions quickly as he states a position and then abandons it. The despair of suffering has a way of affecting the mind and mood of the one suffering. The hope of a trial before God fades and he takes up a lament addressed to God in the second part of his response (10:1-22).[3]

Job's Quest for a Legal Hearing (Job 9:1-35)

The (Im)possibility of a Legal Hearing
Job begins with an apparent concession to Bildad's argument that God does not pervert justice. He states, 'Truly I know

---

1. Hartley, *Job*, 165.
2. Longman, *Job*, 167.
3. Hartley, *Job*, 165.

that it is so' (v. 1). He follows that assertion with a question, 'How can a man be in the right before God?' In other words, how can a person be acquitted when God is the accuser? The question indicates that Job does not think he can win his case against God even if he is innocent.

The possibility, or impossibility, of entering into litigation with God is contemplated in verses 3-13. To present a case before God is not possible because one is not able to answer the questions God would ask the litigant (v. 3). God is full of wisdom and mighty in strength. He is able to move mountains and shake the earth out of its place. He has power over the sun to keep it from rising and over the stars to keep them from shining. God is the great Creator who stretched out the heavens and trampled the waves of the sea (v. 8).[4] He also made the constellations (v. 9). These things only begin to scratch the surface of the marvelous things that God has done (v. 10). Job's words have been described as the 'language of praise' which shows a true hunger for God.[5]

Job reflects on what it would be like to try to present a case before such a powerful, great God. He views God as unapproachable because it is difficult to perceive His presence (v. 11). If God is so hidden, how can one even speak with Him? It is also impossible to challenge God. If He were to carry someone off, who could stop Him or even question His actions (v. 12)? Even the powerful, mythical monster called Rahab submits to God (v. 13).[6] This makes it impossible for Job to give an answer to God. It does not matter that Job is in the right, he still would not be able to find the right words to speak to God. His only option is to appeal for mercy to his accuser (vv. 14-15).

Job feels he is being mistreated by God (vv. 16-18). Even if God answered Job he would have a hard time believing that it was actually God that was listening to him. The reason for

---

4. The sea can be symbolic of chaotic powers hostile to God (Hartley, *Job*, 171). God has subdued everything that stands in opposition to Him.

5. Robert Fyall, *How Does God Treat His Friends?* (Ross-shire: Christian Focus, 1995), 65.

6. Fyall, *Creation and Evil in the Book of Job*, 61. He points out that by the use of Rahab in 9:13 Job is aware of the supernatural forces at work in his situation, but the friends are not aware of such forces.

this pessimism is that God is behind his suffering. God is the one who crushes Job and multiplies his wounds without cause. Job attributes his shortness of breath and his bitterness to God (v. 18). No one can contend with the power of God and no one can summon God to court. Job makes a final plea of his innocence even though it is a useless plea. He fears that before God his own mouth would condemn him and that God would find him guilty (vv. 20-21). Job has no escape, so he vents his hatred for life. The conviction of his own moral purity does not help the sense of meaninglessness he feels because of his suffering.[7]

The next move in Job's argument is significant because he questions the justice and character of God. Job attacks the view of the friends that the righteous are blessed and the wicked are punished by arguing that God treats both of them the same. It does not matter if a person is blameless or wicked because God destroys both the blameless and the wicked (v. 22). It does not matter if a person is blameless because premature, sudden death may still overtake him. When an innocent person dies young, God is mocking him. Wickedness rules the world because God makes the judges blind to righteousness and allows them to exploit the poor and weak. The final question drives the point home: 'if it is not he, who then is it?' If there is only one God, then God must be the cause of injustice.[8]

Job reflects on what the lack of justice in God means for his own life. Job is living a miserable life. His meaningless days pass by swiftly (9:25-26). He has no pleasure in life as there is no good in his life. Job uses several illustrations to show that his life has no purpose. A runner, or courier, is able to endure the run because of the goal before him. A fast boat usually has a destination and an eagle reaches great speed in swooping down on its prey. Job's days are moving by fast but there is no purpose to them or hope that they will end well.

Job could try to change his response (9:27-28). He could put away his complaint, put off his sad face, and try to be happy, but his suffering is so overwhelming that he is not able to

---

7. Hartley, *Job*, 177.

8. Ibid., 178.

make such a superficial change. The reality of his suffering convinces him that God will not find him innocent. Job realizes that his illness makes it look like God is punishing him for some wrong he has committed. His situation is hopeless and there is no possibility of change. His effort to overcome this perception of guilt is doomed to fail because in the end he will be condemned. Even if he would wash himself with snow or lye there would be no change in his situation because God would put him back in the pit where he would become dirty again. Even his clothes would abhor him. Garments in the Old Testament are often associated with a person's moral quality (Job 8:22; Isa. 52:1; 61:10). Jerusalem's desolate condition after her destruction is lamented as a lady clothed in filthy skirts that bears witness to her sin (Lam. 1:8-9).[9] Job's filthy garments would be another indication to people that he deserved his suffering even if he is innocent.

The Need for an Arbiter

Job feels hopeless because he perceives that there is a great barrier between himself and God. Job has already explained earlier in the chapter (9:1-16) that he feels that he will never get an opportunity to present his case before God because God is God and not a human being (9:32-35). Job thus needs someone to come between himself and God to bring them together. He seeks an arbiter who could put his hand on them both and be a mediator between them. This one would take the rod of God away from Job, which would also take away from Job the dread that he has of God.[10] He is not able to speak without being terrified of God. This fear is not because he is losing conviction of his innocence but it is due to the perceived anger of God against him.[11] Job would be fine if God acted toward him in right and not in might. An arbiter

---

9. Hartley, *Job*, 181.

10. Hartley (*Job*, 182) points out that the word for 'rod' (*šēḇeṭ*) is used for a shepherd's staff. God as a shepherd has a staff that can be a comfort for God's people (Ps. 23:4), but it can also be an instrument of punishment (Lam. 3:1; Isa. 10:5; Prov. 22:8). Thinking about God's staff in this way fills Job with dismay.

11. The last line of 9:35 can be translated: 'for I am not so in myself.' Clines (*Job 1–20*, 243) argues that the most straightforward reading of this text is that Job is not aware of anything about his life that should make him afraid of God if God would treat him with justice instead of might.

would help to bring this about. If the rod would be removed, Job could defend himself, free from emotional outbursts and wild accusations.[12]

Job's Lament (Job 10:1-22)

When Job sees little hope of clearing himself before God he laments the horrible nature of his affliction. He asserts that he will speak freely out of the bitterness of his soul. He begins the lament with the words, 'I loathe my life' (v. 1). He appeals to God not to condemn him and to explain to him why He is against him (v. 2). He ponders whether God enjoys[13] sending such affliction in order to despise the work of His own hands and to allow the wicked to prosper (v. 3). In verses 4-5 Job asks questions that probe whether God is any different than a human being. Does God see as a human being sees? Is God limited by time like humans are limited by time?[14]

God seems to be no different than flawed human beings who are limited and misjudge things because of their partial perspective. Such limited human methods cause God to continue to seek and search for his sin. If God would just act like God, He would know that Job is not guilty. It is not possible, however, for Job to escape God's hand. There is no one to deliver him, so he feels trapped by God in his suffering, with no way to relieve himself of his affliction.

Job understands that God is not really limited because God is the one who fashioned and made him (vv. 8-12). There is a personal nature to this relationship which alludes to the way God fashioned Adam in the garden. The very hands of God formed Job from the dust of the ground. Job's conception is described by comparing it to the production of cheese which congeals into a soft substance like an embryo.[15] This substance receives its form from God who clothed Job with

---

12. Hartley, *Job*, 182.

13. The Hebrew *ṭôḇ* ('good') is used here in the sense of pleasure or delight.

14. G. Wilson, *Job*, 102. He understands these verses to be emphasizing that because God is so different from human beings He cannot understand or identify with their suffering. The view argued in this commentary is a little different.

15. The milk may be a reference to semen which is poured into the womb and congeals into a substance that represents the embryo (Hartley, *Job*, 187 and Longman, *Job*, 178).

skin and flesh and knit him together with bones and sinews. Job's very life has come from God Himself. Does it make sense then that God would destroy what He has formed and that He would return Job to the dust through his suffering? But more than life, God has also given to Job His steadfast love, and God's care has preserved Job's spirit (v. 12). Job could be acknowledging that at least God has kept him alive and he has not yet died because of his suffering. And yet, in the context of other statements Job makes in the debate (7:17-19) and in light of the words that follow from Job's mouth, these words are not positive words.

God has preserved Job's spirit so that He can keep close watch on Job's life (10:13-18). There are certain things that God has hidden in His heart that relate to His purposes for Job's life. It is likely that these things include the trials that Job is experiencing.[16] But the reason God has preserved Job's spirit is so that He can keep close watch on his life. Job's perception is that God is looking for sin in his life. Hypothetically, if Job sins, God does not acquit him but continues to watch him.[17] If Job is really guilty, it will be bad for him. But even if God does not find any sin and Job is in the right, it does not really matter. Even then he cannot lift up his head because of his disgrace and affliction.[18] Job's suffering, regardless of whether he has sinned, makes him look like he is guilty. And if Job's head were lifted up, God would make sure it was beaten down again. He would do this in several ways: He would hunt Job down like a lion; He would work wonders against him; He would bring new witnesses against him;[19] He would increase His vexation against Job; and He would bring fresh troops against him. All of this seems like overkill just to keep Job mired in his suffering.

Job ends his lament with thoughts of death (10:18-22). He wonders why he was born. He wishes he had died before he

---

16. Hartley, *Job*, 188.

17. G. Wilson, *Job*, 108. He comments that the statements 'If I sin' and 'If I am guilty' are hypothetical conjectures which are not meant to be a confession of sin.

18. Lifting up the head is a gesture of confidence while a lowered head expresses shame and humiliation (Hartley, *Job*, 189).

19. The new witnesses are not specified. Longman (*Job*, 180) suggests the witnesses may be the friends of Job, while Hartley (*Job*, 190) suggests that each new complication in his illness serves as a witness of his guilt.

came out of the womb. He would have gone from the womb
to the tomb and would have been considered as non-existent.
But that did not happen. Job, however, does feel like his life
is close to the grave. He does not have many days left. He
wishes that God would leave him alone for a few moments
so that he could experience a little cheer before his life is
over. The grave is a place of no return. The place where he is
going is described as a place of darkness without any order.
Job piles up words that emphasize darkness. It is so dark
there that any light is as the darkness. Darkness and disorder
are characteristics of a life devoid of God's presence. God is
light and He is a God of order. In one sense Job is already
experiencing the absence of God because of the disorder that
suffering has brought into his life.

False Perceptions in Suffering

Several issues are raised by Job in this response. Bildad
emphasizes God's justice, but Job questions God's justice in
light of his suffering. The fact of God's sovereignty and that
He is the source of all the events in life is not the problem.
The problem is that Job does not distinguish between God as
the ultimate cause of events and secondary causes.[20] Chapters
1–2 have established God's sovereignty over the suffering in
Job's life, but Satan was the immediate, secondary cause of his
suffering. By not recognizing this distinction Job accuses God
of injustice. God does not mock the calamity of the innocent.
He does not gladly let them vainly cry for help, or struggle
hopelessly until they die, as if He enjoys their suffering. God
does not make the judges blind to injustice (9:22-24). If judges
are blind to injustice it is because of their own wickedness.
God does not make them do wickedness. Although one can
understand Job's frustration, he crosses the line by calling
into question God's justice.[21]

Job feels strongly the impossibility of presenting his case
before God and so he calls for an arbiter that would be able
to bring them together. He needs someone who can lay hands

---

20. WCF 3:1, see note 10 on page 26.

21. Andersen (*Job*, 94) denies that Job's speech crosses the line. This view
makes a difference in the way he interprets certain passages in the book and in the
way he perceives the second response of Job to God (42:1-6).

on both himself and God (9:33). The desire for someone to act on Job's behalf will grow as the debate moves on (16:19 and 19:25-27). There is no hint as to who could act as an arbiter for Job. It is interesting that the Greek translation of the Old Testament translates 'arbiter' with the word *mesites*. This word is used in 1 Timothy 2:5 in reference to Christ as our mediator, 'For there is one God, and there is one mediator between God and men, the man Christ Jesus.' Christ is able to fulfill this role in a unique way. He is a human being so He can sympathize with Job's suffering (Heb. 4:14), but since He is also God He is able to bridge the gap between human beings and God. In a general way He bridges the gap by removing the barrier of sin through His death on the cross. Job's sacrifices in chapter 1 show that he understands the necessity of substitutionary atonement for sin. In a specific way Jesus intercedes for His people by bringing their specific concerns before the throne in heaven. Jesus is exactly the one that Job needs. His words are a testimony to the later work of Christ.

Job also struggles with the fact that suffering brings with it the appearance of sin. Part of the reason Job feels so trapped by his suffering is that it gives the perception that he has done something wrong to bring about his suffering. Perception many times trumps reality. Many wondered how Jesus could be the Son of God and suffer death on a cross. Many today wonder how someone can experience great suffering and also be a child of God. Suffering is never easy but having the example of Jesus helps. He taught His disciples when they confronted a blind man that his blindness was not due to any specific sin but so that the works of God might be displayed in him (John 9:1-7). Jesus rejects the particular connection between sin and suffering.[22] He also reminded His disciples that those who follow Him would suffer persecution (John 15:20). Suffering is not something any one desires but it should be expected to some degree by followers of Christ. This does not make suffering any easier but it does give a perspective that goes beyond the horizon of this life.

22. D. A. Carson, *The Gospel According to John* (Grand Rapids: Eerdmans, 1991), 361-62.

Nothing in Life is Certain but His Mercies are New Every Morning

Nik and I were able to get a few winks tonight. Before drifting off, we said goodnight to Pierce and really just prayed/trusted that God was going to stabilize his levels. It's hard as a mother to not obsess about every little number (at this point, they're all bad because his organs are so underdeveloped) and to lose sight of who it is that is sustaining Pierce. But we went to bed, and God granted us assurance that He was going to grant our request for sleep. And He did. We just checked in on the baby and he is doing better! His levels are slowly creeping down and we have confidence that this is God's hand at work. The neo-natal team has been in a holding pattern, unable to do any kind of intervention (they explained that every level was so out of whack that they couldn't probably treat one without terribly affecting another). But we are so relieved and find that God is answering our prayers for a quiet night.

Our prayer for the day (sometimes these requests will change on an hourly basis) is that God continues to allow Pierce to take a few small steps forward. Today will be a very, very difficult day for us as I will most likely be discharged. I'm so dreading the moment we have to step out of this hospital and leave him, but again, God is gracious. He has proved to us, over and over again, that He is holding/protecting our baby. Our need is that you be in fervent prayer today for us and Pierce.

Also, I know many of you have asked to visit and while we so appreciate the caring, familiar faces and we hope to see and visit with many of you in time, we just ask for privacy today while we try to absorb and process what is going on. We truly feel so loved by so many and God is using every one of you and your encouraging words to lift us up. Please keep the encouragements coming! And know that it feeds our souls.

Thank you for showing us love. And thank you for lifting Pierce up in prayer. It is our heart's desire that, through our pain, God will be glorified. Cling to him. And let our story serve as a reminder that NOTHING in life is certain. Nothing is in your control. All we have in this life is the hope of the Gospel.

We will keep you posted!

Lindsay Franks (4/15/11)

Study Questions

1) Why does Job feel it is impossible to present his case before God?

2) Why does Job question the justice of God?

3) How would an arbiter help Job? How does Jesus Christ meet Job's need for an arbiter?

4) What does Job lament in chapter 10? In what ways does Job wrestle with his perception of God in his lament? How would Christ help with the perception?

5) What does Job teach about suffering and perception? Have you experienced this in your life?

7

Zophar: Interpreter of God's Ways in the World

(Job 11)

Zophar is the third friend to respond to Job. He does not appeal to revelation or to tradition but sets forth an argument of reasoned theology[1] based on the proposition that God's blessing follows obedience and that suffering is a consequence of sin. Zophar is the most antagonistic toward Job in the first round of speeches. He begins his speech with accusations and insults directed at Job. He characterizes Job's words in negative ways. Job speaks a multitude of words and he is full of talk. Many words are an indication that Job is not speaking words of wisdom because a man of understanding speaks with restraint (Prov. 10:19; 17:27).[2] His words are also described as 'babble' and as having the impact of mocking others (11:3). He accuses Job of claiming that his doctrine is pure and that he is clean in the eyes of God (11:4). Job has claimed that he is innocent in chapters 9–10 (9:20-21; 10:7). The word 'doctrine' is used in wisdom literature for teaching or instruction (Prov. 1:5; 4:2; 9:9; 16:21, 23). Job has not claimed to be instructing anyone but has acknowledged that he speaks rash words because of his suffering (6:3). In

---

1. Hartley (*Job*, 193) uses this term.
2. G. Wilson, *Job*, 112.

response, Zophar shows little empathy for Job's suffering.[3] He is more concerned to put Job in his place because if no one answers Job then his words will seem to be right.

In the next section Zophar brings God into the discussion and makes some very pointed remarks to Job about his situation (11:5-12). Zophar has a strong desire that God would speak to Job to show him the secrets of wisdom because he is manifold in understanding. This would put Job in his place by showing him that his punishment is less than he really deserves.[4] This fact must mean that Job has sinned in a greater way than he can imagine. Zophar then asks Job several rhetorical questions concerning the deep things of God (v. 7). It is impossible to discover the limits of God's understanding. It is higher than heaven and deeper than Sheol. There is nothing Job can do or know that can plumb the depths of God's wisdom. Nothing that God does can be turned back. He may imprison or He may summon the court to meet, but He acts in wisdom. It is impossible to escape God's gaze, for He knows worthless men and He will deal with iniquity when He sees it. The implication is that He has seen Job's iniquity and is dealing with it through his suffering. Job is too stupid to understand this and there is little hope that he will change. The stupidity of Job might change when a wild donkey's colt is born a man. In other words, it is hopeless for Job to continue to assert his innocence. Zophar still seems to believe there is hope for Job because he spends the rest of the chapter trying to get him to repent.[5]

The final section of Zophar's first speech is a call for Job to repent so that he can experience the blessings of restoration (11:13-20). He begins with a couple of 'if' statements in verses 13-14 followed by the conclusion ('then') that takes up most of the rest of the chapter. Job should prepare his heart and stretch out his hands toward God (v. 13). The verb 'prepare'

---

3. Clines, *Job 1–20*, 260.

4. The Hebrew of the last clause of 11:6 reads, 'know that God has forgotten some of your guilt.' The point is that God is punishing Job for only part of his wrongdoing, not all of it. This means Job has sinned beyond the extent of his suffering (Longman, *Job*, 187).

5. G. Wilson, *Job*, 118.

(*kwn*) can mean 'to establish' or 'be stable' and can be used in the sense of 'devote' or 'make firm'. The phrase 'prepare your heart' is used in 1 Samuel 7:3 as part of the plea for the people to repent from their idols and serve God only. The phrase is also used in parallel with the concept of trusting God in Psalms 78:8, 37 and 112:7. The spreading out of Job's hands would indicate a changed inner attitude of supplication to God. Also, if there is iniquity in Job's hand or injustice in his tents, he should remove them. In other words, Job should repent of his sin so he can be restored.

The results of restoration ('surely then' in v. 15) are re-counted in verses 15-19. Restoration includes a return of his dignity. When Zophar says that the blemish will be removed, he is probably referring to Job's suffering and the possible disfigurement from his illness.[6] With an end to Job's suffering he can lift up his face again. His confidence will be restored.[7] Job will forget the memory of his suffering and his life will become bright again (vv. 16–17). He will feel secure because his fears will be taken away (v. 15), probably a reference to his dread of God. He will also feel secure because hope will return (v. 18). He will lie down in peace.[8] Many people will again seek Job's wisdom. Repentance could open the flood-gates of blessing for Job.

The speech of Zophar ends with a statement concerning the wicked (v. 20). Those who do not repent will have a horrible end. They will suffer physically, they will experience hopelessness, and they will long for death as their only escape. In many ways Zophar paints the wicked in ways that Job himself has experienced. Job has felt lost and has longed for death. Zophar paints Job as wicked to try to encourage him to repent of his wickedness.

Zophar is confident that he understands how God works in the world and that he can explain it to Job. He is more concerned with proving his opinions than trying

---

6. G. Wilson, *Job*, 119.

7. Longman, *Job*, 190.

8. Hartley (*Job*, 202–203) notes that the verb 'lie down' (*rābaṣ*) is frequently used with sheep (Isa. 17:2). Zophar is directly countering Job's complaint that God is hunting him like a lion (10:16) with the promise that God will lead and protect him like a shepherd.

to understand Job. When a person hurts, their hurt is real regardless of the reasons behind the hurt. Zophar gets caught up in the reasons for the hurt rather than listening to the hurt that Job feels. And so he seeks to interpret the ways of God for Job's life. He offers Job little comfort except for the elaborate picture of the peaceful security of repentant sinners. He believes in the inscrutability of God. God's ways are incomprehensible and so Job should quit questioning God about His ways and submit himself to his suffering. God's ways are full of mystery and Zophar uses that mystery as a cover for exploring what he perceives as the arrogance of Job's verbosity. Zophar thinks he knows the deep things of God. The only way Zophar knows to defend God's justice is to condemn Job. It is hard to have a conversation with someone who does not know how to listen, who always wants to correct you, and who thinks he knows what God is doing in your life.

Staying Strong in the Darkness

The next few days are crucial for Pierce. Right now, he has enough potassium in his body to stop his heart. Because of the need to regulate many other factors in his little body, there is no way for them to bring it down manually at this time. His sodium is high too. Continue to pray for him, for it is working. His electrolytes are only one of many hurdles he is going to have to go through over the next few days. God is good, we have faith as we sit in this darkness…

Pierce is staying stable despite still having high levels of potassium and sodium. They are slowly getting lower, so that is good, but he is still at high risk. The doctor has been surprised that his potassium has been this high for so long and nothing has happened. So, God is good. In fact, Pierce's lungs are getting better which is a major aspect of his recovery. We trust Him to sustain Pierce. We have a great peace in this present darkness. Again, thank you for all the prayers. Keep praying. God is going to bring glory to His name.

Nik and Lindsay Franks (4/14/11, 4/15/11)

Study Questions

1) What is the heart of Zophar's argument (his reasoned theology)? How does this come across in his speech to Job?

2) Why does Zophar want God to speak to Job?

3) What is Zophar's answer to Job's suffering? Why is that not the right answer? In what ways are you guilty of the same presumption in dealing with others?

8

Job: No Help from Friends or God

(Job 12–14)

Job's response to Zophar, which also includes the other friends, is the longest response so far. It includes two complaints against the friends (12:1-12 and 13:1-12) and a reflection concerning God's sovereign rule (13:12-25). Job's second complaint against the friends is followed by a resolve to pursue his complaint directly with God Himself. The friends have been no help, so his only hope is to argue his case before God (13:18–14:22). Job expresses both futility concerning his situation and remarkable assertions of confidence in God.[1]

The Friends' Theology Goes Against Common Experience (Job 12:1-12)

The first complaint against the friends argues that their doctrine of retribution theology is not validated by experience. Job begins the complaint with sarcasm and scorn directed toward the friends.[2] They think that they are the only ones who possess wisdom, but on the contrary, Job is not inferior to them in wisdom. In fact, everyone knows the things they have

---

1. Hartley, *Job*, 241.

2. Daniel J. Estes, *Handbook on the Wisdom Books and Psalms* (Grand Rapids: Baker, 2005), 63.

been asserting. Their views contain nothing extraordinary, new, or profound. They certainly have not offered Job any insight into his suffering.[3]

Job offers several reasons why their explanation of his suffering falls short. He first appeals to his experience (12:4-6). Job used to have a relationship with God and was considered a just and blameless man, but now he is a laughingstock to people. Those who are at ease have contempt for misfortune and they think it only comes to those whose feet slip in some way. This is why they think Job is suffering because of sin. But the reality is that the tents of the robbers are at ease. Those who provoke God are the ones who are secure.[4] In other words, Job is saying that the blameless may be the ones who are suffering and the wicked may be the ones who are experiencing the good things of life. The view of the friends is easily challenged by the experiences of life.

Job also appeals to the animals to argue that even if the friends could ask them about suffering they would agree that the hand of the Lord is behind the anomalies of this world. It is not clear how speaking to the animals would produce an answer. Job may be referring to the fact that wisdom can be gained by examining God's creation because He created the world through wisdom (Prov. 3:19-20; 6:6-8).[5] In light of the sarcasm at the beginning of this chapter, Job could be saying that the wisdom of the friends does not even surpass that of the beasts of the earth, for even the animals know that God's hand is involved in the prosperity of the wicked and the suffering of the righteous.[6] The life of every living thing and the breath of every person are in the hand of God (v. 10). This means that God is sovereign over what happens to everyone who lives on the earth. God's sovereignty over human life should be as obvious as the relationship between the ear and words, between the mouth and food, and between wisdom and the aged. Apparently the friends have not understood what should be obvious.

---

3. Hartley, *Job*, 206.

4. The last clause of 12:6 is difficult. It could be referring to idolatry, to the fact that the gods in their hands are their swords, or to the view that they think themselves to be as powerful as God (Hartley, *Job*, 208).

5. Longman, *Job*, 201.

6. Hartley, *Job*, 209.

God's Destructive Sovereign Power
(Job 12:13-25)

Job demonstrates in this section that God is sovereign over every living person on the earth. He exercises His sovereignty with both wisdom and might so that no one can hinder His actions in the world. If He tears down, no one can rebuild. If He imprisons a person, no one can free that person (v. 14). He can withhold the waters so the land is dry or He can send too much water to flood the land (v. 15). No human being can stand against Him because of His strength and sound wisdom. His wisdom overpowers both the deceived and the deceiver (v. 16).

The other examples given of God's sovereignty show His control over the powerful. He diminishes the wisdom of the court by leading counselors (advisors to the court) away from the court stripped of their dignity and by making the judges into fools (v. 17). God removes the power of kings so that their authority is reduced to nothing (v. 18). The religious leaders, the priests, are not secure even though they deal with things that pertain to the deity. God brings them down (v. 19). The elders are associated with discernment and understanding, but age is no guarantee of wisdom if God takes away their discernment (v. 20). The powerful princes lose their strength and the chiefs of the people lose their way (v. 21). God is sovereign over the light and darkness of creation and He is sovereign over the nations of the earth. He is able to make a nation great or destroy a large nation (v. 22). No power on earth can stand against the power and wisdom of the sovereign God of the universe.

Job rejects the basic argument of the friends. The examples that Job gives shows the destructive power of God at work against the mighty of the earth without any apparent reason.[7] Certainly the world is more complicated than the view of the friends. The combination of wisdom and power creates an aspect of mystery to the events in the world.[8] The implication is that the reason for his own trouble resides with God, not

---

7. Longman, *Job*, 203. The emphasis on God's destructive power is how Job perceives God's power and wisdom in relationship to his life.

8. G. Wilson, *Job*, 129.

with himself. This makes it all the more necessary for Job to settle the complaint he has with God.[9]

The Worthless Arguments of the Friends
(Job 13:1-12)

Job continues his complaint against the friends in 13:1-12 by attacking their arguments against him. He is frustrated with his relationship to the friends because of his apparent inferior position to them. He specifically tells them, 'I am not inferior to you' (v. 2).[10] He is in the same position as they are because his eye has seen it all and his ear has understood it. Thus he knows what they know. The arguments of the friends have not been helpful, so he concludes his only option is to present his case before God (v. 3).

Job first of all characterizes their arguments as morally deficient (vv. 4-5). Their views are lies that whitewash the truth by denying his innocence.[11] The friends are compared to a worthless physician because their words do not help the patient but only make him worse. It would be better if the friends had continued in their silence and had not opened their mouth to speak. They would then be considered wise. Of course, the best course for fools is to keep quiet (Prov. 17:28). These comments are a strong indictment against the arguments of the friends.

Job then charges the friends as speaking falsely on behalf of God (vv. 6-12). They are misrepresenting God by speaking deceitfully. They have not really heard the pleading of Job, who speaks from his suffering, but have assumed certain things to be true about Job. It is dangerous to claim to speak for God when your words are false. God's wisdom can differentiate truth from error and He cannot be deceived by anyone. They should be terrified of God's majesty, and dread should consume them because of the rebuke that will come to those who argue falsely.[12] They have condemned Job not on the basis of evidence

---

9. Hartley, *Job*, 212.

10. The 'you' in this verse is plural referring to the friends.

11. G. Wilson, *Job*, 136.

12. Job accuses the friends of showing partiality toward God and pleading the case for God (13:8). In the context of this chapter this refers to presenting a false argument on behalf of God by distorting God's position.

but only to protect God's reputation.[13] The friends do not have a leg to stand on because their wisdom is fleeting (proverbs of ashes) and their defenses have no substance (defenses of clay). Job is sitting on the ash-heap and his life seems to be insignificant, but the reality is that the arguments of the friends will crumble because they lack substance.[14]

Job's Plea for God to Hear His Case (Job 13:13-22)

The worthless arguments of the friends give Job resolve to continue his pursuit of a hearing before God (13:13-17). He has already expressed this desire in verse 4 and now he tells the friends that he will present his case to God regardless of the consequences. He asks them to remain silent so he can speak without interruption. He is willing to put his life in danger and risk instant death in challenging God to hear his complaint.[15] In a moment of confidence Job expresses the assurance that such a hearing before God could lead to his salvation because the godless do not appear before God. He calls on the friends to listen carefully to what he is going to say when he addresses God (v. 17).

An Affirmation of Perseverance

Before discussing Job's plea with God to hear his case, the translation and meaning of 13:15a needs to be examined. The traditional translation, represented by the ESV, is 'Though he slay me, I will hope in him.'[16] This is a strong affirmation of faith by Job in a context where he could lose his life by speaking to God. The difficulty of this translation is that it is not based on what is written in the Hebrew text (called the Ketiv), but is based on what the scribes would read when they read the text (called the Qere). The difference between the two is the difference between 'to him' (*lô*, לוֹ) and 'not' (*lō*ʾ, לֹא). The other translation options all use the negative 'not'. The RSV translates the verse as an affirmation

---

13. Estes, *Handbook*, 66.

14. Hartley, *Job*, 221.

15. Ibid., 222.

16. See also the KJV, NKJV, NAS, and NIV (1984).

of resignation, 'Behold he will slay me, I have no hope.'
Hartley translates it as an affirmation of uncertainty, 'If he
were to slay me, I would have no hope.'[17] Finally, Habel
translates it as an affirmation of perseverance, 'Yes, though
he slay me, I will not wait.'[18]

The least likely translation is the affirmation of resignation
because Job expresses the hope in verse 16 that 'this will be
my salvation'. The affirmation of uncertainty would fit the
context better as Job moves from a position that he will speak
regardless of the consequences (v. 13) to the strong statement
of the hope of salvation (v. 16). The affirmation of faith could
work in the context as a strong affirmation of the hope he
has even if God slays him.[19] The best option may be the
affirmation of perseverance because it fits the context well. In
verse 13 Job requests silence so he can speak regardless of the
consequences. Verse 14 is difficult but Job seems to be saying
that he is willing to risk his own life by speaking.[20] Job asserts
again in the second half of verse 15 his determination to argue
his case before God. Job's resolve to speak regardless of the
consequences fits in with the first clause in verse 15, 'Though
he slay me.' The debate concerns the nature of the second
clause. Does Job express the hopelessness of resignation, or
of uncertainty, or does he express hope that his seeking a
hearing with God will end well? In light of verse 16 it seems
that Job is expressing hope that the ordeal will end with his
salvation. Thus his hope is in God (affirmation of faith) or he
will not wait to speak because he knows the end product is
his salvation (affirmation of perseverance).

Prepared to Meet God
Job reacts strongly to the friends' mockery and he decides his
only recourse is to argue his own case before God. Job begins

---

17. Hartley, *Job*, 221.

18. Habel, *Job*, 224. The meaning 'wait' is well-attested for the verb *yāḥal*.

19. The fact that the affirmation of faith is based on what is read (the Qere 'in
him') is a negative factor against this translation.

20. Hartley (*Job*, 222) points out that the phrase 'put my life in my hand' is used
in passages where a person is willing to risk his own life in engaging an enemy
mightier than himself (Judg. 12:3; 1 Sam. 19:5). The statement in v. 15 could be
seen as an answer to the questions in v. 14 explaining why Job should take this risk.

by stating that he is ready to meet with God (13:18-22). He has prepared his case and he knows that he is in the right. He does not believe anyone can present arguments that would destroy his case; otherwise he would be silent and die. He requests that God would grant two things to him so that he can speak more freely with God. He wants God to withdraw His hand from him and he wants to be free from the terrifying dread that he has for God. If these two requests are granted, the lines of communication will open up between Job and God. God can call to Job and He will answer, or Job can speak to God and God will reply.

If Job and God are able to speak to each other, several issues can be resolved. Job raises the issue of his sin (v. 23). If Job is suffering because of sins he has committed, then God must list those sins as the basis of the punishment Job is experiencing. If God cannot reveal to him the wrongs he has committed, then he is guilty of inflicting punishment that Job does not deserve.[21] Job also raises the issue of the adversarial relationship that exists between them. He asks God why He hides His face and treats him like an enemy (v. 24). This stance toward Job does not make sense, as expressed in the questions of verse 25. These questions express that a driven leaf does not need to be frightened and dry chaff does not need to be pursued. Job is already experiencing fear and being chased by God in a negative way. The reason he feels this way is because God has not treated him fairly. God has decreed bitter things against Job.[22] God has brought upon Job consequences from the iniquities of his youth. If young people do foolish things during the period of growing to maturity (Prov. 22:15), it seems unfair to bring forward those sins against them. Plus, what must Job have done during his youth to deserve such suffering? God has also treated him like a criminal by putting him in the stocks. God has restricted Job and hedged him in

---

21. Hartley, *Job*, 227. Longman (*Job*, 210) argues that Job believes that he has not sinned and so he is calling God's bluff.

22. The bitter things that God has written against Job are understood by many as God's formal charges that are not made public (Habel, *Job*, 232). Hartley takes it as a contract that God has filled with bitter stipulations (*Job*, 228). God has not written formal charges against Job but He has decreed these events to come into Job's life. The statement is best understood as what God has providentially decreed for Job's life.

by limiting the paths he could take. Job feels trapped in his situation with no way to escape as long as God is against him. He is wasting away like a rotten thing, like a garment that is moth-eaten.

The Nature of Human Life (Job 14:1-22)
In chapter 14 Job turns his attention away from his own suffering to the general condition of human suffering (vv. 1-6). The life of a human being is short and full of trouble. Human beings are like flowers that quickly wither in the heat after a spring rain or they are like a shadow that quickly vanishes. It does not seem fair for God to pay so much attention to human beings whose lives are so short. If humanity is so powerless, why must God keep everyone under constant surveillance and bring such frail ones into judgment?[23] There are certain things that cannot be changed, such as the weakness of human beings born of a woman. Childbirth also brings uncleanness because of the discharge of blood (Lev. 12:1-8). It is impossible for a child to be born clean. The days of human beings are so determined by God that they also cannot be changed. The proper response of God to the general suffering of human beings would be to leave them alone so that they might experience some joy during the fleeting days of life. Job compares this situation to a hired hand that works hard but then is able to rest. Job does not feel that he has had any opportunity to rest because God is constantly watching his life (Job 7:16-19).

More Hope for a Tree than a Man
Job then compares the life of a man with the life of a tree (vv. 7-12). If a tree is cut down, there is hope that it will sprout again. Even if the root lays dormant in the soil and the stump dies, water will cause its shoots to bud and it will put out

---

23. Hartley, *Job*, 231. The ESV and the NKJV translate Job 14:3b as 'and bring me into judgment with you'. The pronoun 'me' seems to be out of place in this passage. The Septuagint reads 'him'. Hartley notes that the writing of a *y* ('me') for a *w* ('him') is a frequent scribal error. And yet, the pronoun 'me' is the more difficult reading. It is easier to understand a scribe changing 'me' to 'him' than the other way around. It is possible to retain 'me' because Job's plight is the plight of humanity and he frequently goes back-and-forth between his own situation and that of all human beings (Clines, *Job 1–20*, 283).

branches like a young plant. Such hope does not exist even for a man of strength and virility. The death of a man is compared to a lake or a river drying up. One way to understand this comparison is that, just as it is impossible for a large body of water or a river to completely dry up, so it is impossible for a man to awake from death.[24] Another option is that this illustration is teaching that when humans die it is as though they are like water that has evaporated because they will remain dead forever.[25] The point of the illustration is the impossibility of human beings to come back from the dead. Humans stay dead until the heavens are no more, which is virtually forever.[26]

In light of the impossibility of being raised from the dead, Job wishes that he could be hidden for a while until God's wrath was past. He actually asks to be hidden in Sheol, the place of the dead, until a set time when God would remember Job again. Job acknowledges God's wrath as the cause of his suffering and that His wrath is only for a short period of time (Isa. 54:8).[27] If resurrection is not possible, then Job is seeking a hiding place in Sheol until God's anger is over. Job is willing to wait out the days of his undeserved suffering ('the days of his service') until his renewal comes. The renewal Job has in mind is a renewal in this life, before death would cut off his life completely. In fact, Job uses the same concept about himself in verse 14 as he used of the plant in verse 7.[28] He too will 'sprout again'. God will eventually desire to re-establish His relationship with Job, the work of His hands. God will call and Job will come out of hiding. Although the interpretation of verses 16-17 is debated, the best way to understand them is to view them as continuing Job's thinking about his renewal.[29]

---

24. Hartley, *Job*, 234 and G. Wilson, *Job*, 153.

25. Clines (*Job 1–20*, 329) understands the comparison to be with water that evaporates, not the lake or river which might fill up again.

26. Ibid., 330.

27. Hartley, *Job*, 246.

28. In v. 7 the verb is used (*ḥālap̄*) and in v. 14 the noun form is used (*ḥalîp̄āh*).

29. The meaning partly depends on how the phrase at the beginning of verse 16, *ki-attah* (כִּי אַתָּה), is translated. These verses are either a continuation of Job's thinking about his renewal ('for then') or they signal that Job has returned to lament his suffering ('but now'). The latter view is taken by Hartley (*Job*, 237-38) who argues that God continues to afflict Job unceasingly. This view must omit the negative in

A more normal relationship with God will be established. God would number Job's steps, which in a normal relationship with God would refer to God's protection and care, not God's scrupulous attention. There would also be a different relationship between Job's sin and God's treatment of him. God would not hold Job's sin against him but would hinder the impact of his sin by sealing it up in a bag or by covering it over.

Hope Destroyed

Job's hope for a different relationship with God comes crashing back to reality with the 'But' of verse 18 where Job turns his attention to the terrors of death (vv. 18-22). God destroys any hope of renewal for mankind by comparing that hope to mountains falling and torrents of water washing away the soil of the earth. Human hope may begin strong but over time it can be eroded by suffering until that hope is gone.[30] God's power is so great that He easily overpowers a human being and sends him away to the realm of the dead where a person's countenance changes. Once in Sheol a person is not aware of any other events happening on the earth. He is oblivious concerning whether his sons succeed or fail in life. His whole existence is centered on himself. The pain of his body overwhelms him so that it is hard to attend to anything other than mourning his own situation.[31]

Job's reflections in these chapters reach the highest point of confidence and the lowest depths of despair. He rejects the counsel of the friends and turns to God with hope that he will be delivered if he can present his case to Him. Yet, that hope of renewal erodes away in light of his suffering that seems to have no end. Such mood changes are not unusual in a person who is suffering greatly.

---

the Hebrew text of v. 16 to read, 'you would keep watch over my sin,' instead of 'you would <u>not</u> keep watch over my sin'.

30. Longman, *Job*, 215. Hartley (*Job*, 239) states that 'Job expresses his fearful thoughts by reciting hymnic lines that recount God's awesome power as manifested in natural catastrophes'.

31. G. Wilson (*Job*, 158) notes that descriptions describing pain and mourning on the part of the dead are highly unusual so that v. 22 is probably referring to what occurs before death.

Job's speech brings to an end the first cycle of speeches (Job 3–14). Job addresses God in his speeches in the first cycle in 7:12, 17–21; 10:3-14; and 13:23-27. His address to God comes at the end of his speeches as if he has to work up the courage to speak to God directly. Job's direct address to God significantly decreases in the second cycle of speeches, perhaps because Job receives no reply from God.[32] There are still strong statements of confidence in the second and third cycles, along with the desire for a fair hearing. He also wrestles with his relationship with God. Suffering has a way of removing hope from a person's perspective, especially if God seems to be distant. Job's hope has been ground into dust by the reality of his suffering. And yet, there will still be flashes of confident hope that break through the darkness of suffering. Christ, in a greater way, wrestled with the darkness of despair in the garden of Gethsemane as He faced the intensity of the suffering of crucifixion and bearing the sin of His people. For a short period of time it looked like He received no help from His disciples (Matt. 26:56, 69-75) nor from God (Mark 15:34; Luke 23:35). And yet, He was heard by His Father and was resurrected to new life. Job eventually hears from God, and all who suffer have the assurance that they too will receive help from God (Ps. 27:1). This hope is even greater in light of the victory of Christ over sin, suffering, and, death (Rom. 8:38).

Confident Hope

We said goodbye to Pierce today and drove off around 3 o'clock this afternoon. I can't even begin to describe the feeling of pain and anguish that you feel when leaving your sick child behind. BUT we want you to know that God has been so gracious. He granted us the strength we needed to physically get out the door (and trust me, there were many moments where we didn't think we could walk one more foot away from his bedside). God has filled our hearts with so much hope, and we trust that He is going to bring Pierce through this. I know we

---

32. Dale Patrick, 'Job's Address of God,' ZAW 91 (1979): 270.

are beginning to sound like a broken record, but we have
been SO lifted up and encouraged by the power of your
prayers. We know that God is using every one of them
to minister to us during this dark time. We are thankful
for the peace He has granted deep down in our soul. We
know that He is the creator and sustainer of life and that
He is our hope.

Love to you all,
Lindsay Franks (4/15/11)

Study Questions

1) How does Job argue from experience against the theology of the friends? How easy would it be to disprove their view from your experience?

2) How does the mystery of God's sovereignty bring comfort to Job?

3) How does Job characterize the arguments of the friends? Why should the friends be concerned?

4) What are the different ways to understand Job 13:15a? What seems to be the best way to understand this verse in context?

5) How can a person like Job express both despair and confidence?

6) How does Christ's experience parallel Job's experience?

9

Eliphaz: Wisdom Destroyed and the Wicked Depicted
(Job 15)

The second cycle of speeches begins. Each of the friends will have a second speech and Job will respond to each of them. This speech of Eliphaz can be divided into two main sections. The first section rejects Job's claim to wisdom (15:1-16) and the second section lays out the woes of the wicked (15:17-35). In Eliphaz' first speech (Job 4–5) he was characterized as a counselor who missed the mark because what he said was generally true but it did not apply to Job's situation. In this second speech, he digs in his heels and continues to miss the mark, but in a way that is more confrontational.

Rejecting Job's Claim to Wisdom (Job 15:1-16)
Eliphaz goes back and forth between rhetorical questions and definitive statements as a way to ridicule Job's position. The first set of rhetorical questions comes in verses 2-3, followed by statements in verses 4-6. These questions expect a 'no' answer. Job's words are again compared with wind. If a person is truly wise he will not answer with 'windy knowledge' and his belly will not be filled with the hot air of the east wind that blows off the desert.[1] A wise person also does not use

---

1. Hartley, *Job*, 244.

words that are unprofitable and useless. And yet, Job is doing this very thing. His words are not the words of someone who fears God and they hinder a relationship with God. Eliphaz repudiates his statement in his first speech that the confidence of Job should be his fear of God (4:6) because he does not believe that Job has any fear of God. Eliphaz does not believe that he is condemning Job because his own words condemn him. Job's words are not the words of a wise man but are words that are deceitful and full of iniquity.

The second set of rhetorical questions comes in verses 7-9 followed by the statement in verse 10. The questions make the point that Eliphaz wants to make and overshadow the brief statement of verse 10. Eliphaz may be responding to Job's claim that his wisdom is not inferior to the friends' wisdom. The questions raise doubts about Job's source of wisdom. If Job was the first man who was ever born, then he could claim a special source of wisdom due to his relationship with God (v. 7). If Job existed before God created the world (v. 7), then he could claim a unique position to acquire wisdom, perhaps even like Woman Wisdom herself (Prov. 8:22-31). If he had access to the council of God like the prophets, then he could claim divine inspiration (v. 8). If none of the above conditions are true, then Job has no advantage over the friends and should not limit wisdom to himself over against them. Eliphaz claims that they know what Job knows (v. 9). The wisdom of the friends is represented by the wealth of wisdom of the aged, who are older than Job's father. Job has no basis to make any claim to wisdom that is greater than the friends. It is ironic that Eliphaz mentions access to the council of God, a situation that the readers of the book have had the privilege of viewing in the first two chapters. They understand that Job is not suffering because of his sin. Eliphaz is speaking of things that he does not know about.

The final set of rhetorical questions is given in verses 11-14 followed by statements by Eliphaz in verses 15-16. The point seems to be that Job does not really appreciate how God has treated him. In verse 11 'the comforts of God' and 'the word that deals gently with you' are in parallel (v. 11). Eliphaz has in view here the consoling advice of the friends which Job has rejected. He questions Job concerning why he would reject such good counsel that comes from God. Of course, Job has not understood the words of the friends as very comforting. Instead, Job has reacted with anger ('your eyes flash') and a heart that moves him further away from God (v. 12). His words show that he has turned away from God. He has become so caught up in his suffering that he has become angry at God and so acts as estranged from God.

Eliphaz reminds Job of the impossibility of being righteous before God with the question, 'What is man, that he can be pure?' This question begins with a familiar query that is identical in Psalm 8:5 and Job 7:17: 'What is man, that...' It is interesting that Eliphaz does not use the question to set forth the exalted position of mankind, as in Psalm 8, but rather he uses the question to introduce the corruption of humanity. Instead of being a little lower than the angels, human beings are much lower than the angels because of their wickedness. The angels' position is not all that good because God does not trust them in light of the impurity of the world. The position of human beings is even worse because they are abominable, corrupt, and drink injustice like water.

These statements take away any possibility of Job's standing before God and his claims to wisdom. Eliphaz could have set forth the exalted position of humanity, as in Psalm 8, as a way to encourage Job to live according to his exalted position. Instead, Eliphaz takes away any hope that Job can have a relationship with God if he continues to speak such arrogant words. In fact, Eliphaz may be speaking directly to Job as the one who is abominable and corrupt in verse 16.[2]

The message of 15:15-16 is similar to Eliphaz' earlier advice in 4:17-19. The similarities include rhetorical questions concerning whether a person can be pure, statements concerning the difficult relationship between God and angels, and a comparison between angels and humans as a way to show the impossibility of a person being pure before God. The difference is that in Job 15 the corrupt nature of human beings is emphasized more than in Job 4.[3] The purpose is to destroy Job's statements of his innocence.

---

2. Habel, *Job*, 256.

3. Habel (*Job*, 255) states that in 4:17-19 the emphasis was on the inferiority and imperfection of mortals made from clay and in 15:14-16 the focus is on the inner impulses that characterize human beings.

An Instruction about the Woes of the Wicked
(Job 15:17-35)

In this section Eliphaz paints a graphic description of the suffering of the wicked. The purpose of this description is to get Job to see himself in the portrait so that he can own up to his wickedness and receive relief from his suffering. Eliphaz introduces the description with an exhortation for Job to listen to his words because what Eliphaz has observed in the world is in accord with the teaching of wise men (vv. 17-19). It is an ancient tradition going back to the fathers[4] when they lived in a land without outside influence to contaminate the teaching.[5] Job should trust what Eliphaz is going to say because it is reliable and he should abandon his own position of innocence.

Eliphaz lays out the sorrows of a wicked man in verses 20-24. He is also identified as a ruthless person, someone who has no compassion and does not care about the pain of others. He experiences his own pain as a constant companion that accompanies him to the end of his life. He is never at peace because he thinks he hears terrifying sounds. Even in prosperity he fears that what he has will be destroyed. He lives with a terrible sense of dread because of the possibility of violent death that awaits him (v. 22, 'marked for the sword') and that will plunge him into never-ending darkness. He lives with a sense of daily doom that overpowers the regular activities of life, such as eating bread. He knows that his end is near and faces life with a sense of terror similar to a king who is preparing for battle. Never able to relax, he has no inner tranquility.[6]

The reason the wicked person lives with such dread and terror is that he lives in defiance of God (vv. 25-26). He runs stubbornly against God with the false sense of being

---

4. The ESV translation, 'what wise men have told, without hiding it from their fathers,' is a literal translation of the Hebrew, but it is hard to know what this means. Other translations omit 'from' and make 'fathers' the subject (Hartley, Longman) or translate the verse in a different way (KJV, NIV).

5. Hartley, *Job*, 251. Longman (*Job*, 227-28) understands v. 19b to mean that no person or situation remains enigmatic to the wise men because they are able to diagnose people's situations.

6. The last sentence is inspired by Hartley, Job, 251.

protected by a shield in battle. The wicked live with a false
sense of security and a false sense of wealth (vv. 27-30). His
presumptuous lifestyle and appearance of health (v. 27,
'fat') conceal the fact that his life is degenerating like the
degradation of cities that will be desolate, or houses that
will not be inhabited but will become part of the garbage
pile. His wealth and possessions will not endure, darkness
will be his constant companion, and he will not be able to
escape the judgment of God. In verse 31 the wicked man is
exhorted not to deceive himself by trusting in futile efforts
directed to a false end[7] because such emptiness will be his
full payment even before he dies. His life will not flourish
but will be like a branch that does not become green, a vine
with grapes that do not ripen, and an olive tree that loses
its blossom. The lives of the godless are barren. The bribes
they use to get ahead will be consumed by fire. The wicked
have no future because they conceive trouble and give birth
to evil.

Eliphaz is so intent on winning the argument with Job
that he does not consider that maybe his counsel to Job is
wrong. Even if Eliphaz is correct in his view of the situation,
instead of digging in his heels he could have tried to change
his approach to Job. His argument is similar to his first
speech, but now he is stronger in his confrontation of Job
and does not hold out hope as in the prior speech. The direct
attack on Job by Eliphaz can be seen in the correspondences
between Job's condition and the description of the fate of
the wicked. These include the mention of fire that consumes
(vv. 30, 34), marauders that attack (v. 21), possessions that are
taken away (v. 29), and houses that crumble (v. 28). Eliphaz'
mechanical view of the deed-consequence relationship must
also impact his view of God. There is nothing in his words
that would indicate that God has any love for sinful human
beings. God sees to it that sinners get paid in full.[8] A false,
mechanical view of how the world works combined with a
false understanding of a person's situation easily leads to a
false view of God.

7. Habel (*Job*, 260) defines emptiness this way.
8. Smick, 'Job,' 4:772.

Still Fighting

Pierce is amazingly three days old today. He was born at 7:42 on Tuesday night. The Lord has sustained him thus far and we pray that He will tonight. His blood pressure is dropping and they are using dopamine to keep it up. I ask you to pray for his heart. Pray that the Lord keeps him strong. He needs to be touched all over, but his heart and his blood pressure are the biggest concern right now. He belongs to the Lord and he is in the Lord's hands. (4/15/11)

Pierce's levels seem to being doing well, relatively speaking of course. His blood pressure has gotten better and with a little bit more improvement they will start weaning him off the dopamine. This is really miraculous! Lindsay's boss is a doctor here at CMC and a good friend of ours is a nurse here. When we told them what Pierce's potassium level was last night they were shocked. Our friend is a strong believer and she started crying because she knew that it was God. Thank you for your prayers. Lindsay and I truly have a peace that surpasses all understanding. Through this, God has made the Gospel more real to us than ever before. In and of ourselves, we don't deserve the incredible grace of your prayers, the peace, and the fact that Pierce is still alive. But, in Jesus, God madly, ferociously, incomprehensibly loves us; unworthy as we are. And He is proving that every second. I myself have never felt the presence of Jesus more powerfully than I have in this trial. Pierce is God's child, he belongs to the Lord. I am so exhausted right now and I do not have time to tell you about all the graces that God has given us since we have been here, but they are numerous towards us and towards Pierce.

Nik and Lindsay Franks (4/16/11)

Study Questions

1) Compare Eliphaz' approach in this speech with his first speech (Job 4–5).

2) How does Eliphaz make the case that Job's wisdom is not superior to their wisdom?

3) What is the significance of the phrase, 'what is man, that...' and how does Eliphaz use the phrase?

4) How does Eliphaz depict the life of the wicked? What is the purpose of this description?

5) According to Eliphaz, what robs wicked men of 'inner tranquility'? Is he right?

6) What clouds Eliphaz' concern for Job? How should this caution our conversations with others? How should Eliphaz' confidence instruct us?

10

Job: Hope in the Midst of Despair
A Heavenly Witness
(Job 16–17)

This section records Job's second response to Eliphaz and it is his fourth response overall. He continues to struggle with his relationship to the friends and with his relationship to God. A level of hope is expressed in this speech but Job also drops back into despair over his situation. He is not able to move to a firm position of hope but has flashes of insight about his suffering that brings encouragement before descending into the abyss again. Job sees no help coming from the friends and little help coming from God. His expressions of hope come in those moments when he sees more clearly the character of God who will not condemn the innocent.

Miserable Comforters (Job 16:1–6)

Job begins his response by telling his friends that they are miserable comforters. The more they speak, the more pain Job feels.[1] There are several things that make them miserable comforters. What they are telling Job is nothing exceptional because he has heard many such arguments before (v. 1). There is nothing special or unique about their counsel that would make Job think that it comes from God. On the contrary, their

---

1. Hartley, *Job*, 257.

words are full of wind (v. 2). Perhaps one could understand why Job's words are rash and windy in light of the extent of his suffering (Job 15:2), but the friends have no excuse for uttering windy words. Something has provoked them (the 'you' of v. 3 is plural) to answer Job with such arguments. Their many words are an indication of their irritation with him.[2] No doubt the friends have been upset with Job's questioning of God's justice and of affirming his own innocence. The reader knows from Job 1–2 that Job is correct about his innocence. Of course, he is wrong about God's justice. This makes it difficult to sort out the arguments because both Job and the friends do not have all the truth in their analysis of the situation. None of them has wisdom to answer this dilemma.

Job wonders what would happen if their places were reversed. How would he speak to them if they were the ones suffering? He envisions that it would be easy to speak to them as they have spoken to him (v. 4). He could be a miserable comforter by speaking against them and by expressing his contempt for them through the shaking of his head. But he also contemplates a different approach (v. 5). Job would use his words to strengthen the one suffering and to try and relieve the pain. Job understands what it is like to suffer and knows what would bring comfort to the one who is afflicted. But in his current situation, it does not really matter whether he speaks or whether he remains quiet (v. 6). If he speaks, the pain does not go away, and if he remains quiet, the suffering continues. In light of the following speech, it is clear that Job chooses to continue speaking because he perceives he does not have much to lose either way. He is in a no-win situation.[3]

A Personal Lament against God as the Enemy (Job 16:7-17)
Job perceives God as his enemy because he believes that God is ultimately behind all the factors that contribute to his suffering. He begins with a general statement that God has worn him out (v. 7). Job is completely exhausted because he has no relief and always feels the affliction of his suffering.

2. Longman, *Job*, 236.

3. Longman (*Job*, 237) uses the phrase 'no-win situation'.

His closest relatives and friends offer him no relief because they also experience desolation because of his situation (v. 7). Also, the ungodly treat Job with contempt (v. 10) because God has given Job over to them (v. 11). The wicked are shocked at Job's suffering and use it to their advantage to torment him while he is down. In this way God is aiding the wicked instead of judging them.[4] God is the one who has brought on Job's illness (v. 8). Job's miserable physical condition is a witness against him because everyone concludes that he has sinned in some way to bring on his sickness. No one believes what Job says because his own body is a witness against him.[5] God is the one who has set Job up as His target, surrounding him with archers, who mortally wound him (vv. 12b-13). Job enjoyed life until God suddenly seized him and dashed him to pieces (v. 12a). Job is the enemy whom God pursues as His prey and against whom God wages war (vv. 9, 14).

The impact of God's relentless attacks on Job is expressed in verses 15-16. Job has mourned for so long that sackcloth, a sign of mourning, seems to be his permanent clothing.[6] The mention of Job's skin also reminds the reader of the horrible nature of his illness. Perhaps he also used sackcloth to cover the loathsome sores, the running pus, and the damage that scraping his skin has caused (Job 2:7-8). Job has run out of strength to keep fighting against God. The word translated 'strength' is the Hebrew word for 'horn' and paints the picture of a wounded animal languishing in defeat[7] (a victorious animal would raise up its head and horn). His face is red because of his weeping and dark shadows surround his sunken eyes. His situation is hopeless even though he has not done anything wrong (v. 17). He has not committed violence and his prayers are pure.

The Heavenly Witness (Job 16:18-22)
It is amazing how hope can burst forth from despair for no reason. Nothing in Job's situation has changed and yet in

---

4. Hartley, *Job*, 261.
5. Habel, *Job*, 271.
6. Lindsay Wilson, *Job* (Grand Rapids: Eerdmans, 2015), 97.
7. Hartley, *Job*, 262.

this section Job expresses hope that his testimony would not go unnoticed and that he has a witness in heaven. In verse 18 Job utters an exhortation that his cry for justice would be heard. His 'my cry' parallels 'my blood' in the first part of the verse. Blood that is unjustly spilled cries from the ground for justice and that is what Job hopes takes place. Like an innocent victim of murder, he petitions the earth not to cover his blood, for he does not want his cries to cease until they have been answered (Gen. 4:10).[8] Job also proclaims that he has someone even now in heaven who will come to his defense and testify on his behalf. He calls this person 'my witness' (v. 19).

The translation of verse 20 is disputed. The NIV (1984) translates as, 'My intercessor is my friend as my eyes pour out tears to God.' This translation identifies the witness in heaven with Job's intercessor who is also Job's friend. The role of the intercessor is then given in verse 21: 'on behalf of a man he pleads with God as one pleads for a friend.' The other way that verse 20 is translated is represented by the ESV: 'My friends scorn me; my eye pours out tears to God, that he would argue the case of a man with God, as a son of man does with his neighbor' (vv. 20-21). Job needs this heavenly witness because his friends are not speaking on his behalf but are scorning him. One of the questions in the ESV translation is the antecedent to the pronoun 'he' in verse 21 ('that he would argue the case of a man with God'). It could refer to the heavenly witness but the immediate antecedent is God. The NAS translates verse 21 as an exclamation: 'O that a man might plead with God as a man with his neighbor!' This puts the emphasis back on Job's desire to plead his case before God. Regardless of the way verses 20-21 are translated, the urgency of the situation is expressed in verse 22 as Job faces the prospect of death. And yet, Job has enough confidence that he wants there to be a continuing witness even after he has died. He even believes he has a witness who now exists in heaven who will speak up for him.

The major question of this passage is the identification of Job's heavenly witness. Several suggestions have been made

8. Hartley, *Job*, 263.

by commentators. One view is that this heavenly witness does not exist. Job may long for a heavenly witness but he realizes that such a witness does not exist.[9] He is a flight of faith[10] or a hypothetical figure whom Job longs for wishfully because of his pain.[11] Such a view does not take into account the growing confidence of Job, even in the midst of despair, that he will be heard by God.

Another view is that the heavenly witness is one of the angels. The one heavenly being that knows Job's situation and could serve as a witness is the adversary ('satan') who interacts with God in Job 1–2. This view would emphasize that the word 'satan' means adversary and that the negative connotations about this figure from later Scripture should not be read into this text.[12] It is hard to conceive that Satan would become Job's witness in light of the negative portrayal of his character in Job 1–2 and in the rest of Scripture.

A third view is that Job's heavenly witness is his own cry or affirmation of innocence. The 'even now' of 16:19 links it to the preceding verse which suggests that it is Job's restless cry that is personified as his witness in heaven.[13] By addressing heaven Job has ensured that the truth of his innocence is on record there as a perpetual witness to his character.[14] If one takes 9:33, 16:19, and 19:23-27 together, Job seems to have in view a person as his witness and not just his words.[15]

A final view is that the heavenly witness is God Himself. This view has been called extremely awkward because the witness would need to speak against God in support of Job.[16] If God is the witness, then God would be speaking against

---

9. Longman, *Job*, 240.

10. Habel, *Job*, 276.

11. L. Wilson, *Job*, 98.

12. Michael Oblath, 'Job's Advocate: A Tempting Suggestion,' *BBR* 9 (1999): 189-201.

13. C. L. Seow, *Job 1–21* (Grand Rapids: Eerdmans, 2013), 739.

14. Clines, *Job 1–20*, 390.

15. Hywel R. Jones, *Job* (Darlington: Evangelical Press, 2007), 141. He argues that the Hebrew word for 'cry' in v. 18 is feminine and the one who is to argue Job's case as witness in v. 21 is masculine, which makes the identification of the two difficult.

16. Longman, *Job*, 239.

God. This view fits with Job's vacillation between confidence in God and despair with the way God is treating him. There are times when Job sees God as his enemy, but there are increasing instances where Job responds with confidence that he will be vindicated by God. Job is not really pitting God against God but he is affirming genuine confidence in God regardless of the way it appears God is treating him.[17]

A Personal Lament (Job 17:1-16)

Job's lament is full of despair with little glimpses of hope. His despair is related to the way he is being treated by others and the glimmers of hope come when he contemplates briefly what God could do and that the righteous will prevail. Job begins with despair over his situation (vv. 1-2). The grave is waiting for him because his spirit is broken and his days are extinct. It is only a matter of time before death overtakes him. The reason his spirit is broken is because he is surrounded by those who mock him. Their constant provocation is taking its toll. It must be difficult to be innocent and to be continually told that you have done something very wicked to bring on such intense suffering.

God is even behind the mockers because He has closed their hearts to understanding. In some way, this gives Job hope because if the friends are wrong in their arguments God will not allow them to triumph. Job views the friends as driven by self-interest (v. 5), which will lead to negative consequences for them. Job requests that God would lay down a pledge for him (v. 3) because such a pledge is not forthcoming from any other source, especially from the friends.[18] Job has another moment of despair when he recognizes that God has made him a byword of the peoples (v. 6).[19] In other words, Job has become a proverb, or an example, of someone who has

---

17. Hartley, *Job*, 264.

18. Both Hartley (*Job*, 266) and Clines (*Job 1–20*, 373) take the nifal verb in the second half of 17:3 as expressing permission. Clines translates 17:3b as 'for there is no one who will stand surety for me'. The implication based on 17:3a is that God is the only one who can do it. Hartley also argues that this verse is evidence that God is the heavenly witness spoken of in 16:19.

19. There is not universal agreement that the 'he' at the beginning of v. 6 refers to God. Some take it to refer to one of Job's friends.

brought suffering upon himself because of a great sin. People have shown their contempt for Job by spitting at him. Such treatment has caused Job great vexation that has made him very weak (v. 7).

Job next describes how someone should react to his situation of injustice, perhaps as a contrast to the way he is being treated by the friends. The upright would be appalled at his treatment and the innocent one would stir himself up against the godless (v. 8). The one who is righteous should not give in to the mistreatment of others but should hold on to his way. This would allow one who has clean hands to grow stronger and stronger. Such a response would bring great encouragement to Job. He knows he will not receive such comfort from his friends. He challenges them to continue to take their best shot at him and to display their lack of wisdom (v. 10). One wonders if Job is describing himself as the one who is innocent in verse 8. Even without such encouragement there are times that Job is convinced, against all appearances, that his situation will turn around because he is innocent. The hope that right will win may grow very dim, but the embers continue to smolder and at times glow strong.

Despair descends on Job once more when he contemplates the reality of his situation (vv. 11-16). He is resigned to the fact that his life is broken, that all his plans and desires are dashed, and that his best days are behind him. Everything is turned upside down and inside out. Job does not share the optimism of the friends who argue that his fortune will be turned to good before he dies if he responds appropriately. They see the turning of his night into day and so believe that light is nearer than darkness.[20] Job, however, sees in his future only the certainty of death, which means that his hope to be vindicated is fading fast. Job wonders if he should embrace death and begin to look at Sheol as his true home. Should he hope for it and accept it by calling the pit 'his father' and the worms that will decay his body as 'my mother or my sister'? If he becomes resigned to death, then he will lose all hope

---

20. Hartley, *Job*, 270. Habel (*Job*, 278) understands the statements about light and darkness in v. 12 as describing the hope in his heart, which Bildad will twist in the next speech.

because it will go to the grave with him. Hope is synonymous with life and can have no existence in Sheol.[21]

Several issues are raised by Job in this section. Job sees his friends as miserable comforters not just based on what they say to him but also based on how they have treated him. The miserable comforter takes no account of the existential situation of the one who is suffering. Job vacillates between despair and hope and so his words are not always consistent. A good comforter tries to understand the condition and emotional state of the sufferer in order to be able to show empathy toward the one suffering. This can be done by imagining what it would be like to be in the situation of the one suffering. Such empathy should lead to sympathy toward the sufferer. If the friends would consider what it would be like to be in Job's situation, they would show more kindness toward him. Jesus Christ can sympathize with our weakness because He did more than just think about what it would be like to be in our situation. He actually became a human being and experienced the temptations, hardship, and suffering of the human condition. He even died an excruciating death on the cross for our salvation. We can, therefore, draw near to the throne with confidence to receive mercy and find grace in our time of need.

The view that God is Job's heavenly witness raises the possible problem that God is called as a witness against Himself. If Job sees God as the source of his suffering, then how can God be his heavenly witness who will come to his aid? This view is not as awkward as some think. Hartley points out that the drama of redemption centers around the tension between God's justice, that is sometimes expressed in wrath toward sinful man, and His love that reaches out to redeem that same sinful man.[22] In the Psalter and in Lamentations the very same God who strikes is the one who delivers (Pss. 6:9-10; 38:22) and in whom one hopes (Lam. 3:21–5:22). God as a witness against God culminates in the cross of Christ where the Son of God, who is God Himself, pleads the cause of His people with God His Father. God the Son becomes a witness on behalf of His

---

21. Hartley, *Job*, 271.

22. Hartley, *Job*, 264.

people with God the Father. Job did not fully comprehend this teaching, but at times his confidence in God led him to believe that God would eventually make things right even if Job did not know how this would happen. We need to have the same confidence in God as we experience suffering.

Completely Broken

Friends, I don't even know how we had the strength to walk back to our room, but we feel God's mighty strength in the midst of our weakness. This morning has been the biggest set-back yet. Since 6:30 this morning, we have begged and pleaded with our God to perform a miracle. We faced many hard decisions and were told right away that there was no hope. They hoped Pierce would make it long enough for us to get to the NICU (our room is about three minutes away). They hoped he'd be alive long enough for us to hold him. The staff had pretty much given up.

There is no way to describe the feeling of helplessness that you have as you are being told that there is no more hope. I wish I could say that I trusted all of the trite Christian things that I so often seem to carry with me, but in that moment, I didn't. Christ brought us to a point of humility today where we learned that regardless of how little or big our faith is, He is the only sovereign, all-powerful one. Not us. Not the doctors.

Before making our decision to hold little Pierce (this seemed like giving up to us), our doctor told us that outside of a miracle there was nothing more that could be done. No more options. Nothing. So we got him out, held him and grieved. But we couldn't stop praying that God would grant him more time with us. I prayed that if God was going to take him, that He would not let him linger or suffer. We expected imminent death. BUT our God is gracious. And Pierce is still with us.

He is, in fact, doing better. While we were holding him, his potassium dropped, his glucose rose (he needed a higher glucose reading to receive insulin to help with the potassium), and he seemed content. We held him for what seemed like a few seconds (of course it wasn't long enough) and over the course of the last few hours, we have held a constant vigil by his side. We see God working. He did not take Pierce this morning. For that, we are so grateful. Pray we make the right decisions. And pray, most importantly, for Pierce. We are so heartbroken right now, and we are just abiding in Christ as He is our only hope.

Love,

Lindsay Franks (4/16/11)

Study Questions

1) Is Job's wavering between hope and despair instructive for the psychology of suffering? If so, how should this inform our expectations in counseling others?

2) What makes the friends into miserable comforters (see also the end of the chapter)? What can we learn about how we should respond to suffering from the friends?

3) Why does Job perceive God as his enemy?

4) What are the various views of the identity of the heavenly messenger?

5) What is the source of Job's despair and Job's hope?

6) What is the difficulty of identifying the heavenly witness with God? How can that difficulty be answered?

11

Bildad: A Diatribe on the Fate of the Wicked

(Job 18)

Although interaction between Job and Bildad continues, the dialogue decreases and angry attacks directed at each other increase. Bildad offers little hope for Job because he wants to persuade him that his questioning of God is wrong and will have bad consequences. The horrible fate of the wicked is what awaits Job if he does not change his ways and repent.[1]

A Complaint against Job (Job 18:1-4)

Bildad, in his complaint against Job, first comments about the argument that Job has been making. Job does not comprehend what Bildad is saying because he is continually hunting for words to express himself. This is evidence that he has deviated from the traditional view which is well-known to everyone and that instead he is trying to justify himself with other arguments. Job should consider the situation and listen to what the friends are saying.

Bildad also addresses Job's attitude toward the friends. He perceives that Job regards them as stupid, even as dumb as animals. Bildad may be reacting to what Job said in

---

1. Hartley, *Job*, 272.

12:7, where he responded to Bildad's comment to ask the ancient generation for teaching (8:8-10), with the statement that he should ask the beasts to teach him.[2] This leads to the conclusion that the friends do not understand Job's situation because they keep setting forth the same old arguments.

Further, Bildad sees Job as torn apart by anger, which can cause someone to lash out at others. It could also be further evidence of his guilt. He certainly thinks Job has become self-absorbed as if the earth should be shaken on his account. Job's desire to be acquitted of any wrong doing without repentance would overthrow the normal way the universe operates just for the sake of one man. Bildad thinks this is a ludicrous position.

The Terrible Fate of the Wicked (Job 18:5-21)

The fate of the wicked is described in several ways by Bildad but he ends his speech with a description of the horrible end of the wicked. The demise of the wicked is described by use of the concept of light (vv. 5–6). Two proverbs show the present condition of the wicked: the first uses plural forms and states a general truth (v. 5); and the second uses singular forms to apply the teaching of the proverb to Job (v. 6). The light of the wicked is put out so that the flame of his fire does not shine. The result of this is that the wicked exists in darkness. His whole life is enveloped in darkness. If light is symbolic of life (3:20), wealth (22:28), and happiness, then darkness represents loss (15:30), sadness, and death (3:5).[3]

The path of the wicked is difficult because he walks into traps (vv. 7-12). A major metaphor for life found in wisdom literature is the 'path'. The wise person walks on straight, smooth paths that lead to life, but the wicked person walks on crooked paths that are filled with trouble.[4] The wicked person falls into traps that are the product of his own schemes. Thus, he stumbles in life. His strong steps are shortened (v. 7) and are not secure (v 8). The word translated 'mesh' is also

---

2. Habel, *Job*, 284–285. He also shows other possible allusions to Job's previous speeches in Bildad's speech.

3. Hartley, *Job*, 275.

4. Longman, *Job*, 250.

used for branches spread over a pit. The wicked thinks he is walking on firm ground but he will fall into a pit.[5] The wicked are trapped suddenly and unexpectedly. Such traps cause the wicked to live in constant terror, which frightens him on every side and continues to pursue him (v. 11). The wicked person lives in terror throughout his life, in fear of the calamity that can bring him down. This takes away his vigor for living (v. 12).

Bildad's speech ends by describing the demise and death of the wicked (vv. 13-21). Death itself begins to do its work on the physical well-being of the wicked. When Bildad says that part of the skin is consumed, it is hard not to make the connection to Job's illness (see the description in chapter 1). The wicked person loses his place of security and is brought face-to-face with death itself (the king of terrors). He loses his place in society when his roots dry up and his branches wither; he loses his vitality and becomes like a dead tree. If the roots of the tree dry up, there is no hope of life springing again from the roots. Bildad removes the earlier hope expressed by Job in 14:7 where a tree that is cut down still has hope of life sprouting again from the roots. The memory of the wicked perishes from the earth so that he has no lasting heritage or posterity. He is plunged into darkness and all those who see his demise are seized with horror. Such an end is what all the wicked should expect to happen eventually to them because they are unrighteous and do not know God.

The friends consistently fall back on a couple of arguments in their case against Job. They offer descriptions of the fate of the wicked to try to get Job to see his suffering as that which the wicked deserve. Eliphaz has already presented such a picture in 15:17-35. He focuses on the mental worries of the wicked and Bildad focuses more on their outward troubles, but the similarities to Job's situation seem clear.[6]

Bildad also emphasizes that the wicked are entrapped by their own schemes (18:7). This is a common teaching in wisdom literature, as expressed in Proverbs 26:27: 'Whoever digs a pit will fall into it, and a stone will come back on him who starts

---

5. Hartley, *Job*, 276.

6. Andersen, *Job*, 187, 190.

it rolling.' This proverb teaches that certain actions may lead to certain consequences. Generally, the proverbs teach that if a person lives a wise life he or she will experience blessings, and if a person lives a wicked life, he or she will experience negative consequences. There is a general relationship between what a person does and the consequences that he experiences in life. This is called the deed-consequence relationship or divine retribution. A problem develops in understanding this relationship if someone argues that there is a mechanical relationship between the deed and consequence, whether that grows naturally out of the deed-consequence relationship or whether God is the one who brings it about. This teaching can lead to the health and wealth gospel or to the teaching of the friends who argue that Job is suffering because of a sin that he committed. This teaching is behind the descriptions of the wicked that the friends put before Job.

A mechanical view of the deed-consequence relationship is a misunderstanding of how a proverb is supposed to work. Proverbs are short sayings, full of meaning, that are meant to set forth examples and principles of how life works in general. Proverbs are meant to be applied to life situations, but it takes wisdom to apply them. Normally, a single proverb is not meant to be universalized in order to apply it to all situations of life.[7] Proverbs are not able to lay out all the extenuating circumstances that might affect the application of a proverb. Even the book of Proverbs recognizes that there are extenuating circumstances in life that impact certain outcomes. Thus, not all poor people are lazy because there is injustice in the world (Prov. 13:23). The better-than proverbs are important for understanding that many of the blessings of life set forth in wisdom literature are not to be understood in an absolute sense. For example, Proverbs 16:8 states, 'Better is a little with righteousness than great revenues with injustice.' Wealth is not an absolute good but a relative good because there are other things more important than wealth. This means that wealth cannot be used as a standard to judge someone's

---

7. Proverbs that use the name of God in an absolute sense (not in a prepositional phrase) can be universalized because God is involved in the proverb (Prov. 11:20; 15:3, 8, 11, 29; 16:4; etc.).

wisdom or standing with God, and illness or trouble cannot be used to argue that someone has sinned.

A better way to approach the proverbs is to see most of them as dependently true sayings that present a slice of life. Generally, if someone lives a life of wisdom, he will experience the blessings set forth in the book of Proverbs. There are many factors in life, however, that might hinder a person from experiencing those blessings. Proverbs 12:21 states, 'No ill befalls the righteous, but the wicked are filled with trouble.' And yet, there are righteous people who suffer trouble and there are wicked people who experience ease and comfort. The solution to this common experience in life is not to argue that a person who is experiencing trouble is not righteous. In that case, not even Christ would be considered righteous. The solution is to understand how a proverb functions. Although proverbs are dependently true now, there is coming a day when these proverbs will be absolutely true for the righteous and wise person. Even in the Old Testament there is life and blessing associated with a relationship with God that goes beyond this life (Pss. 16:11; 49:15; Prov. 24:16[8]). Clearly there is no doubt about this in light of the resurrection of Christ. When Christ comes at the consummation no trouble will ever again befall the righteous but the wicked will be filled with many troubles. In this way, many of the proverbs will be ultimately true for the follower of Christ when the fullness of salvation is experienced in the new heavens and earth.

Ending the Fluff

The other day I was outside with my little boy. He had a tight grip on the 'flower' he had picked for me – a dandelion. I didn't have the heart to tell him it was only a weed. As he sat there studying the dandelion's intricacies, he rubbed it across his cheek, admiring its softness and beauty. There were talks of taking it inside and putting it in a vase. And then, out of nowhere came a giant gust of wind. He watched as the fluffy, white flowery top quickly

---

8. Waltke understands this verse as pointing to the ultimate rise of the believer in the resurrection (Bruce K. Waltke, *The Book of Proverbs: Chapters 15–31* [Grand Rapids: Eerdmans, 2005], 283).

disintegrated, disappearing into the wind. Later it dawned on me that our own theologies can be like that dandelion; they are fluffy and pretty, but do not stand a chance at weathering life's storms.

In college, I took a course on worldviews. The professor challenged almost everything I held to be true. 'Why do you believe the Bible to be true? Why Christianity over other world religions?' he asked. Question after question, the professor crushed my dandelion-like faith. I'd been a Christian for years and yet I couldn't give a basic defense of my faith. It didn't take me long to realize that the countless sermons I had heard, the Christian books I had read, and the Bible studies I had attended had consisted primarily of one thing: *fluff.*

Flash forward a decade. As I sit with a child who has crippling diagnoses, I've been forced again to wrestle through what I believe to be true. It has not been an easy road and there have been more struggles with the truth than resting in it. I'm going to go out on a limb here and believe that many of you can identify with this as you have your own struggles. For years, I've witnessed a large disconnect between the *real* lives – the doubts, pains, struggles and questions – of women I know and the ministry material readily available for them. Blogs, books and speakers that have soared in popularity within the church and yet leave their readers feeling spiritually malnourished. There's a prevailing thought that studying doctrine is something that happens in seminaries; it's boring and not relevant. Combine this assumption with our consumeristic church culture and you get what I have been fed for years and what a large majority of women's studies tend to focus on: *fluff.*

Fluff is pretty. It's emotionally engaging, with its clichés and personal stories and shallow truth statements neatly packaged for us to buy at wholesale. Fluff discourages deep thoughts and theological questions because those things threaten to unravel its pretty little facade.

Fluff relies on moralistic behaviorism, leading us to believe that if we just do more and try harder, God will love us more and things will finally be made right in our lives. Fluff focuses on what we can do instead of focusing on what Christ has done for us. It seeks glorification of self instead of glorification of Christ.

Fluff leads us to believe that the shallow doctrines it proclaims are the destination instead of the tip of the iceberg of our faith journey. Hear me when I say this: It's not that fluff doesn't, at times, have something good or true to say. But fluff only gives us a *microscope* to study God where a *telescope* is needed. Relying on fluff to grow your faith is like putting your toes in the ocean and thinking the whole sea is only that deep. If the power of a lie is how much truth you can pack into it, then isn't it worth considering if the Enemy is not doing exactly what he set out to do by sending teachers who feed us fluff? Yes, Satan sends teachers who offer just enough substance to keep us coming back for more, all the while distracting us from the real source of deep theological truth – the Bible.

And this is where it gets awkward, because we live in world that does not applaud you for saying something is objectively wrong. But what if we, as educated women, began praying for humble discernment when it comes to what teachers/teachings we listen to? What if we decided that we want to go deeper in our theologies, not out of moral obligation or a desire to improve ourselves, but simply because we want to know the One who is pursuing us? What would it look like for us to take the time to learn deep spiritual truths instead of being satisfied with mere rudimentary teachings? Let's go deeper. Let's not be afraid to ask the hard questions. Let's stop using clichés. And let's use our intelligent minds to think carefully about the world through a Biblical lens, letting the Bible guide our beliefs about what we know to be true.

Lindsay Franks (3/18/16)

Study Questions

1) How does Bildad's complaint against Job show the breakdown of the debate?

2) How does Bildad describe the life and death of the wicked?

3) What is the deed-consequence relationship and how do the friends misunderstand that relationship?

4) What is a contemporary misapplication or abuse of the 'deed-consequence' relationship found in some churches today?

5) What is a better way to understand the deed-consequence relationship? What does the phrase 'dependently true now but ultimately true' mean?

12

Job: Hope Born out of Frustration
(Job 19)

In this chapter Job vents his frustration concerning how he is being mistreated by everyone. Not only do the friends and God mistreat him, he also has estranged relationships with his brothers, his relatives, his close friends, his guests, his servants, and his wife. He is even despised by young children. No one has stood with Job, and yet, he is convinced that he has a kinsman redeemer who will come to his aid. He even expresses confidence that he will see God. Even though Job has expressed that God acts like his enemy, there is no one else who can bring about a change in his situation. This chapter has one of the strongest statements of hope in the book. It also closes with a strong warning against the friends.

Frustration with Friends (Job 19:1-6)
Job wonders how long the friends are going to keep torment-ing him with their arguments.[1] Their words have been like sledge-hammers that break rocks in pieces. Their arguments

---

1. Hartley, *Job*, 282. He notes that the pronouns are plural which indicates that Job is addressing all the friends, but that the 'How long' at the beginning of the speech is directed against Bildad who used the same words to begin his two previous speeches. G. Wilson (*Job*, 201) comments that the mutual escalation of frustration is evident in both parties.

have wounded Job deeply. He feels crushed emotionally by their words.[2] They are relentless in their attacks; they treat Job wrongly by criticizing him and expressing their disappointment with him and they feel no shame in their behavior. Even if hypothetically Job has erred in some way (v. 4), it is a matter between him and God, and does not rise to the level of importance that they have made it. Job wonders if the friends have used his situation to magnify themselves while at the same time putting him down in disgrace. If that is the case, the friends need to know that it is God who has put Job in the wrong ('$w\underline{t}$) and is the real cause behind his suffering. Job and the friends agree that God is treating him as an enemy, but the friends think that God is right in doing so, whereas Job believes he is being mistreated.[3] Job's words are a response to Bildad's words that God does not pervert ('$w\underline{t}$) justice (8:3). Job's suffering is out of proportion to any inadvertent wrong he may have committed.[4] He also has not fallen prey to his own folly (18:8) because God has entrapped him.

Frustration with God (Job 19:7-12)
Job here explains what he means when he says that God has put him in the wrong and has enclosed him with His net. He perceives God as his enemy, because he cries out to God, 'Violence,' a cry of someone in desperate need of help,[5] but is not answered. God does not seem concerned that Job is being mistreated. When Job calls for help, there is no justice. He uses justice in a judicial sense because he believes he has been wronged by God. God has also blocked Job's way and darkness covers his path (v. 8). Job is floundering to find direction and purpose in his life which seems to be going nowhere. God has stripped him of his dignity (v. 9)[6] and has

---

2. Longman, *Job*, 255.

3. L. Wilson, *Job*, 103.

4. Andrew E. Hill, שָׁגָה, *NIDOTTE*, 4:44. He comments that the verb *śḡh* (translated 'I have erred' in Job 19:4) can refer to the unintentional commission of wrongful acts or involuntary sin (1 Sam. 26:21; Lev. 4:13).

5. Hartley, *Job*, 285.

6. Two words from Job 19:9 are also used in Psalm 8:6. Instead of experiencing the exalted position of human beings in God's creation, which includes being

broken every aspect of his life so that he has nothing left. His hope is gone, uprooted like a tree (v. 10). Job feels God's wrath and believes that he is under attack from God and His armies. Like a city under siege Job is surrounded and cut off from the normal blessings of life (vv. 11–12).[7] When God is perceived as your enemy, there is little hope that help will eventually arrive. Job is left in hopeless despair.

Frustration with Family and Acquaintances (Job 19:13-20)
Job goes through a list of family and other acquaintances to show that he is being mistreated by everyone. The section begins with God's action of bringing about estrangement between Job and his brothers. The pronoun 'He' at the beginning of verse 13 refers to God, so that ultimately God is behind everyone turning against Job. The focus, however, is on the people whose relationship with Job has been destroyed. Job's brothers have grown distant from him so they no longer enjoy that brotherly relationship.[8] Job's trusted friends, those who knew him well, are estranged from him (v. 13). His relatives have abandoned him and his close friends have forgotten him (v. 14). It is difficult to keep in contact with someone whose situation does not get better because one is always being confronted with the suffering. The guests in Job's house, the very ones to whom he has shown hospitality, and the servants in his house, the ones he has employed, act like they do not know him. He is like a stranger or a foreigner who must degrade himself by pleading for mercy,[9] but is not heard (vv. 15-16). Job is even estranged from the closest of his family members. There is little intimacy with his wife because of his putrid breath, and his illness causes him to be a stench to his brothers and

---

crowned ('*āṭar*) with honor and glory (*kāḇôḏ*), God has stripped these from Job.

7. Habel (*Job*, 301) calls this 'divine overkill' because Job describes God setting siege ramps against his 'tent' (v. 12), which would be easy to destroy.

8. There is some debate whether the word 'brothers' refers to blood brothers (Hartley, *Job*, 288) or to members of his clan (Clines, *Job 1–20*, 446). There is a reference to blood brothers in v. 17, but there is also a possible reference to members of Job's clan in v. 14. There is no reason that each term must have a distinct meaning because there could be overlap between the terms.

9. Habel, *Job*, 299.

sisters.[10] Young children who are not normally bothered by
unusual sights despise Job and talk against him. Job states
again that those closest to him abhor him and the ones that
he loves have turned against him. This section closes with a
statement about his physical condition (v. 20). Even his body
has failed him. There is no place for consolation. It is the
world against Job, with no one standing with him to support
him. The fact that Job has been abandoned by everyone not
only leads to despair, but also makes him realize that there
is only one source from where help can come, even if that
source also seems to be against him.

The Hope of Vindication (Job 19:21-27)
Job appeals to the friends once again and then makes a strong
statement concerning the positive outcome in which his ordeal
will end. His plea to the friends is to show him mercy (vv. 21-22).
As Job argued in verses 1-6, the friends have wounded Job
deeply and have been relentless in their attacks. He pleads
for mercy because the hand of God has struck him. If God has
afflicted Job and pursued him, why do the friends feel that
it is necessary for them to do the same? Isn't God's affliction
sufficient? Why do they feel the need to make things worse
for Job? Shouldn't his physical suffering be enough for them?
Why do they have to add to his emotional pain by attacking
him? The friends are like scavenging animals surrounding the
carcass of the fallen prey, not able to get enough flesh.[11] When
Job pleads for mercy he is not asking for their pity, but he is
asking that they stop verbally persecuting him.[12]

Job expresses a strong desire that his words would be
written down in a way that they would be preserved for all
time. Not only does he want them inscribed in a book, but
he wants them to be engraved in the rock forever (vv. 23-24).

---

10. The phrase in 17b translated in the ESV as 'the children of my own mother'
literally reads in Hebrew as 'the sons of my womb'. Some think this refers to
Job's own children, but they have been killed in chapter 1. The best solution is to
understand this phrase as the sons born from the same womb as Job, that is, his
brothers (Clines, *Job 1–20*, 449).

11. G. Wilson, *Job*, 207.

12. The verb 'pursue' (*raḏap̄*) means to chase, hunt down, even persecute (see
the discussion of Clines, *Job 1–20*, 453-54).

There follows in verses 25-27 a strong statement of assurance that is described as 'a sudden onrush of confidence in a final resolution'.[13] Job is hopeful that things will turn out well for him. There are, however, many questions related to when the things for which he hopes will take place.

Job knows that his redeemer lives (v. 25). The word for redeemer is *gō'ēl*. This word usually refers to a close relative who is willing to act on the behalf of a person who finds himself in trouble. Such actions could include redeeming family property that has been sold due to financial hardship (Lev. 25:25), redeeming a family member who has had to sell himself to pay off a debt (Lev. 25:47-49), and avenging the blood of a family member who has been murdered (Num. 35:19). Later in Israel's history the role of a kinsman redeemer is broadened to include other things (Ruth 3–4 and Jer. 32). Yahweh is also portrayed as a *gō'ēl*. This word is used as a title in parts of Isaiah 40–66 to refer to Yahweh as the one who will redeem Israel from Babylon (43:14; 48:17). Yahweh also acts as a redeemer to defend His people (Prov. 23:10-11).[14]

Job's use of the word *gō'ēl* gives the expectation that he is referring to a close relative or to God. This fact throws doubt on views that argue that the redeemer is not a human being or God. Clines argues that Job's kinsman-champion is his cry of innocence which will go on speaking for him even after his death. This is the same as the witness of Job 16:19. His cry is personified as a witness, advocate, and spokesman on his behalf. Job's redeemer cannot be God because his dispute is with God. Job has even stated that he knows that God is his enemy (6:4; 13:24; 16:7-14; 19:7-12).[15] Job 19 has shown that Job is all alone and that he must rely upon himself. Job's anxious desire is that he should 'see' God enter the courtroom before his death to judge his case while he is still alive (vv. 26–27). But he does not think he will be vindicated before his death.[16]

---

13. Longman, *Job*, 260.

14. Robert L. Hubbard, Jr., גָּאַל, *NIDOTTE*, 1:789-93.

15. It is important to point out that the texts Clines cites where Job knows that God is his enemy do not use the first person singular of the verb 'to know' as does Job 19:25.

16. Clines, *Job 1–20*, 455-59. Michael D. Oblath, 'Job's Advocate: A Tempting Suggestion', *BBR* 9 (1999): 189-201 argues that the heavenly being Satan (the

Clines tries to make logical sense of what Job says, but a person who is suffering does not always make logical, consistent statements. At one point, he may assert that God is his enemy; but at another point of confidence he may see God as the one who will eventually vindicate him. A person who is suffering has periods of despair and moments of confidence. There are conflicting views of God at war in Job's mind depending on his emotional state at any moment.[17] In the remaining speeches Job's struggles continue but there are also statements of confidence, such as God knows the way that Job takes, and when God has tried him he will come forth as gold (23:10). In 27:6 Job states that he holds fast his righteousness and will not let it go. His speeches will end with his confident assertions of innocence in the form of oaths that he will take (Job 31).

Several matters support the identification of the kinsman redeemer with God.[18] The personification of *gōʼēl* as Job's cry would be unusual in the light of its use in the rest of Scripture. The use of the adjective 'living' in 19:25, which could be translated 'I know that my kinsman redeemer is living' (my translation), not only stands in bold relief against Job's fear of dying but also reminds one of the living God (Deut. 5:26; Josh. 3:10; Jer. 10:10).[19] Job has been abandoned by his family and his acquaintances (19:13-20), so it is unlikely that he has in mind any of them as his redeemer. He never expresses strong statements of confidence that a human being will step forward to vindicate him because he realizes that his only vindication can come from God.

Job knows that his kinsman redeemer lives, but how and when he will act on Job's behalf and what the results will be are also debated. There are several important translation decisions that help determine how one views the text. The

accuser) from Job 1–2 is the heavenly witness in chapter 16 and the kinsman redeemer in chapter 19. The character of this heavenly being in the book of Job argues against this identification. Also, no other place in the OT does an angel function as a *gōʼēl*.

17. Hartley, *Job*, 295.

18. A majority of Jewish and Christian commentators from antiquity to the present have identified God as the kinsman redeemer (Seow, *Job 1–21*, 823).

19. Hartley, *Job*, 293.

traditional view argues that Job 19 speaks of the resurrection of Job. His kinsman redeemer will stand upon the earth at the last day and in his resurrected body ('in his flesh') Job will see God.[20] There are some translation difficulties with this view that center around the phrases 'at the last' (v. 25), 'upon the earth' (v. 25), and 'in my flesh' (v. 26). Another important question is whether Job expects to see God in this life or after death.

The phrase translated 'at the last' is the Hebrew word 'āḥărôn and it can refer to the future or to a time that is deferred, as in the phrase 'days to come'.[21] Job knows that his redeemer lives and that at some time in the future he will stand 'upon the 'āp̄ār' (v. 25). This word is translated 'earth' by the ESV. It primarily refers to 'dust', but it can also be used of the material from which the human body is composed (Gen. 2:17; 3:19), of the surface of the ground (Job 30:6; Isa. 2:19), of something that is reduced to powder (2 Sam. 22:43; 2 Kings 23:6, 12, 15), of the debris of human cities that have been reduced to rubble (1 Kings 20:10), and of the grave (Job 7:21; 17:16; 20:11; 21:26; Isa. 26:19; Dan. 12:2). The justification for the translation 'earth' is related to the meaning 'of the surface of the ground'.[22] Based on the use of the word 'āp̄ār in Job, it could refer to the grave. Dust is also used with ashes (Job 30:19), which could refer to the place where Job went after he was struck with his illness (Job 2:8). The options are that at some point in the future Job's kinsman redeemer will stand upon the earth, or the grave, or the place where Job is suffering.

A key question is whether Job expects the redeemer to act before his death or after it. An examination of verse 26 may help answer that question. The first part of verse 26, 'And after my skin has been thus destroyed,' could refer to Job's death and the decomposition of his body. The next phrase is translated, 'yet in my flesh I shall see God'. The meaning of this phrase is debated, based on the use of the preposition

---

20. Thomas, *The Storm Breaks*, 159-65, and Layton Talbert, *Beyond Suffering: Discovering the Message of Job* (Greenville, SC: Bob Jones University Press, 2007).

21. Bill T. Arnold, אחר, *NIDOTTE*, 1:361.

22. Roy E. Hayden, עפר, *NIDOTTE*, 3:472-73.

min. Job could be saying that 'from' his flesh he shall see God, which many take to be a reference to Job in his resurrected body seeing God. Although his body will decompose in the grave, he will yet in his resurrected body see God. Others argue that the idea of the resurrection is not clear in the Old Testament, or that it develops later in Israel's history, and so it is not an option for the understanding of this text.[23] And yet, 'dust' can mean 'grave' and the resurrection is clearly taught in Isaiah 26:19.[24]

Another meaning of *min* is 'without' or 'apart from',[25] and if this nuance is used here the idea would be that even though Job has died, he will still see God, but apart from his physical body. He will be vindicated even if it comes after his death, but apart from the idea of resurrection.[26] Andersen argues for this position on the basis that a written testimony would not be needed if Job expected vindication before death; the word translated 'earth' can refer to the grave, and the word translated 'afterwards' suggests an interval of time and expresses something eschatological.[27] And yet, vindication after death seems rather anti-climactic for the great struggle that Job is enduring from his friends. Job does hope to be vindicated by God, but if it comes after death, who would see the vindication? If Job's sickness leads to his death, then it would seem as if the friends have won the argument.

Another possibility for understanding 19:26 is that Job describes how his illness is destroying his skin. Job 2:8 mentions that he must scrape his skin with a broken piece of pottery. His skin is being destroyed and yet he expresses

---

23. John H. Walton, *Job* (Grand Rapids: Zondervan, 2012), 219.

24. Many scholars would understand Isaiah 26:19 to be from a later time period than Isaiah, but such an argument is circular in that Isaiah 26 must be late because it has ideas that the scholars argue are late ideas.

25. The privative use of *min* marks something as missing or lacking (Bill T. Arnold and John H. Choi, *A Guide to Biblical Hebrew Syntax* [Cambridge: Cambridge University Press, 2003], 118).

26. Matthew J. Suriano, 'Death, Disinheritance, and Job's Kinsman-Redeemer,' *JBL* 129.1 (2010): 49-66. He argues that Job has confidence that his kinsman redeemer, a living human person, will perform the proper rituals on his behalf after his death to preserve his name for posterity. Job's hope of seeing God is explained as some kind of status after death that involves the deity.

27. Andersen, *Job*, 194. Habel (*Job*, 307) and Smick ('Job,' 4:787) also argue that Job expects vindication after his death.

confidence that in his flesh he will see God. In this view Job's expectation is that in his weak, emaciated body he will be vindicated by God before he dies. This makes Job's kinsman redeemer to be God Himself. This thought is so thrilling to Job that he emphasizes that it truly is God whom he will see and that this makes his heart faint (19:27). The verb 'faint' (*kālāh*) can express the meaning 'resolve' (1 Sam. 20:7–9) which would connect Job's desire to have a hearing with God to seeing God before his death.[28]

Although Job says many things in the despair of his suffering, his basic desire is to have a hearing before God so he can present his case to God. Job welcomes death at times because it will end his suffering, but he also knows that death will bring his days to an end without hope (Job 7:6). If he dies, God will seek him, but he will not be found (7:21). There is hope for a tree if it dies, but there is no hope for a man if he dies (Job 14:7-12; 17:13-16). Job believes that if he could argue his case before God it would be his salvation because he believes the godless shall not come before Him (Job 13:16). And, yet, Job is not confident he will have the opportunity to meet with God, so he looks for a way to defend his integrity if he should die (19:23-24). Job's great desire is to be declared innocent by God before he dies. Such a declaration before he dies would be a better defense than a statement written in rock to stand as a testimony after he is dead![29] There is no guarantee that a future generation would give him a fair hearing.[30] Thus, the best understanding of 19:25-27 is that Job is hoping for vindication in this life before death.[31] It is also significant that Job is vindicated by God before the friends at the end of the book (Job 42:7),[32] and that he is also greatly blessed by God after his suffering before his death.

---

28. G. Wilson, *Job*, 209. Other commentators who argue that Job is hoping for vindication before his death include Hartley, Longman, Whybray, Jones, and Konkel.

29. Konkel, 'Job,' 6:132.

30. Thomas, *Job*, 160.

31. Hartley (*Job*, 296) comments that if the resurrection was in view this would be the climax of the book and this theme would be referred to in the following speeches, but it is not treated in any later passage of Job.

32. G. Wilson (*Job*, 209) comments that if the point is Job's vindication after his death, then the remainder of the book is severely undermined, including Job's continued reference to the terror of death (23:17; 26:6; 30:23).

Does the view that Job is vindicated before his death mean that the traditional view of resurrection is completely wrong? Not if Job 19 is understood in light of the whole canon. Job's constant hope is for God to hear his case so that he could be declared innocent and vindicated before the friends. There is an emphasis in the Old Testament that God would immediately vindicate His people before their enemies as a way to show His power and greatness. With the coming of Christ there is more of an emphasis on suffering now for the sake of Christ with vindication coming when Christ comes again. This delayed vindication is more easily understood in light of the clearer teaching on the resurrection of Christ. Our hope of vindication parallels Job's hope of vindication,[33] but our hope is even greater in light of the certainty of our resurrection because of Christ. Thus, Job 19:25–27 can be read in a fuller way as referring to the resurrection hope. The term 'dust' in the Old Testament can refer to the grave, the destruction of Job's skin can refer to death, and the phrase 'in my flesh' can refer to our resurrection body from which we will see God. There is no greater, glorious victory than this.

A Warning to the Friends (Job 19:28-29)
Job ends this speech with a warning to the friends. He presents two statements that the friends have used against him. The first one is 'How will we pursue him!' This statement suggests that the friends are not going to back off but are going to continue to attack him. The second statement is 'The root of the matter is found in him'. This assertion continues to accuse Job of sin as the cause of his suffering. If the friends continue to come after Job with the same arguments they have used before, they should be afraid of the punishment of the sword that represents God's judgment.[34] This is one of the few times that Job pushes back against the friends by bringing into view the judgment of God. In other words, not only are the friends wrong, but they are doing great spiritual

---

33. Hartley (*Job*, 297) states that Job is working with the same logic of redemption as the premise of the NT doctrine of resurrection.

34. This judgment would put the friends in the category of the wicked who pursue the righteous Job, as in Psalm 7:1-6 (Clines, *Job 1–20).

harm to Job and to the cause of God for which they will yet pay the consequences.

A Miracle Baby

We were called in at 6:30 this morning because Pierce's heart was dropping. His kidneys are sliding and they can do nothing to reverse it. Please pray. Jesus can sustain him and we know that if Pierce lives it is because the Lord has rescued him. We are going to praise God in Christ regardless of the outcome. If Pierce lives, he is the Lord's. If he dies, he will be with the Lord. DO NOT give up praying for Pierce! God is able to sustain him.

He's still fighting. Our Lord has answered our prayer today and has sustained little Pierce. We are making it through a new nursing shift and can't wait to bust down the doors in a minute (they kick you out when change over occurs) and see the same nurse who looked at us with weepy, helpless eyes this morning (she, and everyone else fully intended to see Pierce leave this earth early this morning.) We can't wait to proclaim, 'See what God has done!'

I wish God's miracles came quickly. I guess that's the American, fast-food mentality in me. I longed to see him jump into my arms this morning. BUT God is teaching us so much by granting us patience and hope. We have seen God perform a HUGE miracle throughout the course of the day. Pierce's heart has kept beating. And beating strong! Many of his organs are functioning remarkably well, given the gestation age he is at! And the hospital staff literally has no explanation for this! They can't explain why his potassium hit 9.9 – our nurse told us she had never seen it nearly this high without causing the heart to stop immediately – this morning, but yet it has steadily tended downward despite NO medication being given. Nik and I are trying to rest in Christ's mercy in this beautiful moment of peace which He has granted us.

We know God is probably going to put Pierce through many trials before we leave the hospital, but we are trusting in Him to bring home a healthy baby boy in late July/early August. We trust Him to grant us grace and hope when we face the next hurdle. And please, please pray that tonight as we sit with Pierce, that he will make remarkable LEAPS forward in terms of progress. We know that, medically speaking, there is still a slim chance that Pierce will live. But with God, all things truly are possible.

Nik and Lindsay Franks (4/16/11)

Study Questions

1) Why Job is frustrated with his friends and with his family and acquaintances? What does Job want from the friends? How does this give guidance for when you seek to counsel someone?

2) Why is Job frustrated with God? Have you ever felt frustrated with God?

3) What is the meaning of kinsman-redeemer?

4) Why do some people have trouble accepting that God is Job's kinsman-redeemer? What is the evidence that God is Job's kinsman-redeemer?

5) What is the traditional view of Job 19:25-27? What are other ways to understand this passage?

6) What evidence is there that the best view is that Job seeks vindication before his death? How does this relate to the traditional view in light of the whole Bible?

13

Zophar: The Graphic Picture of the Destruction of the Wicked

(Job 20)

Zophar's second speech concludes the second cycle of speeches (Job 15–20). In this speech, he reacts to the words of Job and presents a picture of the fate of the wicked. He does not advance the argument but is stuck in the view that Job's hope is false because he has sinned against God.

An Agitated Reaction to Job's Speech (Job 20:1-3)

Job's warning to the friends (Job 19:28-29) produces a response from Zophar. He is agitated because he has been insulted by Job's condemnation, and is in turmoil due to an inner anxiousness because he wants to answer Job and set the record straight. Thoughts keep coming at him concerning how he might respond to Job. Zophar feels compelled to answer Job and he asserts that 'out of my understanding a spirit answers me' (v. 3). He promises an insightful response and assures Job that his speech will convey wisdom.[1] In fact, he bolsters his claim to wisdom by an appeal to an external, higher authority.[2]

---

1. Hartley, *Job*, 300.

2. Longman, *Job*, 266. Clines (*Job 1–20*, 483) takes spirit (*rûaḥ*) as 'impulse' and understands the appeal by Zophar to be to reason. But the friends have already appealed to external sources, such as ancient wisdom (15:18) or revelation (4:12–16), so it makes sense that Zophar would do the same here.

The Sure Fate of the Wicked (Job 20:4-29)

Zophar paints a picture of the destruction of the wicked to show Job what will happen to him if he does not repent of his sin. He demonstrates that there is no hope for the wicked because everything in their life will turn out for their ruin. Although the wicked may experience joy in life, it does not last very long. In fact, it may look like the wicked have succeeded, but the higher his climb the harder his fall (v. 6).[3] Eventually, however, the wicked will perish forever (vv. 4-11). The perishing of the wicked is described in several ways. The wicked are compared to their own dung,[4] which is a negative way to describe the wicked, but it also emphasizes how short-lived their success is. The wicked will disappear so that people will say, 'Where is he?' He will fly away like a dream and be chased away like a vision of the night. He will be here one day and gone the next. When he is gone, his household will suffer. His children will no longer be cared for, so that they must seek help from the poor. His wealth will disappear and be given back to those from whom he unjustly took it.[5] Job should not be fooled by the youthful vigor of the bones of the wicked because those very bones in the prime of life will lie down in the dust. Job should know this because this teaching has been around a long time (v. 4). He should not be fooled by the momentary prosperity of the wicked.

Those who do evil love the evil that they do; but in the end, they will experience the negative consequences of their evil deeds (vv. 12-23). Wickedness is sweet in the wicked person's mouth. He savors it and does not want to let it go (vv. 12–13). It becomes a part of him like food that is swallowed, but once swallowed it turns sour in his stomach so that he vomits it up.[6] God is the one who causes this sickness (v. 15).

---

3. Habel, *Job*, 304. G. Wilson (*Job*, 214) notes that the wicked go 'from the heights of human glory to the ignobility of human waste'!

4. Clines (*Job 1–20*, 486) argues that the dung is cow dung used for fuel for cooking, which is consumed in a short time.

5. Hartley, *Job*, 305.

6. There may be two scenarios used to describe the demise of the wicked in this section. The main metaphor is that of eating food (Clines, *Job 1–20*, 488). The other scenario is a person bitten by a poisonous serpent. G. Wilson (*Job*, 216) points out that the description is graphic enough to come from the actual observation of someone dying from being bitten by a poisonous snake.

Further negative consequences come upon the wicked person because of his wickedness. He will not live to see the prosperity for which he had hoped and he will not be able to enjoy the fruit of his labor or the profit from his trading. The reason for these negative consequences is that he crushed and abandoned the poor and improperly took over houses he did not build. He was not content with the blessings of life which he enjoyed but sought to greedily indulge himself with the delights of life. He selfishly kept it all for himself and did not care about the plight of others. And so, the prosperity which he enjoyed will not endure. Even though he has everything he needs, he will be in distress. The hands of those who suffer will come against him. More importantly, he will experience the wrath of God against him, even in his own body.

The life of the wicked will end in disaster that will impact every part of his life (vv. 24-29). Although it is true that wickedness carries within itself its own seeds of destruction, God is very much involved with the destruction of the wicked. God pursues the wicked with an iron weapon like a warrior chasing the enemy.[7] The wicked person may flee but he cannot escape the arrows of God which penetrate his body. He experiences both physical and psychological terror (vv. 24-25). Also, his possessions and treasures will be destroyed. The reason for the calamity of the wicked will be made clear to everyone. The heavens will reveal his iniquity and the earth will rise against him. Zophar may be alluding to Job's wish for a trial, but with heaven and earth being called as witnesses against Job in order to reveal his iniquity.[8] There is no hope for a declaration of innocence or an acquittal. The destruction of the wicked is called the day of God's wrath. Destruction is the portion that the wicked has from God and it is the heritage that he receives from God.

Zophar's description of the destruction of the wicked is important in the discussion with Job because the way he frames the destruction is meant to highlight Job's place among the wicked. When he describes God as a warrior pursuing his enemy, he is alluding to Job's earlier statement

7. G. Wilson, *Job*, 220.
8. Habel, *Job*, 309.

that he feels like one who is being chased down by God (Job 16:13-14). Of course, Job believed he was being pursued even though he was innocent, but Zophar is stressing the pursuit of the wicked by God to their destruction. The terms 'portion' (*ḥēleq*) and 'heritage' (*naḥălāh*) are important words used in connection with the righteous. Although both terms can refer to the land which God has given as an inheritance, He is the real portion and heritage of the righteous (Ps. 16:5-6). By using these terms to refer to the wicked, Zophar is stressing that Job should count himself among the wicked.

It is interesting that Zophar does not call Job to repentance and that he will not have a speech in the third cycle of speeches. This is his final word to Job and he does not leave him with any hope because he believes his fate is certain. One scholar raises the question concerning the psychology of a theologian who finds it necessary to invest his belief in retribution with such lurid imaginations.[9] Zophar is an example of a person who gets so caught up in the debate and establishing the truth of his position that he forfeits the personal aspect of the relationship.

Good Friday

Today is Good Friday. Today we celebrate Jesus' going to the Cross and His burial in the tomb. The doctors have told us that this is going to be a marathon and we are starting to feel it. It is getting emotionally and physically draining being at the hospital and driving back and forth between here and home. We really want to take this day and this weekend to reflect on the work of Christ and to pray for Pierce. When Pierce's life was on the razor's edge, I remember asking the Lord to let Pierce still be here on Easter Sunday so that I could tell everyone that Pierce will rise because Christ has risen. Lord willing, that will happen.

This morning, I read Matthew 27 to Pierce in light of today. I want Pierce to celebrate the Cross. Often when we read about what happened to Jesus we get sad. And when we focus on what put Jesus on the Cross we should get sad. Our rebellion is the reason why the God-man

---

9. Clines, *Job 1–20*, 495.

went to the Cross. However, if we can step back a little and see what the Cross is all about, we can learn to rejoice when we hear about the sufferings of Christ. We should rejoice because the mission of God was for Christ to come and take away the guilt of the world by bearing the punishment we deserve. And this mission was accomplished on the Cross.

Every day that passes, the worries over Pierce's death are lessened. Sadly, many premature babies who pass away, die in the first few days. Now, the focus is more on what doctors call morbidity, or getting over illness and trying to avoid long-term defects. For us, we will love Pierce no matter what. We trust that God is going to continue to fully heal, but regardless nothing will change the intensity of our love toward Pierce. It really is a picture of the Gospel. When God looks at us, He does not see physical defects. The paraplegic or the person suffering from Down's syndrome can be hundreds of times more beautiful to God than the most physically attractive, fit person. The defects that God sees in us are behavioral or ethical. He looks down on us and says, 'You've got problems, but I am still dying to love you' (literally, on the Cross). And when all the things that you pursued besides God leave you empty and broken, His level of love never changes and He passionately welcomes you back (see Luke 15, the prodigal son).

Love,
Nik and Lindsay Franks (4/22/11)

Study Questions

1) Why is Zophar agitated at the beginning of this speech?

2) Summarize the picture that Zophar paints of the wicked. What is the purpose of this picture?

3) What is true about Zophar's description of the wicked? What is the problem of this description in relationship to Job?

4) How does Zophar fail as a counselor?

14

The Failure of the Doctrine of Retribution: The Prosperity of the Wicked

(Job 21)

This is Job's sixth speech. He speaks only to the friends and specifically responds to the speech of Zophar concerning his description of the destruction of the wicked (Job 20). Of course, the other friends have been making the same argument. Job challenges their simplistic view of retribution as a way to argue that his own suffering is not an evidence of sin.

An Appeal for a Sympathetic Hearing (Job 21:1-6)

Job appeals to the friends to bear with him and not shut their ears to what he has to say (vv. 1-3). He desires to speak and wants them to listen to him. He may be afraid that the conversation is about to shut down, but he believes what he has to say is important to their ongoing discussion. He has a negative view of their relationship. If they would only listen carefully to his words, this could be their comfort. If they bear with him for just a little while, they can go back to mocking him. These statements show how much the relationship has deteriorated. Job is only seeking a little compassion from his friends.

Job's complaint has not been against any human being, which implies that his complaint has been against God (v. 4).

The reason for his impatience arises from the treatment he has received from God, who has not said or done anything to alleviate Job's suffering.[1] Job responds out of frustration and fear that God may never clear him.[2] Job directs the friends to 'Look at me', which may signify that the friends have lost sight of Job's suffering in the heat of the debate. Job's suffering is so appalling that they should lay their hands over their mouths to express shock. Job speaks of being dismayed when he 'remembers'. Perhaps he is referring to remembering his blessed condition before the onslaught of his suffering. Such memory causes his whole body to shake because the contrast is so pronounced. Job is shaken to the depths of his being because he is innocent and yet he is suffering so deeply. His pain is heightened because his suffering body stands as a witness against his innocence.

Tough Questions about the Doctrine of Retribution (Job 21:7-34)

Job raises important questions that the doctrine of retribution must answer for it to be used as an argument against his suffering. This passage can be divided into three sections with the first section being introduced by the question 'Why' (v. 7), the second section being introduced with the question 'How often' (v. 17), and the third section being introduced with the exclamation 'Behold' (v. 27). The speech ends with a pointed question directed at the friends concerning the emptiness of their argument based on Job's questions.

The first question asks, 'Why do the wicked live, reach old age, and grow mighty in power?' This question introduces verses 7-16 where Job describes the peaceful prosperity of the wicked and their children. Job lists the family and possessions of the wicked to show how many blessings they receive. Their wealth is not so fleeting that that it can never be used for their advantage, as argued by Zophar (20:15-18).[3] Their

---

1. L. Wilson (*Job*, 113) puts forth the possibility that Job's impatience is with the friends for interfering when his complaint is actually against God.

2. Hartley, *Job*, 311.

3. Hartley, *Job*, 313. Habel (*Job*, 325) comments, 'Thus Job's disputation on the wicked is a calculated refutation employing both major themes and key emotive language used by the friends in their portraits of the wicked.'

offspring are well-established so that they live to see many generations (v. 8). They live peacefully in their own homes without fear of human beings or God (v. 9). They do not know the fear of sudden disaster that is supposed to inflict the wicked (Prov. 3:25). Their animals do not miscarry, which means their flocks and herds increase (v. 10). Their children play without any concern of trouble and enjoy the joyfulness of life with their parents, who sing and rejoice in prosperity and peace all the days of their lives (vv. 11-12). They live this life of abundance apart from God. In fact, they deliberately reject the knowledge of God, they do not want to serve God, and they do not see any benefit in praying to God (vv. 14-15). It looks like they are the masters of their own fate (v. 16a). Job, on the other hand, should not be lumped with the wicked because he wholeheartedly rejects their counsel (v. 16b).[4]

A series of questions are introduced in verses 17–18 that raise the issue that the wicked live on without experiencing the judgment of God against their wicked deeds. Their lamp just keeps shining. They do not encounter God's anger against their sin. Without the experience of God's punishment, the wicked become stable and secure. The expectation that the wicked would be unstable and fleeting as straw before the wind or as chaff before the storm is not the reality of a wicked person's life. Perhaps someone might say that God is storing up their iniquity to unleash it upon their children (v. 19). Such a view allows the wicked to escape the pain of their wickedness. What do they care what happens to their possessions after they are no longer conscious of what is taking place in this life? Wouldn't it be better if they would see with their own eyes their own destruction and experience for themselves the wrath of Almighty God (vv. 19-20)?

Job then argues that it is hard to figure out God's ways based on what we experience in this life (vv. 22-26). The friends have described a scenario of quick retribution where

---

4. The translation and interpretation of v. 16 is difficult. The first part of the verse has been taken to mean that the prosperity of the wicked is not in their own hands (Hartley, *Job*, 313), which would be the opposite of the way it is understood by many. The second part of v. 16 has been understood not as a statement of Job's relationship to the counsel of the wicked but a statement concerning God's relationship to the counsel of the wicked (Longman, *Job*, 277).

God immediately judges the wicked. And yet, the experiences of life do not support this. One person dies at ease and secure with an abundance of possessions and health (vv. 23-24). Another person dies after living a hardened, bitter life of poverty without ever experiencing blessing and prosperity. Both men go to the dust and experience the decomposition of their bodies in the grave. There is no connection between how one lives life, how one relates to God, and what the quality of that life is.[5] This is evidence that the friends' view of retribution is a failure because it cannot explain the reality of life.

Finally, Job anticipates what the friends are going to say to him in response to his speech (vv. 27-34). The word 'behold' introduces this final section. Job has learned firsthand how the friends think and how they use their arguments to wrong him. They will deny that experience contradicts their view of retribution. They will ask Job to show them the tent where the wicked live (v. 28). They cannot find such an example of the prosperity of the wicked. Job responds by asking the friends to broaden their horizons and ask those who are seasoned travelers whether the evil man is spared in the day of trouble. Who is there who confronts the evil man with his actions or repays him for his evil (v. 31)? In fact, when such a man dies he is given an honorable burial with many attending the funeral to show him respect (vv. 32-33). Job ends this speech with a question to the friends and then a statement (v. 34). The question asks how such false words of the friends can give him comfort. Job then states that their answers are nothing but falsehood.

Job asks the rhetorical question in verse 4, 'Why should I not be impatient?' The implication is that the friends perceive him as impatient. Job's impatience arises out of the fact that his complaint is against God, and God is not answering him. He gets frustrated when God does not respond to his quest for a hearing and so he believes that God mistreats him. Job is also frustrated with the counsel of his friends that feeds his overall demeanor of despair. It is interesting that the book of James uses the character of Job in a section where

---

5. Longman, *Job*, 279.

believers are exhorted to be patient until the coming of the Lord (James 5:7-11). But was Job truly patient? Has James misunderstood the character of Job?

James exhorts the believers to be patient while they wait for the coming of the Lord. The verb 'patient' (*makrothymeō*) can mean to wait with calm and expectancy.[6] The example is the farmer who waits for the rains to fall so the crop will grow (James 5:7). The next category that James mentions is patience in suffering, with an appeal to the prophets. Within this broad category Job is mentioned, but Job is introduced with a word that emphasizes endurance and fortitude (*hypomenō*). Those who remain steadfast are blessed, says James, even as they have heard of the steadfastness of Job. Looking at Job's overall life, he did persevere until God spoke to him and vindicated him before his friends. James has not misunderstood the character of Job nor has he based his analysis on interpretive traditions of the day that downplayed Job's angry response to God.[7] Part of Job's perseverance in suffering includes his periodic breakthroughs of confidence in the outcome of his life and in his rejection of the teaching of the friends. Job's view of God is more complex than the view of the friends. Life is more complicated than they allow, which gives Job hope for the future.

Perseverance

This is day seven of our hospital stay. It seems like a blur and an eternity at the same time. There is not a word to describe what Lindsay and I felt on Saturday morning. We were suddenly awoken out of a deep sleep by several quick knocks on the door. The doctor makes his way in and sits on the arm of the chair that Lindsay was sitting up

---

6. David P. Nystrom, *James* (Grand Rapids: Zondervan, 1997), 284.

7. Longman, *Job*, 281-82. He argues that James is giving us the Job of the Septuagint or the Job of the *Testament of Job* and that it is wrong to hold up Job of the Old Testament as an example of a proper attitude toward God. Such a view says that James is wrong in his interpretation of Job, which has implications for the trustworthiness and authority of the New Testament. It is better to make the distinction that Job was right in the basic argument with the friends, which is that he was not suffering for a sin that he had committed. He did persevere in that belief and he was vindicated by God. It is also true that in his wrestling with God Job says several things of which he must repent. The latter does not cancel out the truth of the former.

in to sleep, and says 'There is just nothing we can do. I wish he could have stayed on a little bit longer. You should probably get over there and hold him in your arms.' Again, they thought death was imminent, without question.

Well, here we are. Pierce is still alive and our souls and faith have been stretched in ways they never have before. We will never be the same. God has once again shown Himself to be so real to Lindsay and myself. What a grace that is. We have come to know God more intimately within this last week. And we thank Him for that. We can know a bunch of facts about God, but that is nothing like knowing God as a living Father and friend.

We trust God in this situation. He is going to do what is best for Pierce, for Lindsay, and for me. That is just the kind of God He is. I have been praying that Pierce will grow up to do great things for the Kingdom of God. I have prayed that Pierce buries me and his mother, not vice versa. God has snatched him out of the mouth of the lion once and He can certainly do it again and again as we continue down the long road of this trial....

Pierce is nine days old now! Praise the Lord.

Overall, Pierce had a stable, good, quiet day. There have been so many times today when I've been overwhelmed with so many conflicting thoughts and feelings – one minute joy and complete trust, the next anxiety and fear. Although I must say, I'm becoming increasingly aware that NOTHING in life is certain. Any sense of security that I had before April 12th was false. Any sense of security that you have is false as well. The only thing that is secure and steadfast in this life is Christ. So tonight I am resting in His goodness and mercy and praying that He uses every ounce of our pain and struggle to bring glory to His name.

Grace and peace,
Nik Franks (4/21/11)

Study Questions

1) What does Job want from his friends? What does that tell you about people who are suffering?

2) How does Job describe the condition of the wicked in verses 7-21? Is that an accurate description based on your experience?

3) What point does Job raise about God's ways in the world in verses 22-26? How is that more accurate than the view of the friends?

4) What is the possible problem of James' use of Job as an example? What is the best way to characterize Job? Why is it appropriate to understand Job as a positive example?

15

Eliphaz: Just Acknowledge Your Sin and Everything will be Fine
(Job 22)

Eliphaz' third speech begins the third and final cycle of speeches (22:1–27:23). The problems of an incomplete third cycle will be discussed in a later chapter. In this speech Eliphaz will double-down on the view that Job has brought his suffering upon himself because he has sinned and that he needs to repent in order to be at peace with God. In fact, Eliphaz will suggest ways that Job has sinned to seek to push him toward repentance.

Accusations against Job (Job 22:1-11)
Eliphaz begins his third speech by undercutting Job's claims of innocence because such claims do not matter to God. He asks Job a series of rhetorical questions which expect a 'no' answer to show that Job's claims are useless (vv. 2-4). The first question he asks is, 'Can a man be profitable to God?' The implied 'no' answer is emphasized by the contrast in the following statement that a person who is wise is profitable to himself. If a person of wisdom is not profitable to God, how much less is a person who claims to be innocent profitable to God. In other words, it does not benefit God in any way if Job is innocent. The second rhetorical question in verse 3 has two parallel parts to it. This question asserts that even if Job

is in the right or could make his ways blameless, this brings no gain or pleasure to Almighty God. The final rhetorical question assumes that Job is experiencing God's reproof and is under His judgement: 'Is it for your fear of him that he reproves you and enters into judgment with you?' Of course, God cannot be judging Job because Job has the proper attitude of fear and respect toward God. God does not judge those who are pious.[1] Job must be experiencing God's judgment for other reasons, brought out in the questions of verse 5. In light of Job's suffering, his wickedness must be great and there must be no end to his iniquities. Thus he cannot be blameless before God. Eliphaz accuses Job of a worthless argument that covers over the real reason for his suffering.

If Job is not blameless, then he must have committed some kind of evil to bring about his suffering (vv. 6-11). Eliphaz tries to get Job to admit to some form of sin. Surely Job's evil is abundant in light of the depth of his suffering (v. 5). Eliphaz accuses Job with direct statements using the second masculine singular form of the verb:

> You must have been taking pledges[2] of your brothers for nothing.
> You must have been stripping the naked of their clothing.
> You must have been refusing water to the weary.
> You must have been denying bread to the hungry.
> You must have sent widows away empty.

These statements accuse Job of a lack of compassion for the less fortunate. Eliphaz does not bring forward any evidence or witnesses against Job. Perhaps he bases these claims on what he perceives as the arrogance of Job who has tried to force God to hold a trial.[3] The extent of Job's suffering may also be reason for Eliphaz to conclude that Job has sinned. He

---

1. Alison Lo, *Job 28: An Analysis of Job 28 in the Context of Job 22–31* (Atlanta: Society of Biblical Literature, 2003), 97.

2. The translation of the verbs in Eliphaz' accusation follows D. J. A. Clines, *Job 21–37* (Nashville, TN: Thomas Nelson, 2006), 538. All the verbs except one in the list are imperfect verbs, which can stress repeated action. These actions must have taken place in the past as Eliphaz is accusing Job of having committed these actions.

3. Habel, *Job*, 339. He also points out the irony that Job, who has accused God of lacking any genuine compassion for afflicted individuals, is now himself accused of inhuman acts against fellow human beings.

accuses Job of failing to carry out his responsibilities in the social realm. Job has committed sins of omission by failing to respond to people in need, but he has also committed sins of commission by forcefully taking what rightfully belonged to others. There is also an objective statement concerning a man who lived in the land (v. 8). He had power and he was favored. This seems to describe Job's privileged position,[4] but the implication is that he used that position for his own advantage and was not concerned about those who were poor and needy. It follows that Job is being punished because of these wicked deeds. The result is that Job feels helpless and overwhelmed as he is surrounded by snares, overwhelmed by sudden terrors, encompassed by darkness so he cannot see, and covered by a flood of waters.

God's Relationship to the Wicked (Job 22:12-20)

This part of Eliphaz' speech discusses God's relationship to His creation, but more specifically, God's relationship to the wicked. It begins with a rhetorical question that expects a 'yes' answer: 'Is not God high in the heavens?' This question is followed by the statement, 'See the highest stars, how lofty they are!' The visible stars are very high in the heavens, but God is higher than the stars. God is magnificently transcendent over His creation. But then Eliphaz quotes statements from Job that deny that God knows enough about what is happening on the earth to render judgment (v. 13): 'What does God know? Can he judge through the deep darkness?' Eliphaz may believe that Job has used the transcendence of God to bolster his argument that God is not treating him fairly. God walks on the vault of heaven and thick clouds keep Him from seeing what takes place on the earth (v. 14).

Eliphaz believes that such a view of God clearly puts Job in the category of the wicked. In fact, this is a common view of the wicked held from ages past (v. 15). It is a false view because God does see what the wicked do and He acts against them. The wicked are described as coming to a sudden, premature death ('being snatched away before their time') and as having the very foundation of their life washed

---

4. Habel, *Job*, 339.

away. What they thought was secure was unstable. They even had the audacity to tell God to depart from them and they questioned the power of God to do anything to them (v. 17). They were fooled by a momentary experience of the blessings of life. But such counsel from the wicked is doomed to fail. The righteous, on the other hand, see the real downfall of the wicked and they rejoice. The truly innocent mock the foolishness of the wicked. The righteous affirm that their adversaries, the wicked, are cut off and what they have left is consumed by the fire (v. 20).

A Call to Return to God (Job 22:21-30)

The solution to Job's problem is to return to God which will bring an end to his suffering. This makes sense in light of Eliphaz' assumption that Job is suffering because of sin that he has committed. He begins by exhorting Job with several imperatives that lay out a proper response to God (vv. 21-22). Job should 'Agree with God' if he wants peace in his life. This will also lead to good coming back into his life. He should also 'Receive instruction' from God and 'lay up his words in your heart'. Job needs to submit himself to the teaching of Eliphaz who claims to represent God's view of Job's suffering. This means that to agree with God is to agree with the argument of the friends.

Eliphaz lays out what can happen in Job's life if he does return to God (vv. 23-26). Simply put, if he returns to God he will be built up. This promises Job that what he has lost in his suffering can be restored to him. Several other results will follow if Job returns to God. Injustice will be removed far from Job's tents.[5] Even if his wealth is restored, he will come to regard wealth, such as the gold of Ophir, as not very valuable in comparison with his relationship with God.[6] Instead of being at odds with God he will delight in God. Instead of being in tension with God he will lift his face up

---

5. The Hebrew has an 'if' at the beginning of v. 23 but, contrary to the ESV, there is no 'if' before the clause about removing injustice (v. 23b) or at the beginning of v. 24.

6. Some understand the reference to wealth to be Eliphaz' exhortation to Job to put away his wealth so God can be his special treasure (L. Wilson, *Job*, 119). But Job has lost all his wealth. It is better to see the wealth as a result of Job's restoration.

to God. The one thing that Job has been holding onto as valuable is his own innocence. Eliphaz is asking Job to give that up and repent of his sin so that he can be accepted by God again.

Eliphaz ends his speech with several statements that further explain what Job's life will be like if he turns to God (vv. 27-30). His prayers will be answered, his plans will be established and his way will be clear. Job will have the proper attitude of lowliness instead of pride and will become an instrument to deliver others who are not innocent. They will be delivered through the cleanness of Job's hands.

Eliphaz does not understand Job's situation or God's relationship to Job's situation. He is asking Job to repent of sin which he has not committed. Therefore he has no real solution to Job's suffering.[7] When he tells Job that if he repents he will be able to deliver those who are not innocent, he does not realize that at the end of the book he will be the one who is not innocent and must repent through Job's mediation (Job 42:7). In other words, he completely misunderstands Job's situation and his own situation. Job does not need to repent of any sin that has caused his suffering but Eliphaz will need to repent of speaking falsely concerning God.

Some of Eliphaz' misperceptions about God come out in this passage. He implies that God is transcendent and self-sufficient and so does not care that much about people and their claims to being blameless.[8] And yet God seemed to care about Job in chapters 1–2 when He points out Job to Satan and declares him to be blameless. Eliphaz states that there is no benefit to God if Job is in the right. Satan, however, made Job a test case for the gratuitousness of piety. If Job does not remain pious it proves that humans serve God only for the sake of the rewards that He gives. It seems, then, that God does have something to gain from Job's response. Eliphaz has pushed the doctrine of retribution to its logical conclusion

---

7. Andersen (*Job*, 206–207) comments that not everyone's need can be met by simply preaching the gospel. Although such a statement can be misinterpreted and misused, it does seem to apply to Job because the issue with Job is not faith and repentance (justification), but perseverance in the midst of suffering (sanctification). The friends do not understand this and so their solution to Job's problem is not helpful.

8. Longman, *Job*, 287.

and has essentially become a deist with a depersonalized God.[9] A particular doctrine has become more important than God Himself. Job, on the other hand, operates with a personal view of God who exists in all the mystery of His sovereignty. Job pursues God even if he cannot understand how God could bring this suffering into his life.

A Continual Struggle

It seems like we took some steps back today. Pierce keeps on dropping his oxygen levels. They put him on nitric oxide in addition to the oscillator but he still is having trouble. His oxygen on the oscillator right now is set at about 88%, so they don't have much room to go up. Please pray for his lungs and his PDA [patent ductus arteriosus is a heart defect that occurs when the temporary fetal blood vessel that connects the aorta and the pulmonary artery does not close at birth], which is probably contributing to his dropping oxygen levels as well. Pierce will still be in critical condition for some time and our nurse tonight told us this is par for the course.

Today was a struggle for us. It is so hard to see Pierce laying there needing so much help for such an extended period of time. It is only day ten and if all goes really well the earliest he will get out is late July. But still, there are no guarantees – especially for the first month. We are experiencing that now. We will keep trusting and putting our hope in the Lord. This is not going to be easy, but He has proved Himself faithful thus far and we trust He will continue to do so …

Pierce had a pretty rough night and morning. His vitals kept dropping, indicating that his lungs were not tolerating the oscillator (type of ventilator he was on) and that he was fighting an infection. The lab report came back confirming that he indeed does have an infection. Doctors feel confident that the antibiotics can control this. However, they told us that the biggest concern is that Pierce's lungs are just too immature. There is really

9. Clines, *Job 21–37*, 551, 553.

nothing that they can do to help this. Please, please pray that God will touch Pierce's lungs and that they will be able to withstand this battle. It appears that today will be one of those hour-by-hour, sometimes minute-by-minute days where we sit at his bedside and hope and pray. Please join us in praying for healing for our son. We are trusting that God is going to continue working miracles through Pierce's life and that He will grant us strength to make it through today.

Love,
Nik and Lindsay Franks (4/23/11)

Study Questions

1) How does Eliphaz undercut Job's claims of innocence?

2) Eliphaz accuses Job of what kind of sin? What impact does this have on Job?

3) According to Eliphaz, how should the righteous view the wicked? Does Job view the wicked that way?

4) How should Job respond, according to Eliphaz? What would be the results in Job's life?

5) Does Eliphaz offer a real solution to Job's problems? Why not? What can be learned from this?

6) What are some of the ways Eliphaz speaks falsely about God? How is that a temptation to those who are counseling people?

7) Has a particular doctrine about God become more important than God Himself for you? How would you know?

16

Job: Growing Confidence
(Job 23–24)

Job ignores the friends in this speech. He does not respond to Eliphaz' accusations and he does not repent of any wickedness that he has supposedly committed. He speaks directly to God, focuses on the merits of his case before God, asserts strong statements concerning his innocence and acquittal, and wrestles with the injustice that the righteous must endure. Instead of giving in to a false repentance to receive a false peace, he maintains his integrity even if it means that his relationship with God continues to be difficult.

A Statement of Confidence (Job 23:1-17)
Job 23 is called a statement of confidence because Job continues to pursue his desire of presenting his case before God with assertions that the outcome of the case will be to his favor. This attitude does not mean that the struggle is over or that Job has forgotten the reality of his situation. The darkness of his suffering is there but statements of confidence outweigh them.

Job begins by affirming the difficulty of his situation (vv. 1-7). His situation is difficult because his suffering weighs heavily upon him (v. 2). Job has tasted the bitterness of suffering[1] and his agony is so severe that he has to control

---

1. The Hebrew word *mĕr'* means 'rebellious' or 'defiant' and may be a better reading than 'bitter'. Job might be indirectly responding to Eliphaz who would see Job's response as being defiant against God.

himself with a heavy hand.[2] His situation is also difficult because he does not know how to bring his case before God. He does not know where to find the court in which God resides so to bring the arguments of his case to Him (vv. 3-4). If he could only find God, he believes that God would understand his situation and answer him. He does not believe that God would overwhelm him with the greatness of His power. Rather, Job could present his case and God would acquit him of sin. He has confidence that this is the way God the judge would treat an upright man (vv. 6-7).

Job's confidence grows even though God is hidden (vv. 8-12). There is no doubt that God is at work, but everywhere Job looks (forward, backward, on the left hand, to the right hand) he is not able to perceive God. Although he cannot see God, he believes that God can see him. God knows what Job is experiencing, and Job is confident that 'when he has tried me, I shall come forth as gold'. This is a strong statement that his situation of suffering will turn out for his good. He believes that his suffering has the purpose of refining him so that he will emerge victorious. The basis for Job's confidence is found in his integrity. Job has kept the way of God and has not turned aside from God or departed from His commands. God's word has been more important than his own food. Job does not need the exhortation from Eliphaz to receive instruction from God because he already treasures God's word.[3] It is appropriate that Job should characterize his relationship with God in terms of his blamelessness because that has been the issue with the friends. Job clearly asserts over against the charge of Eliphaz that he has not sinned. Job's perception matches God's perception in the first two chapters of the book.

Job expresses confidence even while asserting that he is terrified of God (vv. 13-17). God is not someone to take lightly. He is in a class by Himself[4] and accomplishes all

---

2. Hartley, *Job*, 338. The ESV reads v. 2 as 'my hand is heavy on account of my groaning' but the better translation might be 'my hand is heavy against my groaning'.

3. Hartley, *Job*, 341.

4. The ESV translates the beginning of v. 13 as 'he is unchangeable' but a better translation of *'eḥād* is that God is one or unique (NAS, KJV, NKJV). The point is that God is a God who no one can stand against or hinder His purposes.

that He desires. His plans cannot fail, so He will complete what He has appointed for Job's life. The freedom of God leaves room for the mystery of His ways, but it also leaves Job terrified of God because He cannot be controlled. The darkness of Job's situation presses in on him but he is not silenced by the darkness.

A Complaint about the Unrestrained Activity of the Wicked (Job 24:1-25)

In this section Job wrestles with the injustice that he sees in the world. The wicked get away with oppressing others and God does not seem to be all that concerned. This makes life difficult for those who honor God. This speech is introduced by two questions in verse 1. The first question is, 'Why are not times of judgment kept by the Almighty?' This question wonders why God does not judge the wicked for their wicked deeds. If God never judges them, then they have free rein to continue their wickedness and cause trouble in people's lives. If God would have periodic times of judgment, then the wicked would be stopped and people could see that wickedness does not pay. The second question presents the other side of the coin, 'Why do those who know him never see his days?' This question looks at the lack of judgment on God's part from the perspective of those who know Him. They feel abandoned by God because they do not see Him restraining the wicked and they do not see any evidence that God is on their side.[5]

The Impact of the Wicked on the Poor (Job 24:2-12)

Job gives evidence of the wickedness of the wicked in verses 2-3 to support the view that many suffer because God does not judge the wicked. The wicked take what belongs to others through forcible seizure of property. They move landmarks in order to enlarge their estates. They seize flocks, drive away the donkey of the fatherless, and take the widow's ox for a pledge. The fatherless and the widow are the helpless in a society because they have no one to protect them. The Old Testament

---

5. Hartley (*Job*, 345) understands the phrase 'never see his days' (24:1) as referring to the days of accountability when God judges a person's deeds. This is related to the times of judgement in v. 1 that God has not kept (Longman, *Job*, 301).

commands that they be treated fairly and that they not be taken advantage of because they are vulnerable. The wicked show no compassion for the poor but take what is essential from them so that they are left in a destitute condition.

The impact the wicked has on the poor is laid out in verses 4-12. The poor are afraid so they make themselves scarce by hiding themselves. They must seek food for themselves and their children in areas like the desert that do not yield food very easily. Many of them work for the wicked (v. 6) who take advantage of them. They are without the basics of food, clothing, and shelter as they face the cold and the rain.[6] They have their children and their valuables forcibly removed from them. Even though they are without clothing, food, and drink they are forced to work for the wicked. Many who are close to death groan and the wounded cry for help, but God does not seem to hear their cries. The evidence is that God charges no one with wrong (v. 12b). In other words, the wicked get away with their wickedness because God does not do anything about it.

The Rebellion of the Wicked (Job 24:13-17)
These verses describe those who rebel against the light by flagrantly breaking the laws of society.[7] Rebellion refers to a conscious rejection of something, many times a rejection of God's way. The term 'light' is associated in Scripture with God, who is the source of light. The wicked revolt against the ways of God. They are not acquainted with God's ways nor do they seek to walk in its paths.

Several kinds of wicked deeds are highlighted. The murderer is described as a thief in the night who rises early to kill the poor and needy. He cannot wait to carry out his wicked deeds. The adulterer works at night because he thinks no one will be able to see him in the dark. Thieves also work in the dark so they cannot be seen. On one level this refers to literal darkness as those who do wickedness prefer the cover that the darkness gives them. Light would expose their wicked deeds. On another level, however, the darkness refers

---

6. The law (Exod. 22:25-27) commands creditors to return garments taken as pledges of repayment of debt to their owners at night so they can keep warm (G. Wilson, *Job*, 269).

7. Habel, *Job*, 360.

to the spiritual darkness that is the source of wickedness itself. The wicked do not know the light. The wicked are not able to distinguish the darkness from the light because it all looks the same to them. Deep darkness is no different than morning. In fact, the wicked are so caught up in the darkness that they are friends with the terrors of deep darkness. They are comfortable living their lives in rebellion against God and have accepted spiritual darkness as their friend. These verses demonstrate the point of verse 1 that there are no times of judgment for the wicked.

The Fate of the Wicked (Job 24:18-25)
This section expresses two viewpoints concerning the fate of the wicked. The first viewpoint is expressed in verses 18-20 where the lives of the wicked quickly come to an end. Their quick decline is expressed with the statement 'Swift are they on the face of the waters' (v. 18).[8] Their lot in life is cursed. Their vineyards have no one to tread their grapes so that the fruit is lost. Refreshing waters are snatched away by drought and heat. Sheol, the place of the dead, also snatches away those who sin. In the same way the wicked come to an abrupt end. Both the beginning of life and the end of life are not kind to the wicked. The statement that the womb forgets the wicked may be a description of the loss of a mother's love for the child she bore, a harsh metaphor for absolute abandonment. The idea of abandonment continues in the description of the death of the wicked where the worm finds them sweet. The worm relishes the dead bodies of the wicked like a delicate dessert course.[9] The memory of the wicked is also lost so that posterity does not honor them. The last clause summarizes this teaching by describing wickedness as broken like a tree.

Another viewpoint is expressed in verses 21-24 where the wicked are described as flourishing for a time even though they commit wicked deeds. They take advantage of the weak in society, the barren woman and the widow.[10] God is the one

---

8. Hartley, *Job*, 353. He notes that the first line of v. 18 describes the precarious state of the wicked who are swiftly floating down a river with a strong current.

9. G. Wilson, *Job*, 276.

10. The translation of the ESV as 'they wrong the barren' supports the view that the wicked take advantage of the weak and understands the participle *rō'eh*

who by His power prolongs the life of the wicked. Even when despair comes to them because of the troubles of life, they rise up and are sustained in the midst of despair. God knows their ways and still supports them and gives them security. This security, however, does not last forever because like all human beings the wicked are here for a short time and then they are gone. They are exalted for a little while, but then they die, being cut off like the heads of grain. Job ends this section with a challenge for his friends to prove to him that he is a liar and that what he says is false. He believes that anyone who observes the way the world works will agree with him.

The challenge for this section is that it presents two different viewpoints concerning the fate of the wicked in this life. The first viewpoint (vv. 18-20) expresses that the wicked come to a swift end and would be in line with the view of the friends. The second viewpoint (vv. 21-24) emphasizes that the wicked do not always come to a quick end, but they prosper for a while, even being propped up by God. Scholars have wrestled with how to understand these words as the words of Job since they seem to agree with the view of the friends and disagree with what he has said in 24:1-17. One approach is to deny that Job spoke these words and attribute them to one of the friends. Habel takes Zophar as the intended speaker because of thematic and terminological connections with his previous speech.[11] Others reconstruct a third speech of Zophar with words that are attributed to Job because they seem to affirm the view of retribution of the friends. Zophar's third speech is 27:7-23 with 24:18-24 added to it. Such rearrangement of the text is very subjective and there is no textual evidence to support moving passages to form a third speech of Zophar.[12]

---

as 'feeding' on the underprivileged (Habel, *Job*, 362). Many commentators see this verse as describing the wives of the wicked as barren and as being left as widows (Hartley, *Job*, 353 and Longman, *Job*, 304).

11. Habel, *Job*, 358. The thematic connections include the appointed day of God's wrath (20:28), the allotted portion of the wicked (20:29), and the exploitation of the poor (20:19). Habel speculates that Zophar's name is omitted from this speech because this speech is out of place in the sequence of the friends' speeches.

12. For an analysis of views related to the difficulties of 24:18-25, see Lo, *Job 28 as Rhetoric*, 108-17.

Another approach is to understand Job 24:18-24 as a quotation of the friends.[13] Some argue that only verses 18-21 are a quotation from the friends and that verses 22-24 are Job's reply.[14] The problem, however, is that verses 22-24 are not really a reply because they end with the assurance of retribution on the wicked, and Job argues that experience does not justify this assurance.[15] Others point out that this view leaves these verses hanging as a limp ending with no response from Job.[16] Or if verse 25 is seen as a response from Job, it does not make sense to quote the friends' view and then to challenge them to prove that Job is a liar and that there is nothing in what he says.[17]

Another approach is to accept Job 24:18-24 as the words of Job. Some would understand Job's speech to be expressing what he would wish would happen rather than a description of what does happen.[18] If that were the case one would expect some of the Hebrew verbs to be in the jussive form of the verb.[19] Another approach is to recognize that Job will not remain consistent in his argument throughout his speeches but will at times utter contradictory sayings. Lo finds several examples of contradictory sayings in chapter 23 and argues that chapter 24 shows the conflict between reality (vv. 1-17) and theology (vv. 18-24). The discrepancy between experience and theology is clearly revealed through Job's own suffering (chapter 23) and through widespread social injustice (24:1-17). In 24:18-24 Job defends the moral order with the purpose of supporting his own position and arguing against the friends. Job appears as a righteous sufferer to declare judgment on the wicked. This argument shows the inadequacy of the friends' view of

13. The ESV adds 'You say' to the beginning of v. 18 that gives the impression that vv. 18-24 are a quotation of the friends. It is possible that the quote of the friends includes only vv. 18-20, a view that would support the idea of two viewpoints being expressed in vv. 18-24.

14. S. R. Driver and G. B. Gray, *A Critical and Exegetical Commentary on the Book of Job* (Edinburgh: T. & T. Clark, 1921), 211; see also Lo, *Job 28*, 113-14.

15. H. H. Rowley, *The Book of Job*, rev. ed. (Grand Rapids: Eerdmans, 1980), 167.

16. Habel, *Job*, 357.

17. See the discussion in Lo, *Job 28*, 113-14.

18. Carol Newsome, 'The Book of Job,' in *The New Interpreter's Bible, Volume IV* (Nashville, TN: Abingdon Press, 1996), 511-12.

19. Driver and Gray, *Book of Job*, 211.

retribution to explain Job's situation. The broader truth is that God is to be blamed for withholding the days of judgment and for His indifference to injustice.[20] In this approach, one should not hold Job to consistent statements throughout his speeches as he wrestles with his suffering. There also may be development in Job's thinking and subtle nuances that need to be taken into consideration. Verses 18-24 seem to be expressing two viewpoints with verses 18-20 representing the viewpoint of the friends and verses 21-24 representing the viewpoint of Job that God delays the judgment of the wicked. Although the friends have expressed the view that the prosperity of the wicked does not last (20:5, 11, 21), they have not expressed the view that the prosperity of the wicked is related to the delay of God's judgment. Job is seeking to contrast the friends' view of the wicked with the prosperity of the wicked that anyone can observe. There are many situations where the wicked get away with their wickedness and experience no punishment for it. If such a view of the wicked is accurate, then the simplistic view of the friends is proved to be wrong. The experiences of life support Job's view and, if it were not so, the friends could easily prove him to be a liar (24:25).

Job continues to move from despair to confidence and then back to despair as he wrestles with his suffering. It is interesting that some of Job's strongest statements of confidence come after being accused directly of sin. He affirms that his experience of suffering will turn out for his good (23:10), but such a response does not mean that he remains quiet, especially in light of the argument of the friends who have accused him of sin. Job continues to seek an audience with God. This desire to seek a hearing from God in person is probably a rebuff to Eliphaz' appeal for Job to seek God in repentance.

Job also experiences both the fear of God (23:11-12) and the terror of God (23:16). Those two responses are mentioned by Moses when the people were at Mt. Sinai. When the people saw the lightning and the mountain smoking and heard the thunder they were terrified and trembled before the presence of God (Exod. 20:18). But Moses told them that they did not need to fear because God had come to test them so that the

20. Lo, *Job 28*, 122–123.

fear of God would cause them not to sin (Exod. 20:20). In other words, there was no need for them to be terrified of God, but it was appropriate for them to have a proper fear of God.[21] A proper response to God should bring about the proper attitude of reverence toward God. Job had such a response to God in chapters 1–2. The continuation of his suffering and the argument of the friends have turned Job's world upside-down so that he has lost his bearings. This explains how he can experience both the terror of God and the fear of God. Suffering can remove the bearings of life and cause a person to wrestle with God and even be unsure of his relationship with God.

Jesus Christ Himself faced the loss of the bearings of life to a limited degree. He wrestled with God His Father in the garden of Gethsemane concerning the cup of judgment that He was about to drink. He was counted among the wicked as He hung on the cross. He expressed the problem of His relationship with God with the words of Psalm 22:1, 'My God, My God, why have you forsaken me?' If Christ experienced these things according to His human nature, then we should not be surprised if there are times when His people also experience such a loss of perspective. The power of Christ's work is that He overcame the power of darkness and emerged victorious on the third day in His resurrection from the dead. Any believer may still experience the darkness of suffering and the loss of one's bearing in life, but the hope of victory should eventually shine through the darkness as our union with Christ ensures we will be victorious in Him.

Resurrection as a Way of Life

'Indeed, I count everything as loss because of the sur-passing worth of knowing Christ Jesus my Lord. For his sake I have suffered the loss of all things and count them as rubbish, in order that I may gain Christ and be found in him, not having a righteousness of my own that comes from the law, but that which comes through faith in Christ, the righteousness from God that depends on faith – *that I may know him and the power of his resurrection, and may*

---

21. The same word 'fear' is used in Exodus 20:20. The first use in the phrase 'do not fear' is the verb (*yāra'*) and the second use 'fear' is the noun (*yir'āh*).

share his sufferings, becoming like him in his death, that by any means possible I may attain the resurrection from the dead. Not that I have already obtained this or am already perfect, but I press on to make it my own, because Christ Jesus has made me his own. Brothers, I do not consider that I have made it my own. But one thing I do: forgetting what lies behind and straining forward to what lies ahead, I press on toward the goal for the prize of the upward call of God in Christ Jesus' (Phil. 3:8-14).

In many ways it doesn't feel like the typical Easter for us. We didn't make it to a worship service or celebrate it with anyone else. Nevertheless, we have certainly been experiencing the Resurrection of Christ over the last twelve days. We really have experienced the Risen Lord more this Easter than we have on any other Easter of our lives.

The reason that we can know Christ and say that the things of this world are 'rubbish' is because of Jesus' life, death, and resurrection. The reason why Pierce will rise is because Christ has risen. As Pierce becomes healthier in this life, it is only because of God's love through Jesus. As Pierce is raised up on that Day when Christ makes all things new, it is because of God's love through Jesus. That is what we are celebrating today. The resurrection has transformed, is transforming, and will transform the entire universe. We believe that. That is why the last twelve days have been the best and worst time of our lives.

The Resurrection is a way of life. And as we celebrate Easter today, we are grateful that we have experienced the Resurrection in ways we never before experienced it. By no means have we fully obtained it, but we press on to make it our own, because Christ Jesus has made us His own.

Nik and Lindsay Franks (4/24/11)

Study Questions

1) Show how Job's confidence grows even while his relationship with God remains difficult.

2) How is God's freedom both a comfort and a source of terror for Job?

3) How does Job describe the wicked? Is part of his description accurate? What does he say about God's relationship to the wicked? Is that accurate?

4) What two views of the fate of the wicked does Job present? How have commentators tried to explain these two views? What is the best way to understand this?

5) How might suffering impact a person's life and the way they view life? What are the dangers in how a person responds to suffering? How does the life of Christ help?

17

Bildad's Short Speech: The Collapse of the Debate

(Job 25)

Bildad's third speech is very short. Zophar does not have a third speech. Although many have tried to rearrange chapters 25–28 to extend Bildad's speech and to give Zophar a third speech to complete the third cycle of speeches (see below), the best approach to this problem is to recognize that the debate between the friends has collapsed. No answer has been found to the wisdom debate between Job and his friends. This fact raises the question whether the answer can be found on the human level. God needs to address this problem.

Job 25 is short but is arranged with a chiastic structure with verse 4 standing at the center of the chiasm. This makes verse 4 the focus of this short speech.[1]

A The Greatness of God (v. 2)

    B The Innumerable Heavenly Hosts (v. 3)

        C Humanity's Stance before God:
        How can Human beings be Right before God (v. 4)?

    B' The Lack of Splendor of the Moon and Stars before God (v. 5)

A' The Insignificance of Humanity before God (v. 6)

---

1. Hartley, *Job*, 355.

Bildad's speech begins with a statement on the greatness of God. He is the sovereign ruler of the universe so that people are terrified of Him.[2] His dominion is seen in the peace that results in the high heaven, the place of God's dwelling. God's power is seen in that there is no limit to the heavenly hosts, which are His armies that He commands. God's dominion is demonstrated in the fact that His light shines upon everyone. Bildad's argument of God's sovereign rule answers Job's claim that God rules unjustly (24:1–17).[3]

In comparison with God's power and dominion, human beings seem so small and insignificant. The focus of verse 4 is on human beings' moral standing before God. The rhetorical questions are meant to be answered in the negative. There is no way that a human being can be right before God and there is no way someone born of a woman can be pure before God.[4] These rhetorical questions strike at the heart of the debate between Job and the friends. It is impossible for Job to be right before God and it is impossible for him to be pure before God. In order to support the insignificance of humanity, the splendor of the moon and stars in the presence of God is set forth. Although to human beings the moon and the stars seem bright, they are not bright in comparison with God's brightness: 'the stars are not pure in his eyes.' The brightness of the moon is a poetic image of ethical purity.[5] The payoff of the argument comes in verse 6. If the splendor of the moon and the stars is overshadowed by God's brightness, then how much more insignificant are human beings in the light of God's greatness. In fact, human beings are so insignificant that they are compared with maggots and worms. These terms symbolize a wretched existence and they have the smell of death to them. The frail condition of human beings makes them susceptible to death where the body will be consumed by worms.[6]

---

2. The word *pāḥaḏ* can mean 'fear' but more commonly means 'terror' (L. Wilson, *Job*, 126, n. 204).

3. Hartley, *Job*, 355.

4. The word for 'human being' (*'ĕnôš*) and the phrase 'born of a woman' stress the weakness of human beings (Hartley, *Job*, 357).

5. Habel, *Job*, 369. Eliphaz' earlier speech spoke of the heavenly angels as being impure (Job 15:15), but here Bildad speaks of the heavenly moon and stars as impure.

6. Hartley, *Job*, 357.

This short speech of Bildad leaves little room for mercy for someone who claims innocence before God. It is important to point out that Job never claimed perfection. He has claimed he is innocent of any wicked deed that is the cause of his suffering. The friends have a hard time making this distinction, but it is a distinction that is rooted in the character of Job affirmed by God in the first two chapters. The depth of Job's suffering is what has caused the friends to charge him with wrong. Surely, they argue, no one suffering as much as Job can be innocent of wrong. Perhaps Job's illness reminds them of someone already being consumed in the grave by maggots. In pressing this argument they include all human beings in the category of worms and maggots. It is true that human beings can descend to such low levels because of sin and the way they treat each other. God even calls Israel a worm (Isa. 41:14), but He also speaks of being their Redeemer and helping them become powerful for God again (Isa. 41:15–16). Part of the problem is the way the discussion is presented. It is true that human beings can find themselves in weak and disgusting situations because of their sin, but it is also true that God has given human beings a high place in creation (Gen. 1:26-28; Ps. 8).[7] Sin has defaced human beings but has not destroyed the image of God. No matter how low someone sinks there is hope for redemption and restoration to the high place God has for humans in creation.

The Incomplete Third Cycle of Speeches

Many scholars have a problem with an incomplete third cycle of speeches. Eliphaz has three speeches. Bildad has three speeches but his third speech is very short, unlike the other speeches of the friends. This has led some to argue that there must be more to Bildad's third speech. Zophar only has two speeches and so he does not have a third speech. The text presents Job speaking in chapters 26–31, with headings at chapters 26, 27, and 29. Some of the comments in these chapters sound more like what the friends have argued rather than an argument that Job would make (26:5-14; 27:13-23).[8]

---

7. Longman (*Job*, 309-10) has a section called 'Maggot Theology' where he discusses these issues.

8. Job 26:5-14 is supposed to be very different from the way Job expresses negative aspects of God in his previous hymnic materials and sounds more like the

Thus there are attempts to come up with a complete third
cycle by taking parts of chapters 26 and 27 and adding them
to Bildad's speech to give him a longer speech or by making
a third speech for Zophar.

Hartley argues that the Bildad speech is too short, so
he wants to add 27:13-23 to the end of Bildad's speech to
make it a more normal length. He also argues that 27:13-23
is a restatement of Zophar's teaching that the wicked face
certain judgment. He does not believe that Zophar offers a
third speech. His second speech is significantly longer than
his first speech (56 lines compared to 40 lines) and acts as
a signal that he would not speak again. Zophar is the least
creative of the three friends and nothing is lost if he does
not offer a third speech. Also, the fact that the added section
to Bildad's speech (27:13-23) is a restatement of Zophar's
teaching indicates that the friends have nothing more to say.[9]

Clines takes part of Job 26 and adds it to Bildad's speech
to make it longer and to make it more like the structure of
the other speeches. His reconstruction of Bildad's speech
goes in the order 25:1, 26:2-4, 25:2-6, and 26:5-14. He argues
that 26:1 ('Then Job answered and said') was introduced by
a copyist after the order of the speeches had been damaged.[10]
Job's ninth speech is 27:1-6, 11-12. Zophar's third speech to
complete the third cycle is 27:7-10, 13-17; 24:18-24; 27:18-23.[11]

A better approach to the question of an incomplete third
cycle is to accept the text's presentation of the three cycles.
Trying to rearrange the text to complete a third cycle has
problems. The difficulty of reconstructing a third cycle
is evident in that there is no agreement on how the third
cycle should be completed.[12] This uncertainty does not give
confidence about the attempts at reconstruction. The short
speech of Bildad has a literary structure that demonstrates

---

friends' hymns magnifying the greatness of God (Lo, *Job 28*, 132-33). Job 27:13-23
sounds like the friends' view of divine retribution.

9. Hartley, *Job*, 25 and 355. Hartley discusses Job 27:13-23 in conjunction
with 25:1-6.

10. Clines, *Job 21–37*, 630.

11. Clines, *Job 21–37*, 641 and 651.

12. For a presentation of the different reconstructions of the third cycle, see
Lo, *Job 28*, 127.

unity and argues against the view that it is unnecessarily short and should be added to from the speeches of chapters 26–27. The incomplete third cycle should be accepted because it teaches something significant about the debate. The friends have run out of steam and have not been able to convince Job of their argument.[13] The dialogue has ground to a halt and for all practical purposes the debate is over.[14] Each side has become entrenched in their positions and the debate has deteriorated to hurling insults back-and-forth at each other (Job 8:2; 11:2-3; 12:2; 15:2-3; 16:2-3; 18:2-3; 20:3). Frustration has set in and an impasse has been reached concerning God's justice and Job's integrity.

Some would even argue that the collapse of the third cycle and the fact that Job gets the last word in chapters 27–31 is evidence that he has won the debate.[15] God's statement in Job 42:7 supports this conclusion, but this does not mean that everything Job has said about God in response to the friends is correct. It is also clear that the issue that Job is wrestling with has not been resolved because he is still suffering and he is still seeking a meeting with God. Wisdom has not yet been found and there is a need for God to speak to resolve Job's situation.

God's Sustaining Power

Nik and I were able to stay home last night (yeah!) as Pierce had a great night/morning. We were called in today to meet with the doctor to discuss what we should do about the PDA (open duct near his heart/lungs). Here is the report: the doctors had hoped to be able to administer a medicine to close the PDA, but Pierce has not proven to be a candidate. At this point in the game, they feel it's best to do something as opposed to just leaving it open. In more or less words, they need to act in order for him to get better. That being said, our only option is PDA surgery. It's hard to make this decision when he is seemingly stable

---

13. Longman, *Job*, 309 and G. Wilson, *Job*, 280.

14. Estes, *Handbook*, 89.

15. Jones, *Job*, 189.

… kind of like a 'why rock the boat?' mentality, but we are trusting that God is guiding the doctors and that this is the best choice for our son. Please be in prayer as we meet with the surgeon. Both Nik and I have a peace that this is the best option and we are trusting that God will continue to sustain Pierce's life … (4/25/11)

Friends, we are witnessing yet another medical miracle. We just got in from meeting with Pierce's medical team and they are indeed blown away. Here is how the conversation went:

Nurse Practitioner (after a brief moment of quiet pondering): 'You know, most babies get really sick after this surgery, I'm sure you were prepared. Well, it looks like he is not doing that. In fact, for today, I'm going to give him an "A" in terms of recovery/progress.'

Then enters Pierce's doctor with a BIG grin on his face. He chuckles as he looks at me and simply says, 'Pierce is writing his own book.' He replies to the Nurse Practitioner's comment by saying, 'He gets an A+!' He goes on to explain that God works in mysterious ways … and this amazing recovery is not normal (in fact it is so rare, that he simply is blown away).

So needless to say, God is at work. He is answering our prayers affirmatively and we cannot begin to describe the amount of joy and gratitude that is pouring from our hearts today. We know that God is working and using your prayers. Thank you!

Nik and Lindsay Franks (4/29/11)

Study Questions

1) What does the structure of Job 25 teach about the meaning of Job 25?

2) What does Bildad's speech teach about God and human beings in relationship to God?

3) How does Bildad use the term 'worm' to describe human beings? What is the problem with the way Bildad uses this term?

4) Why do some scholars have trouble with an incomplete third cycle of speeches? What are some of the ways this problem is addressed?

5) What is a better way to approach an incomplete third cycle? What does an incomplete third cycle teach?

18

Job: Who Understands God's Mysterious Ways?
(Job 26)

Attempts to reconstruct the third cycle of speeches impact the way scholars understand Job 26–28. Some attribute parts of Job 26 to Bildad's short speech of Job 25 (see the discussion in the last chapter). Hartley adds Job 27:13-23 to Bildad's speech and understands Job 26:1–27:12 to be Job's response to Bildad. This view goes against the heading of 27:1 ('And Job again took up his discourse') that Hartley ignores because he thinks it is secondary.[1] If one takes seriously the headings in these chapters, then Job 26 has a heading attributing it to Job, Job 27–28 has a heading attributing these two chapters to Job, and Job 29 has a heading that marks Job 29–31 as the words of Job. If one accepts these headings, then Job 26 is Job's response to Bildad,[2] Job 27–28 is Job's reflections on his dialogue with the friends, and Job 29–31 is Job's final speech that ends in strong assertions of his innocence.

The Useless Counsel of Bildad (Job 26:1-4)
Job specifically responds to Bildad in Chapter 26 before responding in general to his situation and the counsel of the

---

1. Hartley, *Job*, 358–362.
2. There is no need to view Job 26–31 as an extended response to Bildad's third speech (G. Wilson, *Job*, 282).

friends in Chapter 27.[3] Job sarcastically responds to Bildad
that his speech offers no help to Job.[4] His emphasis on the
dominion and power of God and the lowly position of human
beings as maggots and worms, full of the stench of death, does
not help someone who is suffering. Bildad has no message
to deliver someone who has no power or strength. Even if
human beings cannot be right before God and are as low as
maggots, where is the help in such counsel for someone who
is powerless and needs deliverance? If Bildad conceives Job
as someone who has no wisdom, then his speech of chapter
25 offers no wisdom or 'sound knowledge' that would offer
hope to the suffering. Wisdom could help someone to rise
above trying circumstances to accomplish God's purpose,[5]
but Bildad's counsel falls short of that goal. Job then questions
the source of Bildad's words, implying that they have not
come from God.

No One Understands God's Ways (Job 26:5-14)

Some scholars have trouble accepting these verses as
the words of Job because the use of hymn-like words is
positive toward God instead of negatively exposing God's
destructive mode of governing as in his other speeches. The
positive tone that emphasizes God's transcendent mystery
and orderly design of the cosmos sounds like the argument
of the friends.[6] Even if Job is more positive toward God in

---

3. The pronouns in Job 26:1-4 are singular and not plural. Job is addressing one
individual and it makes sense that he is responding to Bildad. Normally Job responds
to a speech of one of the friends with plural pronouns because he is addressing the
friends as a group. He will address the friends as a group in Job 27.

4. In Job 26:2-3 each verse begins with the interrogative $m\bar{a}h$ ('what' or 'how'),
followed by a second person singular verb indicating Bildad's ineffectiveness,
followed by a negative prepositional phrase describing the object (G. Wilson, *Job*,
282). These verses could be translated as a question that expects a 'no' answer
or as an exclamation that emphasizes the negative. If a translation has a question
mark, then the verse is a question; and if it has an exclamation mark, then it is an
exclamation (as the ESV).

5. Hartley (*Job*, 363) gives Joseph and Daniel as two examples of individuals
who overcame trying circumstances through God's wisdom.

6. Habel, *Job*, 366. Based on an extensive comparison Lo agrees that Job's
words in 26:5-14 are not negative toward God like Job's other speeches. This should
not be taken, however, as evidence that these words could not have been uttered
by Job. Many apply a test of consistency to Job's words that is unwarranted. Lo's
basic approach is that the author uses contradictory juxtaposition (such as between

26:5-14 these words are a direct response to Bildad that demonstrates that Bildad (and the friends by implication) do not understand the ways of God. If God's ways are mysterious and beyond the understanding of human beings, then Bildad's view that God is punishing Job for personal sin is too simplistic an explanation of the mysterious ways of God.

Job's words in 26:5-14 continue the idea that Bildad's counsel does not help the powerless and the one who lacks wisdom. His counsel does not help because he is not capable of understanding the mysterious ways of God's dominion. Job gives a brief accounting of such mysterious ways. God rules the place of the dead (Sheol). This is an area of God's universe that humans who are alive know very little about. Sheol, however, is not a mystery to God because it is naked before Him. In other words, God knows what happens in the realm of the dead;[7] He sees the dead[8] tremble under the waters[9] (vv. 5-6). God also exercises dominion in the heavens; He is in control of areas of the universe about which humans have little knowledge; at creation, He hung the earth on nothing and stretched out the north[10] over the void of the universe (vv. 7-9). Closer to the earth, God controls the rain clouds and He can hide or expose the full moon by these clouds. From the earth's point of view (vv. 10-11), the horizon that humans see in the distance is the boundary set by God.

Job 25 and 26) in a rhetorical way. Concerning Job 26:5-14, Lo shows that the point of Job 26:5-14 is to demonstrate the limitation of human wisdom in relationship to God's ways (Lo, *Job 28*, 132-66).

7. Abaddon is a term for the underworld that comes from a word that means 'destruction' (*ʾăḇaḏ*).

8. The word for 'dead' is the Hebrew term 'rephaim'. This term refers to those who dwell in the underworld and whose existence is expressed in the translation 'shades'. They are described in the Bible as lifeless before God, as needing rousing, as trembling before Him, and as not being able to travel or participate in banquets. For a fuller discussion of this term, see P. Johnston, *Shades of Sheol* (Downers Grove, IL: InterVarsity, 2002), 127-41.

9. Sheol is presented as a murky, watery existence that lies under the ocean (Hartley, *Job*, 365).

10. The term 'north' seems to be a term for the high heavens, the place of God's throne. In Ugaritic mythology 'north' (the Hebrew 'zaphon') is where the divine assembly of the gods gathered at Mount Zaphon, the dwelling place of Baal (Hartley, *Job*, 365–366).

Since God has created the earth and heaven, the pillars of heaven[11] can be shaken at His rebuke.

God also demonstrates His dominion over the world of the gods (vv. 12-13). The word 'sea' is used in parallel with 'Rahab' to show that the realm of the gods is in view. Yam is the Hebrew word for 'sea', and it can also refer to the sea god. Rahab refers to a mythological creature that inhabits the sea. The stilling of the sea shows God's power over false gods who also represent the forces of chaos in the world.[12] God also destroys the fleeing serpent, probably a reference to Leviathan (Isa. 27:1; Job 3:8; 41:1),[13] to demonstrate His defeat of all the false gods.

The point of Job's words culminates in the main point of verse 14. Those works of God are mysterious because they are the outskirts of His ways that are hardly comprehensible to human beings. If we only hear a small whisper of Him, how much more of God do we not know, much less understand?

The chapter ends on a question: 'But the thunder of his power who can understand?' In light of 26:5-14 the answer is that no one understands God's power and how it is manifest in the world He has created. Such a conclusion is an indictment of Bildad's view. He is unable to understand the ways of God because he only catches a small glimpse of God's ways that are broader and greater than the human mind can comprehend. Drawing conclusions about Job's situation from such a limited knowledge of God is foolish and dangerous. Our knowledge of God is like a whisper in the vast display of the thunder of His power.

The mythological references in this chapter are used to demonstrate God's power and victory over the false gods of other nations. There is no ongoing cosmic battle in the

---

11. The phrase 'pillars of heaven' probably refers to the distant mountains that can be seen on the horizon and appear to be supporting the sky (Hartley, *Job*, 366 and Habel, *Job*, 373). This is a poetic description of the world from the perspective of someone who is looking at the horizon. Such poetic descriptions do not mean that the authors of Scripture are commending an ancient Near Eastern view of the world consisting of a three-tiered universe (for more discussion of this issue, see Richard P. Belcher, Jr., *Genesis: The Beginning of God's Plan of Salvation* [Ross-shire: Christian Focus, 2012], 22–25).

12. Longman, *Job*, 316.

13. Longman, *Job*, 317. For more on Leviathan, see Job 41.

universe to see which of the gods will emerge as the king
of the universe, because God is the king of the universe. He
has no rival, for He is able to defeat all His foes. The fleeing
serpent of verse 13 may be a reference to Leviathan, but it
is also an allusion to Genesis 3:15. There is evil in the world
and spiritual forces of wickedness seek to destroy God's good
creation and hinder the purposes of God. These forces even
attack God's people, as Satan does in Job 1–2.

The rule of God over these forces of wickedness is a comfort
to God's people in that there is nothing in all of creation that
can threaten God's purposes or separate them from His love
(Rom. 8:18-39). God's victory over Satan and the forces of sin
and death fulfils the promise of Genesis 3:15 that someone
would come to crush the head of the serpent. Christ's victory,
through His death, burial, and resurrection, guarantees their
victory so that Paul can affirm that they also will trample on
the head of Satan (Rom. 16:20).

There is so much that Job does not know about God's
purposes in relationship to his suffering, including the
precipitating events of Job 1–2. And yet he is still able to
affirm the mystery of God's rule over His creation and God's
victory over the forces of wickedness. Even Job could see at
times that his suffering could not separate him from God. For
those who understand the gospel, there is an even greater
assurance of hope even although there are many things they
do not understand about the mystery of God's ways. They
see that God, who did not spare His own Son for them, will
also freely provide for them all that they need. This bond
is so secure in Christ that suffering, illness, persecution, or
even death cannot separate them from the victory Christ
has secured for them. The ways of God are mysterious and
wondrous.

Do not be Anxious

Pierce is stable today. I believe this is day 20, so we have
about 11 more days until we hit the crucial month mark.
We have been carried thus far by the grace of God and
we praise Him for that. We were told last night by Pierce's
primary night nurse that he has cleared a lot of hurdles.

There is still a long way to go (if all goes well, he will get out around his original due date which was August 4th), but we are confident Pierce will keep pressing through as he has been. There are so many things that we could sit around and worry about, but we really haven't been fretting. We continue to have a strong confidence and peace from God.

One area that God has used this situation to sanctify us in is the area of worry or anxiety. It is so foolish and prideful to sit around paralyzed by anxiety over things that we can't and don't have control over. Situations like this force us to experience the joy of casting our anxieties on God because He cares for us (1 Peter 5:7). The best perspective on anxiety came from the Lord Jesus Himself, when He said, 'And which of you by being anxious can add a single hour to his span of life?' (Matt. 6:27). Anxiety only displays pride, unfaithfulness, and a foolish desire to prolong life or make it fit to our ideal. I am sure times of anxiety will come for us over the next few months, but I pray that we can remember to cast them on the One who has been more than faithful in this journey thus far.

This week, we are going to attempt to sleep at home every night. We are going to try and establish a schedule that will have us visiting the hospital twice a day. We need your prayers in getting adjusted to this schedule. We need endurance and a peace as we will be daily leaving our son at the hospital. This week, we are also going to try and start addressing all the other things that come with life. In addition to bills, work, etc., this week I am going to attempt to take an exam, read a few books, write a paper, and study for a couple more exams that I have next week.

Fierce Pierce (a friend gave him this nickname) needs your continued prayers for health. Pray that his lungs will grow stronger quickly and that he can come off the ventilation machines sooner than expected. Also, pray that his intestines and bowels mature and grow strong without getting infected or perforated. The intestines and bowels are probably the most serious concern right now. If they get infected it can really affect Pierce's morbidity and become severely life-threatening. And if they get perforated the chance of mortality is high. Nevertheless, we have a strong confidence that the Lord is with Pierce and will sustain him throughout this trial. Also, continue to pray for his brain bleeds. Pierce's ventricles did not swell at all as of the last ultrasound and we praise God for that! Pierce's whole body still needs healing and strength, so please keep praying. God is bringing glory to His name through our little man as only He can. A 1.5 pound baby in a four-month NICU stay isn't exactly the first thing that comes to mind when we think of glory and power. 'But God chose what is foolish in the world to shame the wise; God chose what is weak in the world to shame the strong; God chose what is low and despised in the world, even things that are not, to bring to nothing things that are, so that no human being might boast in the presence of God' (1 Cor. 1:27-29).

We love and thank you all,
Nik Franks (5/2/11)

Study Questions

1) What are the implications if the headings of the text are taken seriously for chapters 26–31?

2) Why does Job believe that Bildad's counsel is worthless?

3) Are the ways of God mysterious? How does this make you feel?

4) Do Christians have any security in the face of God's mysterious ways? Explain.

19

Job: A Warning to the Friends concerning the Fate of the Wicked
(Job 27)

Job 27 begins with its own heading: 'And Job again took up his discourse' (v. 1).[1] This sets chapter 27 apart from chapter 26. In chapter 26 Job responded to Bildad's speech in chapter 25. In chapter 27 Job gives his last response to the friends[2] before making his final statement in chapters 29–31.[3]

An Oath of Innocence (Job 27:1-6)

Job takes an oath that affirms his integrity. In other words, he continues to argue that he has not done anything evil to cause his suffering. He takes the oath in the name of God and the assurance of His existence ('as God lives'), but he adds negative statements concerning God. This is the God who has taken away his right and has made his soul bitter. Here is another example of Job appealing to the very God who is the source of his trouble.[4] He vows by the God who lives and

---

1. Although Hartley sees this heading as secondary, his explanation of why it was added is a good explanation of its original purpose: Job continues to speak because Zophar remains silent (Hartley, *Job*, 368).

2. The 'you' of v. 5 is plural and Job speaks of 'all of you' in v. 12.

3. For how Job 28 fits into these final speeches, see the next chapter where it will be argued that Job 27–28 is his last response to the friends.

4. The appeal to God who is the source of his trouble shows that Job has no hope in a third party to vindicate him (Hartley, *Job*, 369).

gives him life ('the Spirit of God is in my nostrils'), but this God has made life very difficult for him. Job does not renounce God or deny His existence, but continues to assert his own integrity even if it seems like God has wronged him. Job lives in the tension of affirming God while also complaining to God about how God is treating him. He shows resilience in not backing down to the friends or even to God, partly because he has not completely lost faith in God.

The oath asserts that, as long as Job has breath, he will not speak falsehood or utter deceit (vv. 3-4). This means that he will never agree with the friends' view that he is suffering because of specific sin he has committed. He will not affirm that their argument is right because that would deny his integrity. Instead, he will hold fast to his integrity until he dies. Job calls his integrity 'my righteousness' which fits his character as presented in Job 1–2 ('blameless') and as affirmed by God (Job 1:8; 2:3). Job has a clear conscience in affirming his innocence because his own heart does not reproach him for these statements. He truly fits the definition of blameless as one who is not a hypocrite but who lives a whole life dedicated to God.[5]

A Curse against the Enemy (Job 27:7-12)

Job and the friends cannot both be right. Either Job is suffering because he has committed sin or his suffering has nothing to do with any sin he has committed. If Job is right and the friends are wrong, then the friends have treated Job unfairly and have acted toward him as an enemy. They have sinned against Job and they have misrepresented God. Job offers a curse against a singular enemy in verses 7-8 before he addresses the friends as a group in verses 11-12. Anyone who would agree with the position of the friends is an adversary of Job. He requests that his enemy, defined as someone who rises against him, should be treated as the wicked are treated.[6] Each of the friends has risen against Job in their condemnation of him and so he wants them to be treated

---

5. The word 'integrity' (*tummāh*) is related to the word blameless (*tām*) used in Job 1:8.

6. Hartley (*Job*, 371) argues that the enemy is left intentionally vague in order to emphasize that Job is requesting complete deliverance from all hostility.

in the same way because they, unlike Job, are acting in an unrighteous way.

Job raises a series of questions to describe the life of the wicked. What hope does the wicked person have if his life is going to be cut off by God? What hope does the wicked person have that God will hear his cry when distress comes upon him? Does the wicked person always call upon God when he is in need? Does the wicked person take delight in the Almighty so that when trouble comes he has confidence that God will be available? The wicked do not delight in God and so they have no intention of doing His will.[7]

Job turns to the friends in verse 11 to teach them concerning the hand of God, a reference to the way God works in this world.[8] The argument of the friends concerning Job is wrong because they do not understand the ways of God even though they have seen His ways. They have continued in their condemnation of Job and so have uttered meaningless arguments against him.

Instruction concerning the Wicked (Job 27:13-23)
Scholars have doubted that Job utters these words because they sound so much like the friends' argument concerning the fate of the wicked (see the discussion in chapter 17 on the incomplete third cycle). These words are presented, however, as the words of Job and there are reasonable explanations that support this understanding. It is possible that Job quotes the meaningless words of the friends that they have inappropriately used against him. This would see verses 13-23 as an expansion of the meaningless talk that Job mentions in verse 12.[9] Another explanation is that on a general level Job does agree with the argument of the friends concerning the ultimate demise of the wicked. The problem Job has had with the friends' argument is that they have identified him with the wicked.[10] Another possibility is that Job is instructing the friends by turning their argument back upon them, warning

---

7. Hartley, *Job*, 371.

8. Longman, *Job*, 319.

9. Alden, *Job*, 265.

10. Andersen, *Job*, 219–220.

them that what they have argued could happen to them.[11] This view fits well with the emphasis in verse 11 that Job is going to instruct them and it makes sense if the friends are seen as the enemy (27:7) who will receive the portion of the wicked (27:13). The friends have misrepresented God and so have wronged Job with their counsel making their identification with the wicked appropriate.

In verses 13-23 Job lays out what the wicked should expect to receive as a reward from God. Every aspect of the life of the wicked person falls under God's judgment. His descendants will experience the disasters of war, famine, and pestilence.[12] The disasters are so overwhelming that the widow of a wicked person will not mourn his death. The wicked may amass large amounts of money but this wealth will eventually go to the righteous (as in Prov. 13:22). The house of the wicked person is as unstable as a booth or the cocoon of a moth. His wealth can disappear overnight. He lives a life plagued by terror and he can be swept away suddenly by violent destructive forces.[13] The life of the wicked is very unstable and it is just a matter of time before he experiences the consequences of his wickedness. Job would agree with this general description of the wicked and he is also warning the friends that such a description could apply to them because their arguments have misrepresented God and have wronged Job. In this way Job turns the tables on the friends and uses their words against them.[14] The misapplication of theology is a serious offense that could bring God's judgment on them.

Job continues to proclaim his innocence and that he will not let go of his righteousness (27:6). Righteousness has both a forensic aspect and a moral aspect. The forensic aspect refers to Job's standing before God the judge and his desire to argue

11. Talbert, *Beyond Suffering*, 149–150. He combines the quotation view with the idea that this section is an imprecation against the enemies, who would be Eliphaz, Bildad, and Zophar.

12. Lo, *Job 28*, 171.

13. Habel, *Job*, 387. He understands v. 23 to refer to the wind that claps its hands in derision and whistles its sinister mocking sounds through the deserted ruins where the wicked once lived in splendor. Longman understands God to be the subject with the idea that He despises the wicked (*Job*, 320). Some English translations understand the subject to be 'men' (KJV; NAS).

14. Lo, *Job 28*, 194.

his case of innocence before God so that he can be declared righteous. Since Job has been falsely accused of wrongdoing, he should legally be declared righteous in this particular case. And yet, Job has never argued that he is innocent before God on every count. Job recognizes the reality of sin and the need for a sacrifice for sin (Job 1:5). In theological terms, this speaks of the need for justification by faith because no one is righteous before God. A declaration of righteousness can only come because someone else's righteousness has been accepted (Gen. 15:6). When Job is declared blameless in Job 1–2, and when Job continues to assert his righteousness, it refers to the moral integrity of his life as someone who turns away from evil. In theological terms this refers to sanctification and the practical righteousness that is evident in Job's life. It is important to understand basic theology or we might become like the friends and misapply God's truth to a person's life.

Mother's Day

Well it surely wasn't the Mother's Day I had planned. In fact, I hadn't planned on being a mother for this Mother's Day. But I can't put into words how truly grateful I am to have Pierce with us this year. Today was hard, as you can imagine. Going to the restaurant, seeing the moms with their kids, and longing to have mine with me. I found myself growing bitter at some of the moms, even moms in the NICU (neo-natal intensive care unit). It's hard when you go into the NICU waiting room and hear a mom telling about how their full-term, 8 lb. baby is having a 'rough' time because they have to be in the NICU for observation for a few hours. Everything in me wants to scream and say, 'Seriously? A hard time? You don't have a clue.' I know this is totally the wrong attitude to have, but I'd be lying if I didn't say I struggled with this sin. But God is gracious. I am constantly drawn to the verse, 'Humble yourselves, therefore, under the mighty hand of God so that at the proper time he may exalt you, casting all your anxieties on him, because he cares for you' (1 Pet. 5:6-7). This reminds me to lay down my pride. To be humble amidst this trial has indeed been a challenge, and I don't expect that to change. But I am learning that God grants us grace when we are too weak to fight sin. He strengthens us. And He alone brings comfort. I spent a good portion of the day reflecting on the many trials that God has brought us through and how far we have come in three-and-a-half weeks. For that, I am also grateful. I am also grateful for the many ways in which He has worked in my heart, for the ways in which He has used this experience to work in so many of your lives, for how He has brought Nik and I closer together, and for the love He has poured out on the three of us during this difficult time.

Lindsay Franks (5/9/11)

Study Questions

1) What conclusion can be drawn from the fact that Job vows by the very God who Job thinks has wronged him?

2) How can the friends of Job be seen as an enemy?

3) What are the various ways Job 27:13-23 have been understood? How might these words describe the friends? What conclusions can be drawn concerning the seriousness of counseling others or of speaking for God?

4) How does an important theological distinction come into play in this section? Why is it important?

5) How important is theology for the counsel you offer others?

20

The Quest for Wisdom: Who Can Discover Wisdom?

(Job 28)

Job 28 is a tranquil poem that is very different from the heated debate between Job and the friends. Many scholars have a hard time accepting Job 28 as the words of Job. Some of the problems are the peaceful tone of Job 28, the change in literary genre, and the use of Adonai as a name for God.[1] The fact that there is no mention of Job as the speaker in 28:1, unlike 26:1, 27:1, and 29:1, suggests that he is not speaking here.[2] The fact that Job uses the traditional 'fear of the Lord' at the end of chapter 28 means a return to a posture of unquestioning submission that the friends have advocated and that Job has rejected.[3] Thus Job 28 is seen as inconsistent with the words of Job spoken in chapter 27 and chapters 29–31 because it is calm in tone and orthodox in content.[4]

---

1. Smick, 'Job,' 4:823, 829. The change in literary genre refers to the fact that Job 28 is not a speech to the friends.

2. L. Wilson, *Job*, 133.

3. Habel, *Job*, 392-93. He argues that the juxtaposition of chapters 28 with 29–31 shows that Job is no longer seeking traditional wisdom through piety but is demanding direct personal access to God so that his integrity can be vindicated.

4. Lo, *Job 28*, 209-10. Lo has an extensive discussion of the issues surrounding Job 28 and argues they are Job's words through the analysis of the role of contradictory sayings spoken by Job. However, Lo also concludes that Job does not affirm the ideas in Job 28.

A case can be made for understanding Job 28 as the words of Job. Although he has spoken against the friends' view and has protested against God concerning the way he is being treated by God, there is no evidence that Job has completely rejected retribution or the fear of the Lord as the way to wisdom. A person who is suffering may have swings of mood and changing thoughts about God and suffering. Job has already gone from a submissive response of worship in chapters 1–2 to a stance of protest in chapter 3. The speech of the friends helped fuel his protest, and now that the debate has collapsed Job can contemplate his response. He comes full circle to a view that moves from protest to a more reflective attitude of the proper role of wisdom and the fear of the Lord. This speech brings the dialogue to a close and allows Job to make his final plea of innocence in Job 29–31.

Human Skill: Uncovering the Treasures of the Earth (Job 28:1-12)

Gold and silver are very precious metals that human beings take out of the earth through a mining process. Other less expensive metals like iron and copper are also taken out of the earth. The mining process displays human ingenuity in finding these metals in the farthest, darkest regions of the earth and extracting them by going deep into it.[5] Such dark places are not normally exposed to the world of humans. The finding and extracting of such metals are also very different from the normal activities of humans above the ground, like planting wheat and producing bread. Not even the animals have seen such dark recesses of the earth in their roaming over it. Human beings can bring to light such remote places and expose the precious metals of the earth by cutting channels in the rocks and by stopping streams to expose river beds. The point is that human beings can accomplish wonderful things through their ability to figure

---

5. See Hartley, *Job*, 376, n. 26 for a review of the ancient techniques of mining. When v. 4 mentions 'they hang in the air' it is referring to miners who hang from ropes in vertical shafts to dislodge minerals from the side of the shaft. The fire in v. 5 also describes another process of heating rock and pouring water over the rock to cause it to crack. Others think this refers to the activity of volcanoes (Longman, *Job*, 329 and Habel, *Job*, 396).

out how the world works, and then to use that knowledge to their advantage.

Human Skill unable to Find Wisdom (Job 28:12-19)

The search for precious metals through the difficult mining process is a paradigm for the search for wisdom by human beings.[6] The question of verse 12 sets up the parallel: 'But where shall wisdom be found? Where is the place of understanding?' Although human beings show tremendous ingenuity and skill in discovering hidden gems deep in the recesses of the earth, can wisdom be discovered by the ingenuity and skill of human beings? This section answers that question with a resounding 'no'.

This passage falls into two parts based on two questions in verses 12 and 20. The question of verse 12 is answered in verses 13-19. Two problems are highlighted in these verses. The first problem is that wisdom is not a commodity that can be discovered by human beings using their natural abilities. Wisdom is not found in the land of the living (v. 13), nor does it reside in the deep blue sea (v. 14).[7] The second problem is that human beings do not understand the true value of wisdom. Everyone understands the value of gold and silver or the value of precious metals like onyx, sapphire, coral, crystal, or the topaz of Ethiopia. Human beings are willing to expend great energy in seeking for such precious metals (28:1-11). The true worth of wisdom, however, is not understood by human beings. Wisdom is more valuable than gold or silver or pearls. Human beings do not understand the value of wisdom so that there is not a big search underway to find it. But even if there was a human search to find wisdom, the question remains whether human beings could discover wisdom.

The next section raises again the question of the source of wisdom with verse 20: 'From where, then, does wisdom come? And where is the place of understanding?' The answer is that wisdom is hidden from every realm of creation. It is hidden from both humans and animals, with a special

---

6. Habel, *Job*, 396.

7. Hartley (*Job*, 380) notes that the 'deep' is the lowest part of the sea where the entrance to the chambers of the dead was thought to reside. Not even in the deepest sea is wisdom to be found.

mention of birds which have a wider view as they fly high above the earth. Not even the realm of the dead, represented by Abaddon and Death, know where to find wisdom. Those who have died have only heard a rumor concerning wisdom. Wisdom is not accessible anywhere in this world by the living or the dead. Human beings do not understand the value of wisdom, they do not know where wisdom is to be found, and they are unable to discover it by human ability. Although humans can bring hidden things to light in the natural realm, wisdom remains hidden from them.

Only God Knows the Way to Wisdom (Job 28:23-28)
These verses immediately answer the questions that were raised in verses 12 and 20: 'God understands the way to it, and he knows its place' (v. 23). Only God knows where wisdom is to be found. The reason that God knows the way to wisdom is given in verses 24-27. God knows everything and He sees everything. Wisdom cannot escape His discerning gaze. God knows where to look to find wisdom because when He created the world (vv. 25-26) He established wisdom as a part of the creation. God knows the way to wisdom because He established wisdom and understands how wisdom works in the world He created. God then revealed to human beings[8] the essence of what people need to know about wisdom: 'the fear of the Lord, that is wisdom, and to turn away from evil is understanding' (v. 28). Human beings cannot discover wisdom by their own ability so God reveals to them the basic principle of wisdom.[9] The starting point of wisdom is to fear the Lord. A person increases in wisdom by reverence and obedience to God, not by the investigation of the universe.

---

8. The fact that wisdom is revealed to human beings is seen in the statement that 'he (God) said to man' (v. 28). God spoke to human beings this principle of wisdom. The fact of revelation takes care of the problem many see with v. 28 as incompatible with the inaccessibility of wisdom earlier in the chapter (for problems scholars have with v. 28 see Lo, *Job 28*, 11-14).

9. The word 'wisdom' in Job 28 always has the article except for v. 28. The use of the word without the article may distinguish the term from its previous uses where only God understands wisdom, but the fact that the same word is used highlights that this wisdom is available to human beings. Some argue that the practical side of wisdom is in view in v. 28 and others emphasize the difference between the way that wisdom is acquired by God and humans (Hartley, *Job*, 384 and Habel, *Job*, 401).

It is clear from Job 1–2 that Job was characterized as a person who feared the Lord. Even in his suffering he continued to fear the Lord. His honest lament of chapter 3 launched the debate where Job defended his integrity against the friends who accused him of sin. Job also defends himself against God because he feels he is being mistreated by God. The friends do not help Job because they operate with a narrow view of God's relationship to suffering. Job explores the complexity of the nature of God and the mystery of suffering because he does not believe his situation fits the view of the friends. Job does speak about how God is mistreating him and he does call into question God's justice. He also, however, comes to the realization that there is no help available for him except from God Himself. If that is so, then the fear of the Lord is still the beginning of wisdom. Job can affirm this principle intellectually even as his emotional turmoil, as demonstrated in Job 29–31, may not allow him to embrace it fully until after God speaks.[10]

It is still true today. No matter how far human beings have advanced in technical skill and the ability to accomplish great things, the way to wisdom is beyond the reach of human ability. Job 28 is a needed corrective to the friends' view because they think they have God and wisdom figured out. But Job 28 demonstrates that human beings do not have the means of penetrating the mysterious complexity of the universe to understand the events of this world.[11] There is mystery to God's ways in the world, a mystery that cannot be encapsulated by a narrow principle that the wicked always suffer and the righteous are always blessed with material abundance, health, and long life. One of the functions of Job 28 is to show that wisdom has not been discovered so far in the debate. Thus the debate between Job and the friends has come to an end and Job's turning away from the friends to petition God directly is the right response.[12] The reader is also able to pause and reflect on the inability of human beings to discover wisdom and to return to the most important

10. Longman, *Job*, 333.

11. Habel, *Job*, 398.

12. Hartley, *Job*, 384.

principle in relationship to wisdom: the fear of the Lord. If wisdom cannot be discovered on the human level and can only be found by God, then it is imperative for God to speak. Job 28 fosters the desire to hear from God and so anticipates the speeches of God in Job 38–42.

The Wisdom of God's Purposes

Today was a good day for Pierce. He only had one major 'episode' (an 'episode' is typically where he quits breathing or his oxygen saturation levels dip drastically – this is completely normal and expected in preemie world, but still very scary to watch). Pierce weighed in tonight at 2 lbs. even!!! His feeds are steadily increasing – he is currently getting about 1/2 a teaspoon at each feeding.

As we left the hospital tonight, Nik and I were reflecting on how far Pierce has come in one month. It is truly amazing to see how he has grown, how many hurdles he has jumped and, most importantly, how he has been used by God to impact so many lives. I can't even begin to describe the amount of joy and gratitude that fills our hearts tonight.

I stumbled upon this quote this morning and thought it was so appropriate during this trying time. It says, 'God allows in His wisdom that which He could easily prevent in His power.' As I reflected on that today, I had such a peace that God has indeed allowed this for a reason. God is not a distant Father who ignores us in our problems. No, in fact, God *allows* these dark times in our lives for a reason. He has a purpose in all of this. Many of you are probably asking a question that we have wrestled with in the past: what is His purpose? How could a loving God allow our baby to suffer through such gut-wrenching times? The answer is made clear throughout Scripture: to demonstrate the glory and sufficiency of Christ. And how is that demonstrated through suffering? John Piper answers that question in saying, 'Christ is most magnified in us when we are most satisfied in him and when we lose everything but him.' He goes on to say, 'Christ is magnified by being preferred above everything that life can offer.'

Throughout this past month, Nik and I have been forced to deal with the sobering truth that nothing in this life, apart from Christ, is unfailing. Our marriage, our child, our own lives, our possessions – none of those things can or will ever fulfill us. All of them bring joy, but none bring complete satisfaction. It is our prayer that God will continue to use this trying time to make us more like Christ and to bring us into a deeper, more trusting relationship with Him. We also pray that He will do the same in your life through watching our story unfold and by witnessing His hand on Pierce's life. And honestly, if just one of you comes to faith in Christ through this, it is all worth it. Every ounce of pain and suffering is worth your knowing our Lord because, friends, He is truly the only all-satisfying thing you could ever cling to.

We are praying for our readers tonight.

Much love,
Lindsay Franks (5/14/11)

Study Questions

1) Why do some commentators have a hard time accepting Job 28 as the words of Job? How can Job 28 make sense as the words of Job?

2) What example of human skill is given in this chapter? How does that relate to discovering wisdom?

3) What two problems do humans face in seeking wisdom?

4) What is the reason that only God knows how to discover wisdom? How, then, can humans find wisdom?

5) How can Job affirm the fear the Lord even in his suffering? What insight does this give to people who are suffering?

6) What is the function of Job 28 in the book of Job?

21

Longing for the Blessings of
a Glorious Past
(Job 29)

Job 29–31 are the final words of Job. These chapters begin with 'And Job again took up his discourse, and said' (29:1) and they end with 'The words of Job are ended' (31:40). These words are Job's public testimony and they function as his final attempt to prove his innocence and to force God to answer him. In chapter 29 Job gives an account of his glorious past to show how much he has suffered and to demonstrate his own integrity. In chapter 30 Job laments his present condition of humiliation and shame because of his suffering. And finally, in chapter 31 Job asserts an oath of innocence to prove his innocence and to move God to respond to his oath.

Longing for God's Presence (Job 29:1-6)

Job gives an account of his life before he lost everything in his suffering. His opening words, 'Oh, that I were as in the months of old,' express a deep desire to experience again the blessings of his former days.[1] Job begins by showing how wonderful was his relationship with God. He felt protected by God ('God watched over me') and guided by His light through the darkness of life's difficulties[2] (vv. 2-3). The most

---

1. G. Wilson (*Job*, 312) notes that the mention of 'months of old' suggests a brief time of suffering and loss.

2. Hartley, *Job*, 388. He connects darkness to the difficulties of life.

important thing was that Job experienced the friendship of
God that was demonstrated in the presence of God in his life.
Job was in his prime,[3] enjoying the blessings of God in his
children and in all the activities of life. Everything Job tried
was blessed by God. The blessings of life are expressed by
the metaphors of butter and oil that stand for a luxurious life.
Job's life was awash in those blessings. Even the hard rock
poured out streams of oil (see also Deut. 32:13 and Ps. 81:16).[4]
It is clear that God was the source of those blessings and
not Job's own ability or ingenuity. It is also clear that Job no
longer enjoys the friendship of God's presence, a loss that
hurts more than the loss of material goods.

Longing for Community Respect (Job 29:7-17)
Job highlights his prominent place in the community by
mentioning his role at the gate of the city. Legal matters were
determined at the city gate and Job had an important place
among those who heard such cases. Job's reputation was
so great that others deferred to him out of respect. Young
men withdrew from Job's presence, old men rose and stood,
rulers and other important people refrained from talking
in his presence. Job's words of wisdom were respected by
all (v. 11). The reason Job was respected in the community
is because he acted in righteousness toward the poor and
protected them from the unrighteous.[5] He helped the helpless
by delivering the poor, the fatherless, and the widow; he
became eyes to the blind, feet to the lame, a father to the
needy, and a friend to the stranger in trouble. The poor are
depicted as prey in the mouth of the unrighteous whom Job
freed by breaking their teeth. Job's righteousness and justice
were visible in his actions even as a person's robe is visible
to all. Job's description of his life stands in stark contrast to

---

3. The word 'prime' is literally 'the days of my harvest', a reference to the enjoyment of the benefits of his labor (Hartley, *Job*, 388 n.7).

4. Longman, *Job*, 338.

5. The reason (ki in v. 12) that Job was respected by his peers is because of the way Job helped the poor (vv. 12-17). Job is not saying that he believed his former state of blessing was God's reward for his good deeds (contra James Reitman, *Unlocking Wisdom* [Springfield, MO: 21st Century Press, 2008], 115. He understands Job's attitude to express victimization and self-sufficiency).

the view of the friends, especially Eliphaz' claim that Job had ignored the rights of the oppressed (Job 22:5-9).[6] The characterization of Job as righteous and just matches the picture of Job in chapters 1–2 and will become the basis of his oath of innocence in chapter 31.

Longing for a Long, Blessed Life (Job 29:18-25)
Job had every reason to believe that he would live a long life full of blessing. A life of wisdom is a life that leads to great blessing, including long life (Prov. 3:13-18).[7] In verses 18-20 Job expresses the thought of dying in his own home after living many days as numerous as the sand. He presents a picture of the stability of his life which was like a tree with roots spread out to the waters. His life was continually refreshed, as the dew brings refreshment every morning. Job describes a vigorous life that was strong in every respect. The glory and strength that Job experienced in life are expressed in verses 21–25 by his place and respect in the community.[8] Job's wisdom was so highly regarded that others waited for him to speak and after he spoke there was nothing more to be said.[9] His words were like the coming of the winter rains to water the earth, and the community drank wisdom from his words as the ground absorbs the spring rains that bring the crop to a full harvest.[10] Job was also an inspirational leader who did not look down on others with arrogance but encouraged them when they lacked confidence to speak. His role was so prominent that he lived like a king among the people. Job had some authority over the people[11] ('I chose their way') and he acted as a shepherd toward them by comforting those who mourned.

---

6. Habel, *Job*, 410.

7. For how this expectation of blessing that flows from wisdom can be misunderstood, see the end of the discussion of Job 18 (Chapter 11).

8. G. Wilson (*Job*, 321) notes that in vv. 7-11 the emphasis is on the respect that others had for Job and in vv. 21-25 the emphasis is on the impact of his words in shaping and guiding the community.

9. The response of the friends is very different in that they take every opportunity to undermine Job and question his words (G. Wilson, *Job*, 321).

10. Hartley, *Job*, 394-95.

11. Habel, Job, 412. Longman (*Job*, 341) understands the reference to 'way' as a picture of a good sage who gave the people guidance.

Job gives an interesting look at his life before the days of his suffering. It confirms what was presented in Job 1–2 concerning the character of Job as an upright man, who feared the Lord and turned away from evil. It also confirms that Job is right in the debate with the friends concerning the reason for his suffering. Job is not suffering because of sin he committed. The picture of Job in chapter 29 is one of a person who feared God and honored Him. It is a picture of a mature person who demonstrated a life of devotion to God. The righteousness and justice evident in Job's life were a practical righteousness that manifested itself in good deeds that flowed from a fear of the Lord (sanctification). The imagery of a tree is used in other Scriptures to describe the stability and fruitfulness of the righteous (Ps. 1; Jer. 17:8). Although death should always be regarded as an enemy, a righteous person would hope to die a good death, like Abraham, old and full of years, and surrounded by family and friends (Gen. 25:7-8).

The picture of Job's past life may also explain to some degree his response to his suffering. Job understood the legal system and the importance of justice being carried out because he was very involved in rendering verdicts as he sat at the gate. His sense of justice is threatened by the way he is being treated by the friends and by God. The friends have gone out of their way to accuse Job of sin when the readers know that he is not suffering because of sin. Job also perceives that God is not treating him justly. Rather, God has treated Job's hope like a tree that is uprooted and has no hope of being renewed (Job 19:10).[12] Job has also given comfort to those who mourn and he does not believe he has received such comfort from the friends,[13] or perhaps, even from God. Job's wisdom, which was highly respected before his suffering, is now called into question by the friends. His suffering has brought a total reversal to Job's life. Suffering can cause people to question their own lives, their views about life, and their views concerning God; suffering can also be a venue for people to offer guidance that is not helpful to the one who is suffering.

---

12. Habel, *Job*, 410-11.

13. G. Wilson, *Job*, 322.

The debate has shown that answers have not been found on the human level and there is a need for God to respond. God does respond to Job's suffering in chapters 38–41. He also responds to suffering in the life and ministry of His Son, Jesus Christ. Examining the life of Christ can be a way to orient oneself during suffering. Jesus was the Son of God, sent from God to accomplish God's purposes. He lived His life without sin and was innocent of all the charges brought against Him. His experience shows that suffering is not necessarily a result of specific sin that has been committed. Jesus also taught the people wisdom and many times His wisdom left them speechless (Matt. 22:22, 33, 46). And yet, His wisdom was rejected by the people of His day. Jesus' suffering shows that God can work out His purposes through suffering. Jesus' death shows that not everyone who is righteous will live a long life and die a good death. Jesus' resurrection shows that He has conquered death so that Christians should be willing to trust Him even in times of darkest suffering. A person must trust in God in the crucible of suffering and look to Jesus for hope in suffering. Much of the bad theology surrounding suffering, like the health and wealth gospel, can be quickly dispatched by what Christ experienced. The exhortation of Hebrews 12:1–2 is important: '… let us run with endurance the race that is before us, looking to Jesus, the founder and perfecter of our faith, who for the joy set before him endured the cross, despising its shame, and is seated at the right hand of the throne of God.'

Thankful for the Uneventful

Today has been yet another good, quiet day for Pierce. No new changes, only a slight increase on his feeds. Because Pierce was doing so well, Nik and I were able to worship with our church family today. We then snuck by the hospital for a quick visit before heading home for our Sunday nap (quite a tradition at our house).

As I sit here now, in the quietness, my heart is filled with joy and thankfulness. I am so grateful for this day: for an uneventful day, with no new issues to wrestle with, for a peaceful baby, who seems to be resting easy and growing more and more every day, and for a wonderful

NICU and staff (this team truly is amazing and their skill is beyond words).

Indeed, this whole experience has made me treasure the most routine, mundane moments. I am overjoyed at the 'boring' days we have, because I know that the opposite is usually the case because some hurdle has popped up in our way. I am thankful that God has performed many miracles to allow Pierce to see his one-month birthday. And I'm grateful for each one of you, who have so encouraged and blessed us through your words, prayers and giving. Your dedication to following our story and your ceaseless prayers have been so humbling and most encouraging.

Much love to you all,
Lindsay Franks (5/15/11)

Study Questions

1) How does Job describe his life with God and the community 'before suffering'? Is there a connection between suffering and social pain?

2) What does Job 29 confirm about Job's life?

3) How has suffering totally reversed Job's life?

4) How does the life of Jesus help a person understand suffering?

22

Job's Present Humiliation
(Job 30)

In chapter 30 Job turns from a description of his glorious past to an account of his humiliating present. He describes how the scoundrels of society mock him in his suffering. Job 30 has been called a lament and it does contain many lament elements.[1] He struggles with how he is treated by his 'enemies' (30:1-15) and by God (30:16-23). He also wrestles with himself concerning his situation (30:24-31). There is, however, no movement toward confidence that God has heard his prayer or that God will act in his behalf. In fact, Job is troubled by how God is treating him and has not responded to his cry for help. So, there are lament elements in chapter 30, but the laments of Job do not exactly fit the typical laments of the psalms. Job's suffering has so overwhelmed him that he at times perceives God as the enemy who is mistreating him.

Mocked by Fools (Job 30:1-15)
The phrase at the beginning of chapter 30 ('But now,' *wĕʿattāh*) moves Job from his glorious past to his present existence of suffering. This phrase occurs three times in this chapter (vv. 1, 9, 16), twice in verses 1-15. Job is not just living in the past; in

---

1. Hartley (*Job*, 395) identifies Job 30 as a lament. See Richard P. Belcher, Jr., *The Messiah and the Psalms* (Ross-shire: Christian Focus, 2006), 68, for a discussion of the basic elements of the lament psalms. The complaint can focus on frustration with the enemy, frustration with God, or frustration that the psalmist expresses with his own situation.

addition, he is very much aware of how he is perceived by people. He is wrestling not only with the way he is being treated but also with those who are mistreating him. Job mentions in verse 1 that he is being mocked, or laughed at. This idea will be picked up again in verse 9, but the focus in verses 1-8 is on the character and condition of those who are mocking Job. They are described as men who are younger than Job. They show no respect for Job even though he is older than they are. Job is an object of ridicule in the community he once governed with justice.[2] This lack of respect fits their general character, for they have fathers who Job would not even trust with the dogs of his flock.[3] These poor mockers have nothing to offer Job (v. 2). They live in poverty and seek food from the leaves and roots of the trees (vv. 3-4).[4] The futility of their efforts is shown in the description that 'they gnaw the dry ground by night in waste and desolation' (v. 3). These mockers are outcasts to the rest of society (vv. 5–7).[5] They are described as donkeys who bray among the bushes.[6] They are driven out of society because they cannot be trusted to live honorably among other people. Thus they must dwell anywhere they can find a place, in the gullies of the torrents, in the holes of the earth, and among the bushes. The character of these individuals is highlighted in verse 8. They act like fools and they are nameless, a reference to having no reputation or a bad reputation in society.[7] Job is being mocked by the lowest of the low. He is being mistreated by fools who have no moral standing in the community to make fun of Job's situation. The very reason they mock Job is the reason they should keep their mouths shut, for their lives are no better than Job's life. In fact, Job has more integrity even in his suffering than they have in their mocking.

After describing the character and condition of those who are mocking him, Job returns in verses 9-15 to show

---

2. Habel, *Job*, 418.

3. Dogs were not as highly valued in the ancient Near East as they are today. They were not 'man's best friend', but scavengers (Longman, *Job*, 348).

4. Saltwort is a shrub that is very salty and is only eaten by people in dire circumstances (Hartley, *Job*, 398).

5. Hartley (*Job*, 397) calls them 'displaced desert rabble'.

6. Longman, *Job*, 349.

7. G. Wilson, *Job*, 325.

how he is being mocked. This section also begins with the phrase *wĕʿattāh* (translated 'And now' by the ESV). Job has become a song and a byword to them, a laughingstock to them. They taunt him with their songs;[8] they show that they abhor Job by keeping aloof from him or by spitting at him when they are near him (v. 10); they show very little restraint in how they treat him because they perceive that God is behind Job's suffering. The rabble who mock Job do everything they can to disrupt and destroy his life. They are very active in their assault on Job. They rise at his right hand, they push away his feet,[9] and they throw at Job their ways of destruction (v. 12). Their assault on Job is relentless as they promote his calamity.[10] Their mockery leaves Job full of terror, his honor denigrated, and his prosperity gone like a cloud. Often the lowest of society take advantage of the suffering of the wealthy to make themselves feel better about their situation.

Mired by God (Job 30:16-23)

This section begins with the third use of 'and now' (*wĕʿattāh*) as Job describes his suffering and its impact on his spiritual and physical life in verses 16-18. His life is characterized by affliction that has taken hold of him and will not let him go. He describes his soul as being poured out within him.[11] His vitality is gone, leaving only a limp body to fight his illness.[12] Job has no strength left to fight his sickness because he experiences constant excruciating pain with no relief day or night. His illness has impacted his garment, which is disfigured and binds him around the neck like the collar of his tunic. Job feels hemmed in and choked by the confines of his physical pain as though he were in a straitjacket.

---

8. It is suggested that the byword was 'to become a Job', a way to refer to someone who is utterly cursed and worthless (Christopher Ash, *Job: The Wisdom of the Cross* [Wheaton, IL: Crossway, 2014], 302).

9. This phrase may refer to the fact that people were laying snares for Job's feet and trying to trip him up.

10. Some think that verses 12-14 are describing the assault on a city (Hartley, *Job*, 400).

11. Longman, *Job*, 350.

12. Hartley, *Job*, 402.

Job identifies God as the cause of his problems in verses 19-23.[13] God has cast him into the mire (muddy clay) so that his life has become as frail as dust and ashes. He does not answer Job when he calls for help. When Job stands to urgently present his case to the Lord,[14] God only looks at him, but does not respond to him. In fact, it is not as if God is neutral toward Job; instead God has been cruel to him and has used His power to persecute him.[15] Job feels that he is in the middle of a storm, lifted up and tossed about by the wind and roar of the waves.[16] He perceives that God is treating him as an enemy. He has no stability in life and feels trapped by God who is persecuting him. Despair seems to overtake Job in this speech, for he utters the belief that God's actions toward him will lead to his death. Job vents his frustration with the way God is treating him.

Mourning a Dark Life (Job 30:24-31)

Job ends this section with a lament of his situation. There is a shift away from direct address to God to intense personal reflection with the domination of 'I' language.[17] When a person faces disaster and cries out for help, there is an expectation that someone would come and help. In fact, Job himself has wept for those whose life was hard and he has expressed grief for the needy. And yet, when Job faced disaster, no one helped him. He hoped for good, but evil came to him. He waited for light, but darkness overtook him. Anxiety, restlessness, and personal anguish dominate his life.[18] Job's life is overcome by darkness. No one answers his

---

13. This section shifts to the second person singular as Job addresses God directly (Hartley, *Job*, 402).

14. Hartley, *Job*, 403.

15. The verb translated 'persecute' is *śaṭam*. It is possible that there is a word play with the word 'adversary' (*śaṭan*). Job accuses God of being his foe and treating him with animosity (Hartley, *Job*, 403).

16. Habel (*Job*, 421) understands riding on the wind to refer to Job's exalted position before God brought him down.

17. G. Wilson, *Job*, 332.

18. The 'inward parts' mentioned in v. 27 refers to the bowels or intestines and probably refers to Job's inner turmoil (Longman, *Job*, 351). Habel (*Job*, 422) notes that the bowels are the seat of the emotions where personal anguish is experienced at the depths of one's being. Others understand the bowels physically to refer to a description of an internal gastric malady, the noisy gurgling of the stomach and bowels (G. Wilson, *Job*, 333).

cry for help in the assembly. Job compares himself to jackals and ostriches, a way to express his isolation from society and loneliness.[19] Job is decimated physically with his skin becoming discolored. He also suffers with a great fever. The joy of life is gone. Mourning and weeping overwhelm his life.

Job gives the readers an insight into the intense struggles of his life because he has been mistreated by humans and by God. In an earlier speech (19:13-22) he had complained of being abandoned by everyone, including his family and friends. In this chapter Job more generally focuses on the mistreatment he has received using categories that are common in the lament psalms. He has been mistreated by the 'enemy', the lowest of society, who mock his suffering; he has been mistreated by God, the ultimate cause of his suffering, who has cast him into the mire. Job feels trapped because God does not answer his cries for help. Finally, he wrestles with himself over his situation by mourning what he has lost.

The distinctive element of this chapter is not that Job mourns over his suffering or that he complains that God has mistreated him. The distinctive element is that Job is mocked by fools who have no social standing or moral authority. Those who are lowest on the social ladder are more than willing to kick someone who is down and struggling. The reader knows Job is a person of integrity, who is wise and righteous (1:2-3).[20] Here is a clear situation of a righteous person being persecuted and mocked by the unrighteous. The dregs of society made fun of Job's situation. In this sense Job's suffering points to the suffering of Christ. The pure and holy Son of God was mocked by unworthy sinners when He was beaten by the Roman guards (Matt. 27:27-31) and as He hung on the cross (Matt. 27:38-44). He was crucified with criminals, one of whom railed against Him on the cross (Luke 23:39). Jesus' suffering is greater than Job's suffering in that His suffering led to His death that was part of God's plan to redeem His people.

19. Jackals and ostriches inhabit ruins (Longman, *Job*, 352). Habel (*Job*, 422) connects the sound of these animals with the mourning cries of the next verse.

20. Although Job does call into question God's justice from the context of his suffering, it is clear from Job 1–2 that Job is not suffering because of a sin he has committed.

Christ's suffering carried out a redemptive purpose because in His death He bore our sins and received the judgment that we deserve for our sins. But was Job's suffering redemptive? Is it appropriate to speak of our suffering as redemptive? It depends on how one defines the term 'redemptive'. Certainly Job's suffering was not redemptive in the sense that he was suffering in place of someone else to purchase someone else's release. Job had lost much of his family and he was left all alone to bear the load of his suffering. If redemptive means that something good comes out of his suffering, then Job's suffering can be seen as redemptive.

Longman speaks of shame being redemptive because it drives a person to God.[21] Ash uses the term redemptive to argue that Job's suffering makes redemption possible for others. In this way Job anticipates the suffering of Christ.[22] But is that too broad of a concept of redemptive? It is important how the term 'redemptive' is defined. Job lived before Christ and he can serve as a type of Christ in that he suffered unjustly in many ways that foreshadowed Christ, but to use the term 'redemptive' can be misleading because Job did not suffer to redeem anyone.

Paul's statement in Colossians 1:24 should also not be understood in terms of redemptive suffering. There Paul states, 'Now I rejoice in my sufferings for your sake, and in my flesh I am filling up what is lacking in Christ's afflictions for the sake of his body, that is, the church.' The focus is not the complete satisfaction that Christ has made to His Father by His death, a redemptive theme, but the relationship of the members of Christ's body to His sufferings. Calvin writes: 'Christ has suffered *once* in his own person, so he suffers *daily* in his members and in this way there are *filled up* those sufferings which the Father hath appointed for his body by his decree.'[23]

Although it is misleading to use the term 'redemptive' to speak of human suffering, the sufferings of others can be encouraging and inspiring.[24] Suffering can also be transforming

---

21. Longman, *Job*, 352-53.

22. Ash, *Job*, 177.

23. John Calvin, 'Philippians,' in *Calvin's Commentaries* (Grand Rapids: Baker Book House, 1996), 21:164.

24. See the account of the death of Coptic Christians by ISIS in *World Magazine* 30.25 (December 2015).

when seen in the broader context of God's purposes in history that will climax at the coming of Christ. It helps move God's purposes forward toward the consummation of the kingdom. Suffering reveals Christ to a glory-starved world because true glory is revealed in weakness.[25] In the weakness of suffering Christ transforms us by His grace that we might demonstrate that grace to others.

A Peace that Passes Understanding

There are many ideas, philosophies, and 'things' that offer peace. When the savings account is looking good, we have peace. When we get a clean bill of health from the doctor, we have peace. When we feel like we are accomplishing our life's purpose, we have peace. And those are all fine and good, but all these things offer us a peace that is understandable. On the other hand, when the doctor tells you there is a significant risk that the right side of your son's heart could eventually wear out and kill him, and despite your fear and anguish, you are overwhelmed with a sense of joy, it is a peace that surpasses understanding.

And that is the news that we got today. We knew that we were not completely out of the woods, but this is the first time that we had ever heard that there is a possibility that Pierce's heart could shut down. In micro-preemies, especially at 23 weeks, their lungs are very immature and the right side of the heart has to work a lot harder to keep blood flowing to them. The right side of the heart is only supposed to 'lift light things', we were told. And when it has to work so hard to push blood to Pierce's lungs, it can wear out, thus causing heart failure. And as we were told, there is simply nothing they can do to prevent right-side failure of the heart.

When I was told this, for some reason I wasn't scared. Of course, if I dwell on this threat I would soon go crazy. And one thing this experience is doing is teaching us not to be anxious. Anxiety will suffocate you. I have also

---

25. Michael R. Emlet, 'When It Won't Go Away: A Biblical Response to Chronic Pain,' *JBC* 23 (Winter 2005): 24-25.

been angry and frustrated. Sometimes it is hard to get an accurate answer about what is going on. Three different people will tell us three different things. Then we will do research and get a different take. On top of that, we have witnessed miscommunications between the different shifts. It makes it hard to comprehend what's going on when you can't get a unified answer and the team coming in doesn't have an exact knowledge of what went on with Pierce three days before. However, we know that the medical team is one of the top in the country and that God is sovereign despite any human errors.

However, most of my reflections have produced peace. God didn't let Pierce's heart stop when it was pumping for seventy-two hours with a potassium level of nine, eventually reaching a level of ten (miracle!), and I just don't believe that He is going to let him die now. God has consistently answered our prayers to sustain Pierce, and we are trusting in His character. As James 1 reminds us, God's character does not change over time. In light of this, we really do have a peace that surpasses all understanding. We are not lying and it is not denial. It is the grace of the living God at work in us.

Love,
Lindsay Franks (5/21/11)

Study Questions

1) How is Job's lament in this chapter similar to laments in the psalms, but also different from them?

2) Who are the people mocking Job and how are they mocking him? What can be learned from this?

3) How has suffering impacted Job's physical life and his view of God?

4) How does Job's suffering point to Christ's suffering? How is Jesus' suffering greater than Job's suffering?

5) Should our suffering be regarded as redemptive? Why or why not? What is a better way to describe our suffering?

23

Job's Oath of Innocence
(Job 31)

This is the final speech of Job – chapter 31 ends with the statement: 'The words of Job are ended' (v. 40c). Job dramatically asserts that he is innocent of all charges brought against him by using an oath. He declares his innocence by calling down curses on himself if he has committed any of the forms of wicked behavior he lists. Job's purpose is to give God no option but to answer him. This oath is a legal challenge offered in a court that demands a response from the other party in the case.[1] Job desires that God will respond to his oath with justice by declaring him innocent of the charges. Job desperately wants to hear from God.[2] If God remains silent and the curses do not fall upon Job, then his innocence will be established.[3]

The oath is expressed with 'if' statements (called the protasis) introduced by *'im*. The 'then' clause (called the apodosis) is not always stated, leaving many of the oaths without a clearly anticipated consequence.[4] Sometimes Job will give the reason for his rejection of such behavior. In the legal setting of the chapter, the obvious result of being

---

1. G. Wilson, *Job*, 334.

2. Hartley, *Job*, 408.

3. Habel, *Job*, 431. He goes on to say that if God remains silent, God will be seen to be the guilty party.

4. L. Wilson, *Job*, 149.

convicted of the sin expressed would be for Job to lose his case.[5] There is disagreement among scholars how many oaths of disavowal Job expresses.[6] There are seventeen 'if' statements, but no one argues for seventeen oaths of avowal. Any analysis of the number of oaths must group some of the 'if' statements together. Hartley finds fourteen sins listed, but he must combine several 'if' statements (vv. 19-20 and vv. 24-25) and separate several 'if' statements that seem to go together (vv. 16-23 all seem to deal with the poor, but he lists three separate sins).[7] The approach taken here is a thematic approach that groups several 'if' statements according to theme. This approach yields the following list:

1. Lust (vv. 1-4)[8]
2. Falsehood (vv. 5-6)
3. Covetousness (vv. 7-8)
4. Adultery (vv. 9-12)
5. Mistreatment of one's servants (vv. 13-15)
6. Mistreatment of the poor (vv. 16-23)
7. Trust in wealth (vv. 24-25)
8. Idolatry (vv. 26-28)
9. Rejoicing at a foe's misfortune (vv. 29-30)
10. Failure to extend hospitality to a sojourner (vv. 31-32)
11. Concealment of a sin without confession (vv. 33-34)
12. Abuse of the land (vv. 38-40)

Just before the final sin listed Job appeals to God to give him a hearing and he seals the oath with his signature (vv. 35-37).

Lust (31:1-4)
Job begins his final appeal with an affirmation that he has made a covenant with his eyes. The commitment to be careful

---

5. G. Wilson, *Job*, 334.

6. See Clines for a list of the different proposals (*Job 21–37*, 1013). Many find fourteen oaths as double the number of perfection to point to Job's faithful adherence to the entire law (Hartley, *Job*, 409).

7. Hartley, *Job*, 408-09.

8. The opening verses do not begin with an 'if' statement but with a statement of affirmation (Hartley, *Job*, 409).

what he allows his eyes to see is a commitment to purity.[9]
He asks the question, 'how then could I gaze at a virgin?'
This question must refer to looking at a virgin with lustful
desires. Job has made a covenant that he will not lust after
other women. The danger is what the lustful desire might lead
one to do.[10] The seriousness of this sin comes out in verses 2-4.
Such a sin would destroy his relationship with God and would
take away his inheritance from God. Job also highlights the
negative consequences that would come from such a sin. Those
who do iniquity are looking disaster in the face. Calamity
overtakes the unrighteous. The consequences show that the
sin is more than just a lustful look and must include some
action on Job's part because the result is the ruin of the person
who commits the sin. Job cannot hide his sin from God because
God sees Job's ways and numbers his steps. God knows his life
intimately. This knowledge means that God knows whether
Job has committed sin as the reason for his suffering and gives
Job hope that God will declare him innocent.[11]

Falsehood (31:5-6)
The first use of an 'if' statement occurs in verse 5, followed
by a statement that confirms Job's integrity. There is no
'then' statement, unless verses 5-7 are combined with the
'then' statement in verse 8. But the sins in verses 5 and 7
are different sins. The sin in verse 5 is falsehood or deceit.
For a person to 'walk with falsehood' describes a life that
is committed to treachery and lies. This is a description of a
person's whole life, but it would also include a person's quick
tendency to lie in specific situations. In verse 6 Job expresses
a mild imperative[12] that his life would be weighed in a just
balance that would result in God knowing his integrity. Job is
not aware that God has already declared him to be blameless
and upright. Job is not a hypocrite and his life is not full of
deceit. Job's testimony fits God's testimony from Job 1–2. The

---

9. Habel, *Job*, 432.

10. Hartley, *Job*, 409.

11. Hartley, *Job*, 408. G. Wilson (*Job*, 334) asserts that the fact that God is able to render justice makes Job's experience of suffering even more acute.

12. The verb forms are 3ms imperfects that function as jussives.

angst that Job has felt is partly due to the fact that he is not aware of this knowledge because God has not responded to his cries for help.

Covetousness (31:7-8)
In verse 7 there are a series of statements that are governed by the opening 'if' particle, followed by a 'then' statement in verse 8.[13] The first and third clauses refer to the feet ('step') and hands with the middle clause focusing on the heart. The middle clause is the key clause because the heart is the seat of a person from which actions flow. The specific statement about the heart is '(if) my heart has gone after my eyes'. This statement describes a person who pursues something that the eyes desire or covet. If a person's mind is controlled by lust, it can negatively impact actions that a person takes.[14] If a person pursues things that belong to other people, or desires what other people have, his steps can easily turn aside from the right way and his hands can become dirty. Covetous desire, also called greed, can destroy a person's life. The consequence or 'then' statement in verse 8 follows naturally from the 'if' statements of verse 7. If a person pursues what another has, then it is appropriate that what the covetous person has acquired would be taken by other people. If Job has acted in this way, then whatever he sows another person should eat, and whatever he grows as a crop should be rooted out by others. Although the emphasis in these verses seems to be on the produce of the land, the word for 'crops' (*ṣeʾĕṣʾ*) can also refer to human offspring (Job 5:25; 21:8; 27:14).[15] Job may be referring to the tragic events described in chapters 1–2 where he lost his crops and his children. He is clearly stating that he is innocent of the charge of covetousness as a basis for his loss.

Adultery (31:9-12)
In these verses Job describes the sin of adultery. The sin itself is presented with the protasis (the 'if' clause) of verse 9, the

---

13. Sometimes 'then' statements are introduced by the conjunction *waw*. Here the clause begins with the first person imperfect cohortative ('let me').

14. Hartley, *Job*, 412.

15. Hartley, *Job*, 41 and G. Wilson, *Job*, 338.

consequences of the sin with the apodosis (the 'then' clause) of verse 10, and the reason for the consequences (introduced by *kî*) is given in verses 11-12. Job describes a situation where his heart is enticed toward another woman so that he waits for her at her door. In other words, strong desires to have a neighbor's wife are acted on, leading to adultery. This sin breaks the trust between neighbors and violates the covenant of marriage.[16] If Job has so acted toward another man's wife, the consequence is fitting that his wife would also be involved in adultery. The apodosis of verse 10 is rather jarring, 'then let my wife grind for another, and let others bow down on her.' The verb 'grind' (*ṭāḥan*) could refer to grinding grain and so could be a description of Job's wife being reduced to menial slave labor (Exod. 11:5).[17] She would be under the control of a new master who may also take advantage of her sexually. The verbs 'grind' and 'bow down' also describe the sexual relationship. One should not conclude that Job is without feeling toward his wife and that he glibly offers her for the sexual pleasure of others.[18] He is saying that if he has taken advantage of someone else's wife, then it is just punishment if someone else takes advantage of his wife. The reason that he offers for this consequence in verses 11-12 shows that he understands the serious nature of the sin. He calls adultery a heinous crime that deserves to be punished by the judges. He also describes the devastating consequences of the power of sexual lust as a fire that consumes everything, even as far as Abaddon, a term for destruction that refers to the place of the dead.[19] Lust is a fire that would burn to the root or foundation of everything that Job possessed. This description of the power of the sin of adultery fits very well with statements in the book of Proverbs that also lay out its consequences (Prov. 6:28-35).

---

16. Hartley, *Job*, 413.

17. The results of adultery can include monetary consequences (Prov. 6:31-35) that might result in the wife being reduced to poverty and having to sell herself into menial slave labor.

18. G. Wilson (*Job*, 340) comments that although the language is harsh, Job is so certain of his own innocence that he never anticipates that the consequences would be realized.

19. G. Wilson, *Job*, 340.

Mistreatment of Servants (31:13-15)

In this passage Job states the sin with a protasis but does not
state the consequences with an apodosis. Instead, he hints
at the disastrous consequences of the sin and gives a reason
for the heinous nature of the sin. The sin itself is stated in
verse 13: 'If I have rejected the cause of my manservant or
my maidservant, when they brought a complaint against me.'
It is clear from chapters 1–2 that Job has a large estate that
requires many servants to care for it. The sin is to ignore a
complaint[20] that one of his servants brings against him. This
response would show a callous attitude toward his servants
and could lead to a denial of justice. Although Job is in the
superior position he is obligated to hear the cause of his
servant. The reason this sin is important to Job is because he
must give an account to God (v. 14). Job will have no answer
to give to God, his superior, if he ignores the complaint of
his servants. Job then elevates the position of his servants by
recognizing that God has created both him and his servants
(v. 15). Even though Job may be in a superior social position
he is no better than his servants because he shares humanity
with them (Prov. 22:2). Human beings made in God's image
have a dignity that no one can take away from them.[21] Job
has honored that dignity by hearing the complaints of his
servants. The way Job has treated his servants is the way
he wants God to treat him. In fact, this is a testimony to his
innocence because what guilty person would seek such a suit
with God?[22]

Oppression of the Poor (31:16-23)

Job mentions several possible sins in this section introduced
by a protasis. The sins all focus on the mistreatment of the
poor. An apodosis introduces the consequences that would
fall upon Job, stated in the form of self-imprecation (v. 22).
The section ends with a reason for the judgment (v. 23).

---

20. The word for 'complaint' is the word *r'ḇ* showing that what Job has in mind
is a legal complaint in court and not the informal grumbling of his servants (G.
Wilson, *Job*, 341).

21. In the ancient Near East, slaves were treated as chattel, but Job regarded
his servants as human beings with legal rights (Habel, *Job*, 434).

22. G. Wilson, *Job*, 341.

In a list of several sins related to the mistreatment of the poor Job mentions the most vulnerable among the poor – the widow and the fatherless. These members of society lacked protection from exploitation[23] and the provision to meet their needs that a husband and a father would provide. The law specifically condemns this (Exod. 22:22-24). Job describes this sin in a general way as having 'withheld anything that the poor desired' (v. 16).[24] Concerning widows, the sin is stated as 'caused the eyes of the widows to fail'. The failing of the eyes probably refers to giving up hope because of being turned away so many times (Ps. 69:3).[25] Concerning the fatherless, Job has not acted as a miser by hoarding his food;[26] instead he has abundantly shared his food with them. In verse 18 Job gives a reason for these actions (introduced by *kî*). The fatherless and the widow have always been a part of Job's life from his youth. He has acted as a father toward the fatherless and he has guided the widow. In verses 19-20 Job shows that he has blessed the needy and protected them from the cold by clothing them. In verse 21 Job comes back to the fatherless and speaks of the sin in such a way that sets up the self-imprecation that follows in verse 22. The sin is 'if I have raised my hand against the fatherless, because I saw my help in the gate.' Job refers here to the fact that he has not abused his position as a judge at the gate to intimidate people and undermine the cause of the poor.[27] The mention of 'help in the gate' may refer to someone who could sway the legal decision in Job's favor rather than allow a case to be judged on its own merits.[28]

The consequence of mistreatment of the poor is given in an apodosis in verse 22. The consequence picks up on the action of verse 21. If Job has raised his hand against the fatherless,

---

23. Longman, *Job*, 361.

24. The 'desire' of the poor here refers to basic necessities of life. Food and clothing are specifically mentioned (G. Wilson, *Job*, 343).

25. Hartley, *Job*, 416 and L. Wilson, *Job*, 152. G. Wilson (*Job*, 343) understands the phrase to refer to the approach of death.

26. G. Wilson (*Job*, 344) notes that the word 'morsel' (*paṯ*) refers to a fragment of food and could be understood as scraps. The picture would be of a friendless miser who hoards his scraps and eats alone.

27. Hartley, *Job*, 417 and G. Wilson, *Job*, 346.

28. L. Wilson, *Job*, 152, n. 274.

the self-curse is that his shoulder blade would fall from his shoulder and that his arm would be broken. This judgment would prevent Job from mistreating the poor because he would not be able to raise his hand against them any longer. The reason Job offers this self-imprecation (*kî*) is that he is in dread of God's judgment against him. He would rather suffer a broken arm than be in terror of calamity from God. He understood the majesty of God and did not want to face God with sin in his life.[29] Job's assertions of innocence in this section respond specifically to the accusations that Eliphaz made against him (Job 22:5-9). He also may be alluding to the way he feels he has been treated by God, whose hand has oppressed and intimidated him (10:7; 12:9; 13:21; 19:21). The irony is that Job acted in justice toward the fatherless because he feared calamity from God. Even though he is innocent he has experienced calamity from the hand of God. And yet, his acknowledgment of God's majesty gives him hope that God will do what is right in his situation. Job ultimately believes in the justice of God.

Trust in Wealth (31:24-25)
These two verses describe the sin of trusting in one's wealth. There are several 'if' statements that deal with an improper view of wealth followed by two clauses that explain the 'if' statements. In verse 24 the focus is on making wealth the source of one's confidence or trust. Such an attitude has a distorted view of life because God should be the source of such confidence and trust. Someone who is rich, however, feels secure that their wealth can help them meet any trial. Wealth brings power, prestige, and the desire to increase the wealth.[30] The clause of verse 25 describes an attitude of rejoicing, followed by two clauses that give a reason for the rejoicing (*kî*). The reason is that a person has an abundance of wealth. Job denies that he rejoiced over his former wealth, an attitude that is consistent with his response in 1:21.[31]

---

29. Hartley (*Job*, 417) asserts, 'A profound awareness of God's majestic holiness guides a person to pursue righteousness and to shun evil.'

30. Hartley, *Job*, 418.

31. G. Wilson, *Job*, 348.

Idolatry (31:26-28)
There is no apodosis ('then' clause) laying out the consequence
of Job's behavior in the two verses on wealth. The very next
verse continues with a protasis ('if' clause) that shifts the
focus to idolatry, with a statement of the consequence of
such activity in verse 28, introduced by 'this also' (*gam-hû'*).
The close relationship between wealth and idolatry may be
the reason these two subjects are discussed back-to-back
without any break between them.[32] The focus in verse 26 is
on looking at the sun or the moon as an object of worship.[33]
The seductive pull of idolatry comes out in verse 27 with the
mention that the heart can be secretly enticed by idolatry.
The reference of the mouth kissing the hand probably refers
to an act of homage to the idol.[34] The consequences of such
actions come in verse 28. If Job has done any of the idolatrous
activities mentioned in verses 26–27 he would be liable to
be punished by the judges for his iniquity. The basis for his
punishment (*kî*) is that he would have been false to God if he
had participated in any form of idolatry. Job has not betrayed
God in this way but has remained true to Him.

Rejoicing at an Enemy's Misfortune (31:29-30)
The structure of the rest of the chapter has been called
convoluted. There are a series of 'if' statements without a
'then' clause in verses 29-34. The 'if' statements resume in
verses 38-39, followed by a 'then' statement in verse 40. The
list of sins is interrupted by verses 35-37 when Job expresses
his longing for an audience with God. Although some want to
restructure these verses by relocating verses 38-40 and ending
the chapter with verse 37, it is better to let the chapter stand
as it is. The convoluted structure could be due to the urgency
of Job's desire for vindication.[35] The rest of the chapter will be

32. Hartley (*Job*, 418) comments that the wealthy may be tempted to have their gold cast into an idol.

33. The worship of the sun and the moon was prevalent in the ancient Near East (Longman, *Job*, 362).

34. Hartley (*Job*, 419) comments that this action may refer to a pagan practice of kissing the hand and throwing the kiss to the heavenly bodies.

35. L. Wilson, *Job*, 153. Longman (*Job*, 363) attributes the structure to Job's excited state of mind as he finishes his final speech.

covered in the same fashion as the prior verses by focusing on each individual sin mentioned by Job.

The sin is stated with the characteristic protasis in verse 29, followed by a statement of affirmation in verse 30. The sin focuses on how Job should respond when an enemy, defined as someone who hates him, experiences ruin or calamity. The natural human response is to rejoice when bad things happen to someone who is trying to destroy you.[36] Job affirms in verse 30 that he has not treated any of his enemies in this way (Prov. 24:17-18). He has not sinned with his mouth by calling down a curse on his enemy to try and seek the end of his life. There is no apodosis laying out the consequence of such a sin.

Failure to Show Hospitality (31:31-32)

These two verses are very much like verses 29-30 in that there is a protasis in verse 31 followed by a statement of affirmation in verse 32. The sin discussed is not showing hospitality. People who needed hospitality are sojourners and travelers. Although the sojourner (*gēr*) can describe an alien who has a particular status in the land that includes special treatment, here it may be used in a general way to refer to any foreigner.[37] The traveler describes a person who is on the road passing through the city. The 'if' clause focuses on the behavior of the servants of Job. Hospitality toward those in need is so much a part of Job's way of life that even his servants are concerned with the plight of the sojourner and the traveler. Job is culpable for this sin even if his servants have not been concerned with showing hospitality. The affirmation in verse 32 affirms the fact that Job has shown hospitality by not only feeding the sojourner or traveler but also by providing a place for them to lodge.[38]

---

36. Longman (*Job*, 362) notes that the concern must be with someone's personal enemy because there are examples of the nation of Israel celebrating the downfall of their enemies after victories, such as in Exodus 15, Judges 5, and Esther 9.

37. See A. H. Konkel, גּוּר, in *NIDOTTE*, 1:837–838. The sojourner is many times placed alongside the widow and the orphan as those who are vulnerable in society and need special help (Deut. 10:18; 14:28; 16:11).

38. See Genesis 19:1-3 and Judges 19:16-21 for how hospitality might work in this situation. Travelers would seek refuge at the plaza of the city where they could

Concealment of Sin (31:33-34)

These two verses are structured a little different from the previous four verses that cover two different sins. The sin is stated with a protasis but instead of a statement of affirmation there is a reason given for why someone would commit such a sin. The specific sin is that Job has concealed his transgressions by hiding his iniquity in his heart. The word 'transgression' is a strong word that refers to acts and attitudes of rebellion. It is a natural, sinful reaction for people to try to cover up their sin rather than confessing it.[39] This cover-up of sin includes the attitude of the heart because the heart is the source of a person's feelings, thoughts, and actions. The reason a person would conceal their sin is stated in verse 34. The reason focuses on how others would view Job because of the sin he committed. Job greatly feared public opinion and how others would treat him. Such results could keep someone silent and isolated from the community. Job has been accused by the friends of covering up his sin but he denies that he has kept sin hidden from others.

Sealing of the Oath (31:35-37)

Job abruptly interrupts the list of sins to express his longing to meet with God. He expresses a strong desire that someone would hear his cause (v. 35). In a series of exclamations, he expresses his willingness to seal the oath with his signature,[40] his exhortation that Almighty God would answer him, and his strong wish that God, his adversary, would present to him a written indictment. Job does not fear such an indictment; rather, he would carry it around on his shoulder and wear

---

stay the night. The usual custom was for a citizen of the city to invite the traveler to stay the night and to provide care for the traveler's animals, a meal, and a place to sleep (Hartley, *Job*, 420).

39. The Hebrew reads *ʾāḏām* that could be understood as a reference to Adam or a reference to human beings in general. The comparison with Adam would refer to the way Adam hid himself from God after he had sinned. Some English translations use 'Adam' in this verse (KJV, NKJV, NAS) and some commentators use this comparison (Andersen, Delitzsch, Habel, and Clines). Most see this as a reference to the common human response of trying to cover up sin to avoid the consequences of sin. Of course, this response did originate with Adam.

40. The Hebrew word for signature is *tāw*, a reference to the last letter of the Hebrew alphabet. It can refer to a mark or a signature confirming a document. Job probably personally signed the oath (Hartley, *Job*, 424).

it as a crown. This would give Job confidence to approach God to give an account of his life. He would approach God with honor 'like a prince'. Job is confident of his vindication because he is innocent. His words are a culmination of many statements throughout his speeches of his desire to have a meeting with God. At times, such a desire has seemed very unlikely because Job has not figured out a way to make God listen to him. His final oath is a way to try to seek a response from the hand of his accuser. He still is not sure that such a meeting will happen, but he expresses his desire for such a meeting in a strong series of exclamations. There is nothing more that he can do. It is up to God to respond.

Abuse of the Land (31:38-40)

Job returns to his list of sins laid out in a series of 'if' statements (vv. 38-39) followed by result clauses that state the consequences of the sin. The focus of this last sin is Job's treatment of his land. The land is personified as crying out against Job with the furrows of the land weeping together. The specific abuse of the land is not stated in verse 38, but verse 39 mentions mistreatment of those who work the land. Job denies benefiting from the harvest of the land without paying those who work it. He also denies treating the owners of the land in a way that causes their desperation, or even death,[41] perhaps by making them work very hard. The result of such sin is presented in a jussive form of the verb (a mild third person imperative). If Job has committed the sins listed, then the consequence should be that the land would grow thorns instead of wheat, and foul weeds would grow instead of barley.[42] In other words, Job would not be able to enjoy the fruits of the land. The chapter ends with the phrase, 'The words of Job are ended.'

Job 31 is a remarkable passage because Job proclaims without compromise his innocence. It is impressive that even as Job

---

41. G. Wilson (*Job*, 354) takes the phrase using 'breath' (*nep̄eš*) to refer to desperation or grief but Hartley (*Job*, 422) takes it as a reference to death. The reference to 'owners' seems to be a reference to tenants who work the land (both G. Wilson and Hartley), but it is possible that Job is referring to ending the life of the owner of the land so he could take over the land (L. Wilson, *Job*, 155).

42. Habel (*Job*, 440) connects the thorns and weeds to the sin of the first Adam that resulted in the curse of the earth.

suffers physically, emotionally, socially, and spiritually that he expresses his innocence in such a magnificent way. The clarity of his conviction shows that he has risen above the self-centered perspective and the deep despair of the curse-lament in chapter 3.[43] His oath of innocence is also spoken against the friends' view that Job has sinned in some way to bring on his suffering.[44]

Job's words are also directed to God because he longs for a meeting with God. The way Job declares his innocence is understood as a way to force an accuser to present written charges against the accused.[45] It seems that God must either verify Job's oath or activate the curses it contains. If God remains silent, then everyone will know that Job is innocent.[46] Job would rather have a session with God to present his case and be declared innocent by God. The reader waits with anticipation for God to speak.

The picture of Job as a righteous man in chapter 31 fits the characterization of Job in chapter 1 as a blameless man who turns away from evil. This characterization of Job's character is also affirmed by God in the first two chapters (1:8; 2:3). Thus it is clear that Job is correct in the debate with the friends concerning the reason for his suffering. He is not suffering because of sin he has committed. And yet, there is evidence that Job has called into question God's justice because he believes God has mistreated him (7:11-21; 16:7-17; 19:7-12). Job's situation is complex. This makes the possibility of God answering Job interesting because one wonders how God will handle Job's argument over against the friends and Job's claim that God has mistreated him. It is helpful as a reader to distinguish the major issue between Job and the friends

---

43. Hartley, *Job*, 426. Longman (*Job*, 364) notes that this is a new Job who is no longer a defeated man longing for the grave.

44. Longman (*Job*, 358) argues that Job is still operating with the same view of retribution as the friends because he protests his innocence as a way to show that he does not deserve suffering. It is better to see Job arguing against the view of the friends who have charged him with wrong. Job has already begun to explore in his earlier speeches the mystery of God's sovereignty and has called into question the view of the friends as speaking falsely for God.

45. Michael Brennan Dick, 'The Legal Metaphor in Job 31', *CBQ* 41 (January 1979): 37-50. He argues that 31:35 is the defendant's official appeal before a third party for a civil hearing at which the judge would compel the plaintiff to formalize his accusations and to present any supporting evidence.

46. Hartley, *Job*, 424.

concerning the cause of his suffering from the situation of how Job responds after he is experiencing the suffering.[47]

In Job's declaration of innocence, he is a model of what a person who fears God looks like (Job 28:28), a model of a blameless, righteous person. Job proclaims his innocence both in his outward actions and in his inward attitudes.[48] He is a picture of sanctification, a picture of a person growing in his holiness and living out a practical righteousness in his life. The character of Job's life matches up with other passages that speak of a person who is blameless and righteous, such as the person who seeks to worship God (Pss. 15, 24). On this level Job is a model of righteous behavior.[49] And yet, in the total message of the book of Job, Job fails when he calls into question God's justice. He is a reminder that no matter how much we grow in our sanctification or how much we are innocent of false charges brought against us, we are unable to keep the whole law of God with our minds and our actions. In this way Job points us to the One who was blameless in every way, the One who kept the law in its entirety, the One who was tempted in all ways as we are yet without sin, the One who is fully righteous and can stand before God in His own righteousness. This One was also an innocent sufferer. He did not need a mediator because He is our mediator before a holy God. This is the One in whom we trust.

The Baby Bird Flew

One of Pierce's doctors told us his philosophy: 'sometimes you just have to kick the baby bird out of the nest and let him fly.' While I was a little concerned

---

47. For an example of the results of a view that does not recognize these two situations see Georg Fohrer, 'The Righteous Man in Job 31', in *Essays in Old Testament Ethics*, eds. James L. Crenshaw and John T. Willis (New York: KTAV, 1974), 3–21. His conclusion is that 'Job 31 describes the man who considers himself to be righteous before God because of his ethically perfect conduct, and therefore must be rebuked by God' (p. 21). Job does not consider his conduct 'perfect' and although Job will be rebuked by God for calling into question God's justice, he will also be vindicated by God before the friends (42:7).

48. For a discussion of Psalm 26 in which the psalmist declares his innocence see Belcher, *Messiah and the Psalms*, 89–93.

49. Elders must also be 'blameless', translated by the ESV as 'above reproach' (1 Tim. 3:2; Titus 1:6).

(thinking that many a bird has fallen to the ground that way), I'm pleased to tell you that this is exactly what is happening. Pierce is flying! He was taken off the vent on Monday and hasn't looked back since! P is loving his new-found freedom – being able to breathe completely on his own, whenever he wants. He has his moments where he holds his breath or forgets to breathe, but so far, he's self-recovered every time. We are so proud of our little guy. Today and yesterday have been the two best days of his life! It's taken us seven LONG weeks to get here, so as you can imagine, we are beyond thrilled! Today the NICU was buzzing as everyone discussed our little guy's progress. And on rounds, the doctors had to make sure they had the right kid (they're not used to such an easy, short report for our boy!). Thank you all for your prayers and support.

Today, I've spent so much time reflecting on God's goodness and mercy. I am flooded with memories of how He has repeatedly sustained Pierce's life throughout these past seven weeks. And still, as today is one of our best days yet, I'm filled with bittersweet thoughts. Once you've tasted how fragile life truly is, it becomes hard not to dwell on the 'what ifs' and 'whys'. I constantly find myself wondering why we still have our son with us, while several of our friends have not been so fortunate. And then there's the 'what if' – like what if he gets _____ or what if ____ happens. But God is gracious. He has reminded me not to be anxious about anything. It hit me today that even if Pierce leaves the NICU with little to no complications (which we are praying fervently for), his life will still be fragile. All our lives are fragile. They're all hanging by a thread. We just fool ourselves into thinking that, when things are good, we have complete control. But we really don't have any control, do we? So tonight, I'm praying for faith; asking for a faith that grants me the ability to trust in God, because I know all too well that trusting in God is much easier said than done.

One last thing. Tonight we were able to hear Pierce cry for the first time ever!!! It was a squeaky cry, almost like a puppy makes when it's first born, but oh, was it ever music to our ears! We only heard it once, because apparently, Pierce is a pretty content baby these days. We tried for a few minutes to make him mad again so that we could hear it once more (aren't we wonderful parents, making our baby cry?!), but nothing worked. Pierce just kept quiet, gazing around his isolette (an incubator for a newborn baby).

Thanks for praying with us on this journey.

Love,
Lindsay Franks (6/1/11)

Study Questions

1) Describe the structure and the purpose of Job's oath of innocence.

2) Describe the various sins that Job lists in his oath. Which one of these sins gives you the most trouble? Could you take this oath of innocence?

3) What hope comes through as one reads through Job's descriptions of these sins?

4) What is remarkable about Job's oath of innocence and what does it say about Job?

5) How should Job's oath of innocence be understood in theological terms?

24

Elihu: Friend or Foe?

(Job 32:1-5)

Introduction to the Elihu Speeches

The discussion between Job and his three friends has come to an end. After Job's oath of innocence in chapter 31 the expectation is that God would respond to Job. And yet, instead of hearing from God, we hear from another individual who inserts himself into the debate. Elihu is angry at both Job and the friends and he is frustrated that the debate has come to an impasse. It will become apparent that Elihu promises a different approach to Job than the friends. He will try to tone down the rhetoric of the debate by acknowledging that his involvement is not personal and he will try to identify with Job (32:14; 33:6-7). He promises to use different arguments than the friends used (32:14). He will quote from the words of Job and then give an answer (33:8-11; 34:5-6; 35:2-3). Elihu seeks to further the discussion by treating Job kindly and by using different arguments.

The main question concerning Elihu is whether his arguments are that different from the argument of the friends. Does Elihu operate with the same principle of divine retribution with which the friends operate? Is Job suffering because he has committed sin? This chapter will lay out the different ways that Elihu has been understood so that the different approaches to Elihu can be evaluated as his speeches are examined.

Different Views of Elihu

A Negative View of Elihu

Some scholars see Elihu as a negative character. Following Job's oath of innocence in chapter 31, the question is whether God will defend Himself or remain silent. Elihu assumes that God will not answer Job because for God to appear before a human court is improper. So Elihu steps forward to take charge of the case himself and to bring the case to an orderly close. In the introduction to the Elihu speeches he is presented as a hothead whose anger has flared up over the debate. Elihu sees himself, however, as wise and patient. He claims to be one thing but his language reveals his true nature. He is a hypocrite and a brash fool. He thinks he can fulfill the role of an arbiter and defender of God, but he comes across as untutored in the ways of wisdom.[1] Others see Elihu as pompous, opinionated, brash and verbose,[2] partly because he associates his knowledge with God's knowledge (36:4; 37:16). He comes across to some as self-important and banal (not saying anything new or original).

A Positive View of Elihu

Others take a positive view of Elihu. His anger is a righteous anger and he contributes something important to the argument. Unlike the friends, Elihu is given a genealogy that indicates weight and significance.[3] The fact that Elihu is given six chapters and four speeches (one more speech than any of the friends) leads to the conclusion that his argument must be important.[4] Why would so much space be given to someone who does not contribute to the argument and only repeats what the friends have said? Also, the failure of the

---

1. Habel, *Job*, 443–447. He sees hypocrisy between the way Elihu is presented in 32:1-5 and the way Elihu presents himself in 32:15-17.

2. C. S. Rodd, *The Book of Job* (Philadelphia, PA: Trinity Press International, 1990), 63.

3. Ash, *Job*, 326-28. He argues that Elihu claims inspiration from God and so is a true prophet.

4. Hartley (*Job*, 427) specifically mentions the four speeches of Elihu. He also comments that Elihu's verbose, overly apologetic style offers comic relief to the atmosphere created by Job's oath. He comes across in a boastful way so that his stature has suffered greatly in biblical interpretation (427, 449).

friends' argument leaves the divine proceedings open to censure without a response.[5] In other words, one could draw the conclusion that God has mistreated Job. This would leave God open to accusation of wrongdoing in Job's situation. Elihu's speeches answer this charge.

Many argue that Elihu gives a partial solution to the problem and that he sets up God's response. First, God governs justly without exception. Elihu's speeches emphasize God's sovereignty. If God had answered immediately after Job's oath, it would look as if Job's oath had compelled Him to answer. Second, God disciplines a person to turn him from the error of his way. So Elihu does not assume, like the friends, that all suffering is punishment for past sin. Misfortune may befall a person to awaken him to a wrongful attitude or an unconscious error, and so keep him from a wrong course. Suffering may be an expression of God's mercy more than His wrath.[6] There is a divine purpose in suffering because God seeks the sufferer's purification and improvement. The friends had argued that suffering might have a chastening purpose, but Elihu argues that God has a beneficial design in suffering.[7] Thus, Elihu's arguments are not the arguments of the friends.

Another angle under the positive approach to Elihu argues that Elihu may not be flawless but that he refocuses the debate and thus shifts the argument. Instead of arguing that Job is suffering because of his sin, Elihu observes that Job is sinning because of his suffering.[8] Elihu's argument focuses not on Job's sins as the cause of his suffering but on Job's words in response to his suffering (32:12; 33:8ff; 34:5ff; 35:2ff). He recognizes that the righteous may suffer (36:7), but suffering should not necessarily be linked to God's justice, a view not held by either the friends or Job.[9] The narrator's perception of Elihu is important. Elihu is introduced as possessing a correct

---

5. William Henry Green, *Conflict and Triumph: The Argument of the Book of Job Unfolded* (Carlisle, PA: The Banner of Truth Trust, 1999), 118.

6. Hartley, *Job*, 427.

7. Jones, *Job*, 226.

8. Talbert, *Beyond Suffering*, 164 and Jones, *Job*, 226.

9. Talbert, *Beyond Suffering*, 170.

perception of Job's problem (32:2: 'he justified himself rather than God'). There is also a similarity between the arguments and concerns of Elihu and the arguments and concerns of God in His speeches.[10] And finally, there is no response to Elihu from either Job or God that leaves the impression that the words of Elihu are accepted by both.[11]

A Mixed View of Elihu

Others take a mixed view of Elihu's speeches. This view argues that he states some things differently than the friends do, but that he does not move beyond their argument. Some of the different emphases in Elihu include the views that God disciplines a person to turn him from the evil of his way, that God always governs with justice, and that God uses suffering for restoration. This is a more positive view of suffering because not all suffering is punishment for past sins and suffering may be more an expression of God's mercy than of His wrath. This view also argues, however, that the disciplinary nature of suffering was not completely absent among the three friends (5:17-22) and that Elihu sees only one recourse for Job, which is to repent and be restored.[12] Thus Elihu operates with the same view of the friends concerning suffering and sin. This means that Elihu would agree with the friends' view that Job is suffering because of sin he has committed.

Another angle to this approach is that Elihu has a different role than the three friends, but that he operates from a flawed foundation. In the dialogues, Job has shown that his righteousness has not been motivated by potential material

---

10. Talbert, *Beyond Suffering*, 172–173. He lists several similarities between Elihu's arguments and God's arguments, including an emphasis on Job's words rather than his actions, on Job's defense of his own righteousness at the expense of God's righteousness, on the glory and incomprehensibility of God, and on questioning Job's knowledge of God's ways in creation.

11. Talbert, *Beyond Suffering*, 168–169 and Jones, *Job*, 227.

12. Longman, *Job*, 63. Longman comments that Elihu represents a different approach than the friends to the foundation of wisdom. The wisdom of the friends is based on their experience and tradition, which contains the wisdom of their ancestors. Elihu is young and represents 'charismatic wisdom', a spiritual wisdom, grounded in the spirit of a person (32:8). His wisdom is not affirmed in the book, which means that his view of wisdom is rejected. It is a false spirituality that leads to error rather than insight (pp. 367–368).

benefits. And yet, Job's challenge to God's policy that He allows righteous people to suffer remains unaddressed. Elihu will address this aspect of Job's argument in the debate. He does not advise Job to confess to past sins, nor is he concerned about Job's motive for being righteous. His accusation does not identify something in the past or something that is hidden in Job as the cause of his suffering, but he accuses Job of a self-righteousness that is so extreme that it impugns God's character. Elihu is not impressed with Job's oath of innocence and his advice to Job is that he should abandon his self-righteousness. He believes that Job lacks the humility that characterizes true righteousness. So he is not arguing from the same perspective as the friends concerning divine retribution, but offers a modified form of the principle. His variation is that judgment may precede the offense since it can have the purpose of drawing out the offensive behavior. Job's offensive self-righteousness that undermined the justice of God was not evident until he began to suffer. His suffering was necessary to reveal the problem. Elihu defends God's policies, but he does so from a flawed foundation because when God speaks, not only will Job's motives be vindicated but his righteousness will be affirmed, even though his self-righteousness will be condemned. So God's actions in the world are not yet properly understood by Elihu.[13]

The above views of Elihu should be kept in mind as each of his speeches is examined. It seems that a key question is whether Elihu's attacks on Job are limited to Job's statements about God's justice during the debates with the friends, or whether he also brings into the discussion the sin of Job as the reason for his suffering. In other words, does Elihu argue the same principle of divine retribution as the friends and thus believe that Job is suffering because of sin he has committed?

---

13. John H. Walton and Tremper Longman, III, *How To Read Job* (Downers Grove, IL: InterVarsity Press, 2015), 70-72. Also see L. Wilson for a similar view (*Job*, 156-57). It will become important to specify how Job's motives and righteousness are affirmed and how his self-righteousness is condemned in the speeches of God and their aftermath. The main issue with this view is that it raises the question of whether Job's self-righteousness existed before his suffering. This would not fit the view of Job in Job 1–2 of a blameless man and upright man.

The Introduction of Elihu (Job 32:1-5)

Elihu will give four speeches (32:6–33:33; 34:1-37; 35:1-16; 36:1–37:24), but before his first speech there is a prose introduction of him. His name means 'he is my God' and it is similar to the name Elijah ('Yahweh is my God').[14] He is identified with a genealogy: 'the son of Barachel, the Buzite, of the family of Ram' (v. 2). There is not agreement concerning whether Elihu is an Israelite or a non-Israelite.[15] Readers are also given information concerning the debate and the reasons why Elihu enters the debate. The debate has come to a standstill with Job's oath of innocence. The three friends cease to answer him because he was righteous in his own eyes. The friends view Job as self-righteous[16] because they could not get him to acknowledge sin as the reason for his suffering. Job's oath of innocence is not a statement of self-righteousness,[17] but is a statement that he is innocent of all the charges the friends have brought against him. Job puts himself on trial in chapter 31 by focusing on his own integrity (31:6) and not making God's treatment of him the major issue.[18]

Elihu gets involved in the debate because he is angry with the arguments presented. He is angry at Job because he justified himself rather than God. Job's assertion of his own innocence at the expense of God's character has raised the ire of Elihu. Elihu is angry at Job for questioning the justice of God. He is also angry at Job's three friends because they

---

14. Hartley, *Job*, 429.

15. The argument that Elihu is an Israelite understands Ram as a descendant of David (Ruth 4:19; 1 Chron. 2:9, 25) and Buz as the brother of Uz (Gen. 22:21), a nephew of Abraham (Longman, *Job*, 381). The argument that Elihu is a non-Israelite understands 'Buzite' as an inhabitant of Buz, a place and people associated with areas around Edom in Jeremiah 25:23 (G. Wilson, *Job*, 361).

16. A similar phrase 'wise in his own eyes' is used in Proverbs 3:7; 26:5, 12, 16; 28:11 in a negative way marking a person as arrogant and unteachable. This is how the friends view Job (G. Wilson *Job*, 361), but to claim that this is the narrator's view of Job or that Job is almost claiming to be sinless before God (Jones, *Job*, 230), goes against the view of chapters 1–2 (see also the conclusion to Job's oath of innocence in Job 31).

17. Contra Reitman, *Unlocking Wisdom*, 118-19. He comments that Elihu's speeches expose Job's self-righteous presumption.

18. William P. Brown, *Wisdom's Wonder: Character, Creation, and Crisis in the Bible's Wisdom Literature* (Grand Rapids: Eerdmans, 2014), 103-04.

were not able to answer Job. Their main, and only, response was to declare that Job was wrong even though they had no real evidence for the charge. These arguments have made him angry and have motivated him to enter the debate. The silence of the friends makes it appear that Job has won the debate.[19] Elihu did not enter the debate earlier because he is younger than the participants in the debate. In that culture, youth would give way to age as more experienced and wiser. His anger that the friends have not been able to answer Job motivates him to offer his own thoughts.

The anger of Elihu is not necessarily a bad thing because anger is not always wrong.[20] There is a righteous anger, called righteous indignation, that is a response to what people do or say. Righteous anger focuses on how people's actions and words foster injustice or false views of people or of God. God's anger is always righteous because He responds to people's sinful actions, words, and attitudes. Christ also expressed righteous anger because people turned the temple from a house of prayer into a marketplace of buying and selling (John 2:13-17), because the Pharisees taught the law in such a way as to make people slaves to it (Matt. 23:16-24), and because the Pharisees acted in ways that were self-righteous and hypocritical (Matt. 23:1-6, 25-28). Paul also expressed righteous anger in Athens when he saw the city full of idols (Acts 17:16).

The problem with righteous anger is that human beings are sinful and it is easy for righteous anger to become self-righteous anger. God's people should become angry at sin and its results.[21] We should become angry when we hear the God that we worship maligned or called immoral.[22] How we respond is important. Righteous anger does not need to lead

---

19. Hartley, *Job*, 428.

20. For discussions of anger, see Stuart Scott, *Anger, Anxiety, and Fear: A Biblical Perspective* (Bemidji, MN: Focus Publishing, 2009) and David Powlison, *Anger: Escaping the Maze* (Carlisle, PA: P&R Publishing, 2000).

21. The 2016 videos of Planned Parenthood personnel discussing the harvesting of baby parts from aborted babies should fill Christians with deep remorse, but there should also be outrage at the total disregard for life and the law.

22. Many use the Old Testament to argue for an immoral God, such as Christopher Hitchens, *God is Not Great: How Religion Poisons Everything* and Richard Dawkins, *The God Delusion*.

to angry outbursts. We must be honest with people concerning the negative consequences of sinful behavior and attitudes, but we must also with humility and a winsome spirit present the glorious message of the gospel of Christ. The only hope of hardened sinners who hate God and the morality that comes from His Word is the transforming power of Christ.[23]

Questions, Anger, and God's Goodness

The following is the first blog on Lindsay's new website (www.lindsayfranks.com). The blog was originally entitled 'Questions'.

Will he be able to walk? Will he be able to talk? Will he be able to learn? Hear? See? And run? These questions continue as if I've pressed the repeat button on the thought player that is my mind. Literally, every day, it is not long before one of these questions enters my mind. Then, what usually follows is a series of intense emotions: fear, pain, grief, sadness, anger.

I find myself growing bitter towards those who have healthy children. They never have to worry about those things. They go about their day, posting casual photos on Facebook. 'Oh, Johnny found his toes.' Great. 'Johnny is rolling over.' Great. 'Johnny is walking.' Great. Great. Great. It's SO embarrassing. Really, I shouldn't feel this way. But I do. And I regret having to confess this.

So many of my readers have children who have had less than perfect starts. Their lives have been filled with struggles, and while little Johnny was finding his toes, our children were struggling to stay alive. You know what it's like to wrestle with these intense emotions. And maybe you're like me, finding yourself confused as to how to process these emotions in light of your faith.

People casually say things like, 'Look how far he's come,' and 'He's going to be just fine.' And yet, those nagging questions continue to play repeatedly in my mind. Over and over. Again and again. Never-ending.

---

23. See the story of Rosaria Butterfield, *The Secret Thoughts of an Unlikely Convert* (Pittsburgh, PA: Crown & Covenant Publications, 2012).

We know how blessed we are that Pierce has overcome great odds. But we are also so very aware that we are still in the beginning stretch of a marathon. We have come so far, yet have so far to go. So many of the above questions will not be answered for several years. Some days it feels like we are in an airplane, circling the ground, unsure of where we will land. Will it be hot? Cold? Bumpy? Smooth?

I guess what I'm trying to say is that the fear of the unknown can be very overwhelming.

But God is graciously teaching me not to fear the unknown, because *not fearing the unknown demonstrates your trust in Him and in His goodness.* So often I get stuck in the mindset that this world is it, so I better make it the best it can be. But that's not so. This world is not final. And because of Christ, this world is the *worst* that I will experience. *So to fear something that is so temporary, so fleeting, reveals the disbelief in my heart.*

As I've wrestled through this, I've found my questions have started to subside. They're not gone, and I don't anticipate they will ever be. But they're not as terrifying. They're less intrusive. And instead of the questions, I'm remembering the Truth – *that God is good, He does good and He works things for good.* So, whatever struggles He allows us to endure, I am trusting that He will grant us the grace to make it through. And while I definitely think that the character of God demonstrates that it is okay to want the best for your child, I also find that it shows that God loves Pierce more than I could possible imagine and He wants what is best.

But here's the kicker, perhaps my definition of 'what's best' has been *wrong* all along? If Pierce can run, jump, laugh, and play, but he doesn't know Christ, what good is that (Matt. 16:26)? So tonight, as I tuck Pierce in, my prayer will continue to be the same that I have prayed since he was born: that God would heal his entire body – his brain, his lungs, his heart, his eyes, his bones, *but more importantly, that my son would never know a day apart from Christ.* That is my prayer now and always.

Lindsay Franks (3/5/16)

Study Questions

1) How does Elihu approach Job differently than the friends?

2) Summarize the various views that commentators take concerning the character of Elihu. What is a key question that must be kept in mind when reading Elihu's speeches?

3) Why is Elihu angry?

4) Is anger always bad? How can it be a good thing? What are the dangers that come with anger?

25

The First Speech of Elihu
(Job 32:6–33:33)

God is Greater than Man

Each speech of Elihu is introduced with a form of the phrase 'Elihu answered and said' (34:1; 35:1). The last speech uses the phrase 'Elihu continued and said' (36:1) and the first speech uses an extended statement that identifies Elihu: 'And Elihu the son of Barachel the Buzite answered and said' (32:6). This breaks down Elihu's speeches into four speeches: 32:6–33:33; 34:1-37; 35:1-16; and 36:1-37:24. The identification of Elihu in the first speech may be to lend authority to his words because of his youth.[1]

An 'Apology' to the Friends (Job 32:6-22)

Elihu begins by offering an apology for why he is entering the discussion between Job and the friends.[2] He gives reasons for why they should listen to him. In the first part of the apology (vv. 6-14) Job is addressing the friends (evidenced by the plural 'you'). In the second part of the apology (vv. 15-22), Elihu speaks of the friends in the third person ('they'). He is probably speaking to Job here, but clearly he speaks to Job directly in chapter 33.

---

1. Hartley, *Job*, 433. Longman, to the contrary, takes the repetition of the identification of Elihu as evidence that he is pretentious. He argues that Elihu is self-centered in this speech, a young man bursting to express his opinion (*Job*, 382).

2. Hartley (*Job*, 433) notes, with examples, that apologies are well attested in the ANE when one assumes a role not rightly his by position, status, or age.

Elihu states in the first part of the apology (vv. 6-14) why they should listen to him. The basic reason is that the friends could not answer Job (vv. 11-13). Although Elihu was patient and listened closely to the arguments of the friends, they were not able to refute the arguments of Job or give an answer to him. Elihu contends that no arbiter has risen to process Job's case with God and to answer his charges, something that Job himself had requested (Job 9:33).[3] Thus, the debate has ceased without resolution. Elihu will seek to fulfill this function for Job. He anticipates an objection from the friends, which is that they have offered wisdom and now it is up to God to answer Job (v. 13).[4] On the contrary, the friends could not answer Job because they do not possess wisdom. Elihu has not spoken up earlier because he is young. Conventional wisdom of that day would argue that the aged are wise because of their experience. Thus, Elihu has been timid and afraid to speak because of his youth. He waited to hear the wisdom of his elders, but after the debate he concludes that 'It is not the old who are wise nor the aged who understand what is right' (v. 9). The true source of wisdom comes from God who makes people understand, regardless of age or experience (v. 8).[5] The result of this conviction is that the friends should be willing to listen to the opinions of Elihu (v. 10) Plus, he hints at taking a different approach to the questions raised in the debate. There is no personal animosity between Elihu and Job because Job has not directed any of his words against Elihu. Also, Elihu is going to use different arguments than were

---

3. Habel, *Job*, 452. Both Job 9:33 and 32:12 use the term *môḵʾah*.

4. The thought here may be that the friends have given up on convincing Job and have turned the situation over to God. Job has stubbornly rejected their wisdom, so it is up to God to change his thinking (Longman, *Job*, 383).

5. The phrase 'spirit in man' parallels the phrase 'breath of the Almighty', so that the reference is to the insight the human spirit receives from the Spirit of God (Hartley, *Job*, 434). This statement is not necessarily referring to the special revelation of divine inspiration but could be referring to knowledge that is available to anyone who is endowed with wisdom from the Spirit of God (Thomas, *The Storm Breaks*, 257). God may give insight (*bʾn*) in ways other than by divine revelation. On one side, Habel's understanding of v.8 (*Job*, 450-51) as referring to the spirit of wisdom in all humans by virtue of being created by God is too general and negates the special role of the fear of Yahweh as the beginning of wisdom. On the other side, to present Elihu as uttering prophecy reads too much into his statements at this point (Ash, *Job*, 333).

used by the friends. Thus, there is hope that progress will be made in the debate.

Elihu explains in the second part of the apology why he feels compelled to declare his opinion (vv. 15-22). He feels compelled to answer because the friends are dismayed and have nothing more to say to Job. He will fill in the void with his answers and thus fulfill the role of the arbiter (v. 18).[6] Elihu also feels compelled to speak because he is full of words that are about to burst forth from him. Up to now his spirit has constrained him, but the compulsion to speak is like a new wineskin that has not been vented and is ready to burst. He must speak to find relief. He promises that his words will be honest words that will not show partiality. God his Maker is his witness that he will not flatter; otherwise, God would be angry with his words and take him away.

An 'Apology' to Job (Job 33:1-7)

Elihu speaks directly to Job and implores him to listen to his words. He gives several reasons why Job should listen to him. Elihu claims to speak from the uprightness and sincerity of his heart. He approaches Job honestly without any agenda other than speaking what is truly on his heart. Thus, his words are trustworthy.[7] He also asserts that he is no different than Job because the source of his life is the breath of God and he is made from clay just like Job.[8] Elihu and Job share a common humanity so that Job should not feel threatened by Elihu. With the heat turned down in the discussion Job should be able to give an answer to Elihu. He should have the freedom to set forth a rational argument so that they might have a discussion of the issues. Elihu also presents himself as the arbiter of Job's legal case with God. He uses three imperatives (v. 5) to encourage Job to prepare his case before him ('answer me,' 'set your words in order before me,' and

---

6. Konkel, 'Job,' 6:193 and Habel, *Job*, 472.

7. Hartley, *Job*, 438.

8. The statements in vv. 4-6 reflect Genesis 2:7. If the point is that Elihu and Job share common humanity, so that Elihu and Job are on equal footing, then the reference to the Spirit of God and the breath of the Almighty would not be a statement of divine inspiration, but that the work of creation provides human beings with intellectual ability (Konkel, 'Job,' 6:196).

'take your stand').[9] His hand will not pressure Job as he has felt such pressure from God (13:21).[10]

A Refutation of Job's Claim of Innocence (Job 33:8-33)

Elihu seeks to answer Job's claim that he is innocent before God and that therefore God has mistreated him. In the process of answering this claim, he will also deal with some of the other arguments of Job. Elihu also gives an indication of how he is going to approach Job. He has heard Job present his arguments to the friends and he is going to begin his discussion with Job by quoting his own words.[11] This approach is very different from the way the friends approached Job. Elihu may be trying to avoid the problem of people talking past each other. The benefit of quoting the words of Job is that it cuts down on misunderstanding and gives them common ground for the discussion. At least he is going to try to answer the specific words of Job.

Elihu sets forth the central claim of Job in his argument against the friends by quoting Job's own words (vv. 8-11). Job has claimed that he is pure and clean, without transgression or iniquity. In addition, Job has argued that God still counts him as an enemy by the way He treats him. God seeks to make Job's life miserable by finding occasions against him (6:4; 16:12-14). He punishes him without cause ('puts my feet in the stocks') and He scrutinizes Job's life ('watches all my paths'). God's scrutiny of Job never allows him a moment of rest so that he might catch his breath (Job 13:27).[12]

Elihu's answer is direct and simple, but it also takes several turns. The direct answer to this claim is that Job is wrong because God is greater than man (v. 12). What Elihu means by this statement comes out in the way he develops his argument

---

9. Habel, *Job*, 464-65. He emphasizes the legal aspect of Elihu's words, but the parallel he draws between Elihu and Lady Wisdom seems forced.

10. If 'my hand' (ESV 'my pressure') is the word in 33:7 (L. Wilson, *Job*, 161, n. 304, identifies it as a possible variant form), then this would support the concept of an arbiter (Job 9:33).

11. Although the 'you say' of v. 9 is not in the text, it has been added to make clear that Elihu is quoting Job.

12. Hartley, *Job*, 440. The verb 'watch' (*šāmar*) normally refers to God's providential care but here it refers to God's spying on Job as a dangerous foe, what Habel calls 'satanic surveillance' (*Job*, 467).

against Job. He believes that Job is being contentious[13] toward God because he asserts that God will not answer any of the words of man, much less his own claim against God.

Elihu presents several answers to this declaration of Job before he comes back to the assertion of Job's innocence. He states three things in response to the statement that God does not answer man. He wants to show that God speaks to humans in a variety of ways that may not be perceived by them. First, God speaks to people in dreams or visions of the night while they are sleeping (vv. 14-18). He may give them understanding by opening their ears, He may terrify them with warnings, He may turn aside a person from some action, or He may keep[14] pride from a person to protect his life from perishing by the sword.

Second, God may speak to a person through the pain of illness (vv. 19-22). He may use the physical difficulties of sickness to rebuke a person. The hardship of illness is presented as a lack of appetite in loathing food, as an emaciated body that shows all the bones, and as a life that is close to death.

Third, there is the possibility that God would provide an angel[15] to be a mediator to declare to a person what is right for him (vv. 23-28).[16]

It is possible that God would show mercy to the person who is suffering by delivering him from death through a ransom. Such mercy would lead to a restoration of the person in every way. His emaciated body would become as the body of youth and his energy would return. He would pray to God

---

13. The word 'contend' in v. 13 is the Hebrew word $r'\underline{b}$ that is used to refer to God's covenant lawsuit against His people for breaking the covenant (Hosea 4:1; Micah 6:1-2).

14. The word 'keep' means 'to conceal' (ksh), as translated by the ESV. The idea seems to be that the warnings which terrify people keep them from pride.

15. There is debate about the identity of this angel. The Hebrew word $mal'\bar{a}\underline{k}$ could refer to a messenger. The phrase 'one of a thousand' is also debated. If this phrase refers to the uniqueness of the mediator, then the mediator could be the angel of Yahweh (Hartley, *Job*, 447), or even Elihu (G. Wilson, *Job*, 377). If the phrase refers to one messenger among many, then the messenger could refer to any number of heavenly angels. Longman (*Job*, 389) believes Elihu is referring to a heavenly angel and understands the provision of an angel for mediation to be unique.

16. This statement may refer to the right way a person should take, the way that will lead out of suffering back to God (Hartley, *Job*, 446).

and God would accept him and restore him to righteousness. The restored one would see God again and would sing for joy. He would recognize that he had sinned and perverted what was right, but God took away the consequences of his sin and redeemed his soul from death by bringing him back to life. In fact, God continually acts this way toward people to restore them and to allow them to live in the light (vv. 29-30).[17] The actions of God are both preventative and affirmative. God seeks to prevent people from going down to the grave and He seeks to illumine people's lives with the true light that leads to a full, meaningful life.[18]

Elihu ends his first speech with an invitation for Job to respond to his words (vv. 31-33). He encourages Job to pay special attention to what he has said so that he will be able to provide an answer. He wants Job to speak because he desires to justify him. Elihu's desire is to help Job be acquitted, so he can be restored to God.[19] This vindication of Job would include an admission by Job of his own faults.[20] If Job decides not to speak, he should be silent and listen to the wisdom that Elihu will teach him.

Evaluation of Elihu's First Speech

There are many different reactions to the first speech of Elihu. Some argue that the wordiness and repetition of segments of the speech are an indication that he is an arrogant windbag.[21] The key issue is the argument of Elihu and whether he agrees with the view of the friends that Job is suffering because of his sin. This can be answered only be an analysis of what Elihu says to Job.

His response to Job is based on his quotation of what Job has said (vv. 9-11). The first question is whether he has quoted Job correctly. It is interesting that there are statements of Job that match verses 10-11, but not verse 9. Job has said that

---

17. The use of 'twice, three times' refers to God's continual efforts to turn people from the error of their ways (Longman, *Job*, 390).

18. Hartley, *Job*, 448.

19. Hartley, *Job*, 448.

20. Longman, *Job*, 390.

21. G. Wilson, *Job*, 366. Hartley (*Job*, 435) points out that it is difficult at times to evaluate Elihu because we cannot hear the tone in which he speaks his words.

God is acting toward him as an enemy (13:24; 16:9; 19:11) and verse 11 is a quotation of what Job says in 13:27. The words of verse 9, 'I am pure without transgression; I am clean, and there is no iniquity in me,' are not words that Job has spoken. Job claims that he is blameless (9:20-21), but not that he is pure, without transgression, or clean without iniquity.[22]

This discrepancy raises the question of whether Elihu is quoting Job correctly. It sounds as if he is accusing Job of claiming moral perfection even though Job has never claimed that he has never sinned. In light of the fact that verse 11 quotes 13:27, many find in 13:23 evidence that Job has tacitly denied sin.[23] Job's statement in 13:23 is a response to Zophar who has accused Job of sin as a reason for his suffering (12:14). It is not a statement that he is sinless. If Elihu misquotes Job, then his argument against him has no foundation.

The other important aspect about verses 9-11 is that it is difficult to limit these words to Job's response to his suffering. If one appeals to chapter 13 as the source of the quotation of verse 9, then it is clear that Elihu is arguing the same point as the friends because that is the issue in chapter 13. There is no evidence that Elihu is trying to limit the discussion with Job to his statements after suffering has overtaken him. At best, he is ambiguous concerning the matter. Words of wisdom are meant to clarify situations which Elihu fails to do in chapter 33. One of Elihu's solutions is that the sufferer should repent in order that he can be restored (vv. 26-28). Even some who argue for a positive view of Elihu acknowledge that his argument in these verses sounds very much like the argument of the friends (bad behavior leads to destruction).[24] In fact, Elihu's accusation that Job asserts that he is 'clean' is the same accusation that Zophar had made against Job in 11:4.[25] It is

---

22. Job does use the word 'pure' in reference to his prayer (16:17), but not in reference to his life (Hartley, *Job*, 440).

23. Jones, *Job*, 239 and Arden, *Job*, 324.

24. Arden, *Job*, 327. Jones (*Job*, 240-41) also acknowledges that the friends had pointed out that when God speaks to people in dreams He is calling a person to repentance for sin that brought judgment.

25. The word that Zophar uses (*bar*) is different than the words Elihu uses (*zak̲, ḥap̄*), but the words express the same concept. Exegesis is not limited to the word level but can appropriately be done on the concept level.

difficult to avoid the conclusion that the starting point for the discussion is the same starting point as the friends.

Once it is recognized that Elihu's starting point in this speech is the same as the friends' starting point, other matters become clear. Although there is hope that Elihu will use a different approach with different arguments, the first speech falls short of that expectation. The fact that Elihu does not want to make it personal and does not want to use flattery or be partial in his approach are good things, but the first attempt at answering Job not does advance the argument. Therefore, it is appropriate to take a negative view of the character of Elihu. He claims to speak wisdom, but it is a false claim in relationship to the major point of contention. His compulsion to speak (32:18-20) has been compared to Jeremiah as evidence that his words are prophetic.[26] But the difference is that Jeremiah did not want to speak, but had to speak because of divine compulsion, even against his will, whereas Elihu's compulsion to speak arises from a burning desire to speak.[27] He wants to enter the debate and impart his wisdom. If such wisdom falls short, it can hardly be called prophetic.

The argument that Elihu presents a different view of the purpose of suffering has some merit. Elihu does correctly quote the words of Job that he thinks God is his enemy who has treated him harshly (33:10-11). Job has also questioned whether God would ever answer his words and give him a hearing (9:32-33; 16:20-22; 23:3-9). Elihu responds that God does answer in many ways that are not perceived by people. Part of the purpose of dreams is to warn people to turn aside from the wrong way (vv. 15-18). God also speaks to people through the pain of illness. The impact of illness on a person's life fits very well the physical effect of Job's illness on him (vv. 19-22). God may also mercifully provide a mediator who offers a ransom with the result that the person turns to God, confesses his sin, and rejoices in his redemption. Elihu's desire to 'justify' Job (v. 32) is that Job would confess his

---

26. Ash, *Job*, 334.

27. Longman, *Job*, 384. Habel also notes that Jeremiah pronounced his oracles against his will (Jer. 20:9) whereas Elihu delighted in venting his views (*Job*, 454).

sin and be restored. The divine purpose of discipline is to strengthen a person's piety and thereby lift him to a higher spiritual sphere. The fact that God can use affliction for gracious purposes is alleged to be a new doctrine that moves suffering beyond the discussion of punishment for sin. God's purpose from the beginning was to bless Job through this trial.[28] On one level God's discipline is preventive to warn people, but the mention of the confession of sin means that there must be an element of punishment also involved.[29] Both aspects can be part of discipline.

Elihu also mentions that God can provide a mediator for Job (33:23). Job has several times longed for someone who could act as a mediator on his behalf (Job 9:33; 16:19; 19:25). This mediator could be an angel, but the word *mal'āk* could also mean a messenger. He will declare what is right for Job in his suffering. He will show mercy and deliver him through a ransom. The right response of Job is to repent of his sin and be restored. If Job would respond in this way, then he would be accepted by God and see His face. Elihu is acting as the mediator for Job by teaching him the purpose of suffering and telling him how he should respond to God. This role of Elihu is why Job must listen to him so he can teach him wisdom (v. 33). The role of Elihu as mediator, however, will fail to bring about the desired outcome for Job. Job has also expressed a longing to see God, but not through a confession of his sin that would lead to restored health. Job longed to see God even in his suffering because he believed his kinsman-redeemer would vindicate him (19: 25-26). Elihu in his first speech may emphasize more the disciplinary aspect of suffering, but he fails as a mediator because he does not have the wisdom nor the power to bring God and Job together. Job's situation will be solved by God's intervention. In time the one mediator approved by God for sinners, Jesus Christ, will come and He will not fail as a mediator (1 Tim. 2:5).

---

28. Green, *Conflict in Triumph*, 122–134. It is significant that this purpose for Job's suffering is not mentioned in Job 1–2.

29. Jones (*Job*, 241) argues that God's discipline was preventive but not punitive.

Important Steps: Taking Nothing for Granted

Pierce is 65 days old. He weighs 3 lbs. 7 oz. and is around 15 inches long. He is growing like a weed!!! I can't tell you how thrilled I am that he is now starting to fill out his preemie outfits. And pretty soon, he will likely be moving from his heated condo (aka incubator) to a big boy bed (bassinet).

Two weeks ago, Pierce was on the vent; I was beginning to wonder if he'd ever get off and thinking that even if he did, there was no way we'd ever be leaving the hospital near his due date (Aug. 4th). Ok, flash forward to tonight – Pierce is off the vent. He's now regulating his temperature fairly well, and is able to wear clothes!

Pierce is progressing so rapidly that tonight his Nurse Practitioner took me on a tour of the step-down nursery. That's right folks, I said it – the step-down nursery! The step-down (or progressive care nursery) is for low-maintenance babies who just need to feed and grow before leaving the hospital. We never thought our child would be considered 'low maintenance'.

In NPCN (Neo-natal Progressive Care Nursery), Pierce will be given a new list of tasks. You see, up until this point, Pierce's main goal in life has been to keep breathing (and for the first seven weeks, a machine did this for him!). When he moves to NPCN, he will not only do those 'basics', but he will also have to regulate his own body temperature (he will move out of his nifty plastic womb and into a regular crib), learn to eat from a bottle, pass a car seat test and much, much more. Needless to say, this is a *big* step for the lil' man. Nik and I are shocked at how fast he is progressing. I think he is in a hurry to get home.

God has been SO good to us along the way. Today I found myself reflecting on the many times God has intervened and performed miracles to save Pierce's life. Medically speaking, our son should not be here. I don't ever want to take for granted God's grace and every night I pray over Pierce that he would never know a day apart from Christ. I get so excited when I think about reading him stories from the Bible about how God saved those He loved. And then what really excites me is how I will be able to close the Bible and tell my sweet son the story of how God saved *him*. I want to thank each of you for your continued prayers. God has heard them and He is the one who has brought us to this point. Please continue to pray for us as Pierce makes his big move tomorrow.

The above account was taken from a couple blogs over a several-days period in June 2011.

Nik and Lindsay Franks

Study Questions

1) Why has Elihu waited to enter the debate? Why should the friends listen to Elihu? What role does he claim to fulfill?

2) How is Elihu's approach to Job different from the friends' approach?

3) Does Elihu quote Job correctly? What are the implications if he has not quoted Job correctly?

4) Does Elihu differ from the argument of the friends? What is the evidence for your response?

5) How does the first speech of Elihu fail in its purpose? How is Elihu's view of the purpose of suffering different than that of the friends?

26

The Second Speech of Elihu
(Job 34:1-37)

A Defense of God's Justice

Elihu's second speech is going to focus on the righteous rule of God.[1] He will address the 'wise men' in the audience, which no doubt includes the friends, in verses 1-15. He will specifically address Job in verses 16-33 before he again addresses the 'men of understanding' in verses 34-37.[2]

A Summons to Listen (Job 34:1-4)

Elihu begins his second speech by exhorting the wise men to listen to his words. The parallel structure of verse 2 identifies the wise men as those who know. Knowledge and the application of knowledge is the business of the wise men. The friends of Job have failed to offer wisdom and so Elihu invites them to hear what he has to say.[3] The reason (*kî*) he exhorts them to listen to his words is given in verse 3: 'for the ear tests words as the palate tastes food' (a proverb used by Job in 12:11). This is a proverb that compares the ear and the mouth. Everyone understands that 'the palate tastes

---

1. Hartley, *Job*, 449.

2. The change concerning the addressees can be seen in a change from plural pronouns (vv. 1-15) to singular pronouns (vv. 16-33) and back to plural pronouns (vv. 34-37).

3. The fact that Elihu uses imperatives in v. 2, which issues commands, may signify that he does more than invite them to listen.

food'. In a similar way 'the ear tests words' by examining arguments and statements that people make. The wise man should be able to understand, examine, and offer wise advice concerning what people say. The goal of such discernment is to choose what is right and to know what is good (v. 4). Wisdom has the practical benefit of helping people evaluate different arguments so to live with understanding and knowledge. The friends have not offered such wisdom to Job (32:3). Elihu suggests that he will be able to offer wisdom to Job. The wise men should be able to judge between his views and Job's views concerning which view is right and good.[4]

A Refutation of Job's Claim against God (Job 34:5-33)

A Summary of Job's Claim (Job 34:5-9)
Elihu continues to address the wise men through verse 15 but he begins his refutation of Job's argument by quoting what Job has said (vv. 5-9). The words of Job are quoted in verses 5-6 and 9 with a commentary on what he has said in verses 7-8.

The quotation from Job emphasizes the word 'right'. Job says 'I am in the right'. The verb is ṣādaq in the first person which Job used in 9:15, 20; 10:15; and 13:18. Job has continually claimed that he is in the right, and that he has a just case to present before God. He believes that God has not treated him fairly. Job is quoted as saying, 'God has taken away my right' and 'in spite of my right I am counted a liar' (vv. 5-6). The word for 'right' is the word mišpāṭ. If God has taken away his right, then God has treated him unjustly. God even counts him a liar before his case has been heard. The failure of God to respond has led Job to believe that he is being mistreated by God ('my wound is incurable though I am without transgression') and that there is no benefit for a person to 'take delight in God'. Although the latter quotation is not an exact rendering of a specific statement of Job, it

---

4. Longman, *Job*, 391. Nothing specifically is said to identify the wise men addressed by Elihu. Hartley (*Job*, 450) denies they include the three friends because of Elihu's attitude toward them in chapter 32. He surmises the elders who sit in the gate are in view who will decide this dispute, but there is no evidence to support their involvement. In the context of the book of Job, the friends should be included, but Elihu may also be appealing to any and all sages (G. Wilson, *Job*, 381).

does express Job's claim that God destroys both the blameless and the wicked (9:22) and that God favors the designs of the wicked (10:3) so that they escape punishment (21:7, 15).[5] Thus, Job asserts his own integrity at the expense of God's justice. In this case Elihu has correctly presented Job's position.[6]

Elihu comments on what Job has said in verses 7-9. He puts Job in the category of a hardened sinner. Job is a person who drinks up scoffing like water. As often as people drink water, so Job's words reflect a scornful attitude indicative of foolishness.[7] Job travels in company with evildoers and he walks with wicked men.[8] Job's whole life is characterized as full of wickedness, from his words to his companions. Elihu's characterization of Job is broad and does not highlight any aspect of his life. All of Job's words and life are characterized as wicked because he has called into question God's justice.

A Response to Job's Claim (Job 34:10-30)
This section can be broken down into two parts based on the argument of Elihu and who is being addressed. In verses 10-15 Elihu continues to address the wise men and he sets forth the basic thesis that he wants to argue concerning the just rule of God over the world. In verses 16-30 he addresses Job directly as he defends his thesis that God governs the world with justice.

The Thesis: God Rules the World with Justice (Job 34:10-15)
Elihu begins the statement of his thesis with an exhortation for the men of understanding to hear what he is about to say. He begins with the word 'therefore' (*lākēn*) to show that he is responding specifically to the words of Job. The basic thesis is that God does not act wickedly nor does the Almighty do wrong (v. 10). He does not just assert the thesis but he states it in such a way to emphasize the impossibility for God to do

---

5. Konkel, 'Job,' 6:201.

6. The only quotation that does not represent anything that Job has said is v. 6: 'though I am without transgression.' See the discussion of similar words attributed to Job in the previous chapter.

7. Hartley, *Job*, 452.

8. Longman (*Job*, 392) characterizes the description of Job as reminiscent of the description of the wicked in Psalm 1:1.

wrong ('far be it from God').[9] The reason that God does not do wrong is that He repays a person according to his work. God ensures that whatever happens to a person will be in accord with the way he lives his life (v. 11). God judges every deed to render to a person a just reward. This statement counters Job's position that God acts as He wills whether people are innocent or wicked (9:22-24; 24:1-12).[10] In order to be sure that there is no misunderstanding, Elihu states his thesis a second time, emphasizing that it is the truth. God will not do wickedly and He will not pervert justice (v. 12). This thesis is reinforced by a rhetorical question and then a conditional statement to show God's power and authority over the earth. The rhetorical question is 'Who gave him charge over the earth, and who laid on him the whole world' (v. 12)? There is no one who is above God who delegated to Him charge over the world. The implication is that God has charge over the world because He is its sovereign ruler. God's power and sovereignty are demonstrated in the fact that He could at any time cause the breath of man to return to Him. The result would be that all flesh would perish and that human beings would return to dust. A person should be very careful in calling into question God's rule of the world because all life depends on Him.

A Defense of the Thesis that God Rules with Justice
(Job 34:16–30)

In verse 16 Elihu again exhorts Job to listen to what he has to say by the use of the word 'hear' (*šāmaʿ*). In verse 10 the plural form was used because Elihu was addressing the men of understanding. In verse 16 the singular form is used because Elihu is addressing Job. If Job has understanding, he should listen to what Elihu has to say.

Elihu begins with a series of questions to support the thesis that God does not pervert justice. The first question, 'Shall one who hates justice govern?', states that justice is

---

9. Hartley, *Job*, 453. Norman Whybray, *Job* (Sheffield: Sheffield Academic Press, 1998), 146-47, calls the phrase *ḥālilāh lĕ* ('far be it from') an extremely strong expression having the force of an oath that declares something to be unthinkable because it is contrary to the speaker's moral character.

10. Hartley, *Job*, 454.

essential for governing. This question is further explained by the questions in verses 17-19. The opening words 'Will you condemn' goes with several of the questions that follow and these questions expect a 'no' answer. The initial defense of God's justice highlights two things. It is absurd to condemn someone who is righteous and mighty (v. 17b).[11] It also does not make sense to condemn someone who demonstrates justice by not showing partiality in judgment. God does not show partiality to those who hold power but He renders just verdicts, such as 'worthless one' to a king, or 'wicked man' to a noble. God does not regard the rich over the poor because they are both the work of His hands. He does not need to show partiality to the rich because God does not need anything that the rich could offer Him. In fact, any person, rich or poor, could experience death 'in a moment'. Even the mighty die apart from human agency because God is ultimately the sovereign ruler of the world.

Further evidence for God's just rule of the world is given in verses 21-30. God governs impartially because He sees all things. He sees everything that a person does (v. 21). Nothing is hidden from Him, so that not even deep darkness can hide the actions of evildoers (v. 22). God does not need to convene a court to find out the evidence in a case because He already knows the case fully. Thus, God can shatter the mighty without an investigation. He can put people in their place, to crush them in the night by overturning them, and to strike them for their wickedness (vv. 23-27). Here is confirmation that God repays people for the wickedness they have committed and He does it in a public place for all to see the outcome of wicked behavior. Part of the rationale of a public display of the consequences of wicked action is that such wickedness included oppression of the poor and the afflicted who cried out to God (v. 28). If Job truly believes in God's justice, then he would not condemn God when He seems inactive or when He hides Himself and a godless person ends up reigning for

---

11. Hartley (*Job*, 457) points out that the logical connection between justice and power makes more sense in the ancient world because these two were considered united in an ideal ruler. If God does not rule justly, then Job's claim that God is all-powerful is invalid. Elihu would affirm that God is both righteous and mighty, so that Job's suffering is justly deserved because of his sin (G. Wilson, *Job*, 388).

a period. God's slowness to act does not deny His justice or sovereignty.[12]

A Call for Job to Make a Decision (Job 34:31-33)

Elihu calls on Job to respond to his argument concerning the just rule of God in the world. He begins with a series of general questions that are addressed to God ('has anyone said') and which focus on a person's iniquity (vv. 31-32). Both questions assume that the person has come to see his iniquity and will not do it anymore. These statements could be possible confessions that Job could offer to God.[13] In the first question the person will not offend anymore because 'I have borne punishment'. The person has learned his lesson through the consequences of sin and will not continue in it. In the second question the person will not do iniquity anymore because he has been shown his iniquity ('teach me what I do not see'). Such responses would be elements of true repentance.[14] And yet, it seems that Job has rejected both responses and that he is calling upon God to repay him for his trouble. In other words, Job has rejected both positions because he is not willing to recognize any sin he has committed (v. 33a). The reader knows that there is nothing for which Job needs to bear punishment and there is nothing for which he needs to be taught because he has not committed any sin to bring on his suffering. Elihu, however, states that Job must choose what stance he is going to take and he should declare what he knows.

The Judgment of the Wise Men (Job 34:34-37)

Elihu ends his second speech with a judgment that he thinks the wise men will render now that they have heard the evidence. Their basic verdict is that Job answers like a wicked man. His words are without insight. The reason for this verdict is that he adds rebellion to his sin. This is a key conclusion that has implications for how one evaluates

---

12. Hartley, *Job*, 459.

13. Hartley, *Job*, 460. G. Wilson (*Job*, 392) comments that Elihu is setting forth hypothetical situations where a guilty person could acknowledge his sin, return to God, and sin no more.

14. Hartley, *Job*, 460.

Elihu's argument. In addition, Job also clasps his hands among them[15] and multiplies his words against God (v. 37).

Evaluation of Elihu's Second Speech

Elihu establishes the justice of God by declaring that God repays a man according to his work (v. 11). God is the sovereign who does not show partiality to anyone. He omnisciently knows what people are doing so that He can shatter them without any investigation. He strikes people for their wickedness for all to see. These words are meant to apply to Job's situation. God has repaid Job for his sin and all people can see the results of God's action.[16] Some try to distinguish Elihu's position from the friends by limiting his words to Job's response to his suffering. In other words, Elihu is not speaking in this speech about a sin that brought on Job's suffering.[17] The problem with this approach is that Elihu condemns not just what Job has said, but he condemns what Job has done. He even offers Job a possible confession related to his deeds: 'if I have done iniquity, I will do it no more' (v. 32). The wicked are the cause of the cry of the poor (v. 28) because of how they treat the poor. Elihu also highlights that the words of Job are without insight, that he speaks without knowledge, and that he answers like a wicked man (v. 35). Both Job's deeds and his words come under condemnation.[18] Thus the statement that 'he adds rebellion to his sin' (v. 37) must include both Job's actions and his words.[19] The rebellion is specifically connected

---

15. There is a lot of ambiguity concerning what the phrase 'claps his hands among us' means. L. Wilson (*Job*, 169, n. 325) understands the clapping as a way to summon God. Others seek to emend or rearrange the consonantal text that would omit the gesture (see Hartley, *Job*, 461, n. 5 for different possibilities).

16. G. Wilson, *Job*, 391 and Habel, *Job*, 485.

17. Jones, *Job*, 244–245. Talbert comments that the friends argue that Job had become one of the wicked while Elihu argues that Job is becoming like the wicked by what he is implying about God (*Beyond Suffering*, 182).

18. L. Wilson (*Job*, 166) seeks to limit Elihu's condemnation of Job to his words in his suffering, but she must acknowledge that Elihu does focus here on Job's deeds.

19. Ash (*Job*, 352) tries to limit Elihu's condemnation of Job in v. 37 to his words by defining sin as what Job had said and by defining rebellion as undermining piety in others and thus encouraging them to rebel against God. The context, however, does not emphasize Job's influence on others and it has been shown that Job's deeds are in view in Elihu's condemnation.

to what Job has said in the statements of verse 35 and at the end of verse 37: he 'multiplies his words against God'. This leaves the sin to which Job adds his rebellion to be referring to the original act of wickedness that brought all this suffering upon Job. Thus Elihu's view of divine retribution is not any different from the view of the friends.

Seasoned by the Trials of Life

We are seventy-nine days into this journey. Some days go faster than others. Now that we've seemed to hit a plateau, most days only seem boring and uneventful. We like those kind of days.

Pierce is doing well and working on his bottle-feeding skills so that he can come home with us soon. He is now up to three bottles a day and he gets 40 mL at each feeding. Today he is thirty-five-weeks corrected age. That's right, just five weeks shy of the magical forty-week mark. It's hard to believe that had he not come early, I would have been waddling around anxiously awaiting his birth. Sometimes I find myself daydreaming about what that would have been like. What would it be like to have the nursery and our house prepared for him? To attend my baby shower and be uncomfortably large? And what about those late night cravings and Braxton-hicks contractions (periodic uterine contractions that start about six weeks into pregnancy)? Oh, the dreams. But then I snap out of it. I remember how blessed I am. Those meaningless little things I sometimes long for, they're worthless. If I had carried Pierce to full-term, we wouldn't be where we are at today. Quite frankly, we wouldn't be the people we now are. We wouldn't be as mature, or as grateful. We've been seasoned by the trials of this life, and have come out with a different outlook on things. I'm sure that if Pierce were to be a standard forty-weeker, I would have been complaining about stretch marks, breastfeeding and lack of sleep. But what an appreciation for life we have now!

Thank you all for your continued prayers and support. We continue to be blown away by everyone's generosity and love.   Lindsay Franks (7/1/11)

Study Questions

1) Who are the wise men that Elihu addresses and what is the role of wisdom?

2) What part of Job's argument does Elihu address in this speech? What is Elihu's view of Job?

3) How does Elihu answer Job's argument? What does he emphasize about God? What evidence does he present?

4) How does Elihu think Job should respond to his speech?

5) What is the relationship of Elihu's views to the view of the friends that Job is suffering because he committed sin? What is the reason for your answer?

27

The Third Speech of Elihu
(Job 35:1-16)

Job's Claim of being Right Questions God's Justice

In his third speech Elihu focuses on Job's claim that he is right before God and that God has mistreated him regardless of whether he has lived a life of sin or lived a righteous life. The implication is that God is unjust because He treats both the righteous and the sinner the same way. Elihu will quote the words of Job (35:1-3) and then he will answer Job in two ways (35:4-8 and 35:9-16).

Job's Claim: 'What Difference does it Make?' (Job 35:1-3)

Elihu follows his normal procedure of quoting the words or sentiments of Job so that he can respond to them. He begins by asking a question concerning justice: 'Do you think this to be just?' He then quotes Job as saying, 'It is my right before God.' Some translations translate this clause as 'My righteousness is more than God's' (KJV, NAS).[1] Although Job has not uttered those exact words,[2] Elihu believes that this is a natural conclusion based on Job's claims of innocence (9:15) and his claim that God is treating him unjustly (9:20). Job

---

1. The comparative sense is justified by the comparative use of the preposition *min* attached to the word 'God'.

2. Whether one accepts the comparative translation of the NAS or the non-comparative translation of the ESV, the point that Job makes is that he is right in his claim against God, and that God is therefore wrong in the way He is treating him.

257

does not believe that God is willing to listen to his concern that he is suffering unjustly. It is a matter of justice for Job that God would listen to his cries for help and respond by hearing his cause. The lack of a response from God explains the questions Job has raised about there being no advantage for the righteous and that it does not matter whether someone lives a righteous life or a life of sin. Job is not any better off for living a righteous life. He may as well have lived a life of sin considering the way he is being treated by God. Job has questioned the value of moral behavior (9:22), but he has also put those questions in the context of not being able to understand the wisdom and mystery of God's actions in the world (9:2-13). Elihu contends that Job has sought to assert his own righteousness, but in the process, he has called into question God's justice. He stacks the argument in his favor by asking the rhetorical question as to whether Job is more righteous than God. Of course, no human being is more righteous than God. Elihu also leaves out the part of Job's argument that explores the mystery of God's sovereignty.[3]

Elihu's Answer: God's Sovereign Justice (Job 34:4-16)

Human Actions have No Impact on God (Job 34:4-8)
Although Elihu primarily speaks to Job, he also speaks to the friends (v. 4).[4] He exhorts Job to look at the heavens and observe that the clouds are higher than him. This view sets the tone for what Elihu is going to say about God, who is so far above human beings that human actions do not benefit or take away anything from God. On the one hand, if Job has sinned, or even if he multiplies his transgressions, this does not negatively impact God (v. 6). On the other hand, if Job is righteous, this does not benefit God either (v. 7). Job's actions of wickedness or righteousness only impact himself or other humans. God is so great that humans, like Job, are of no concern to God and their actions make no difference

---

3. Hartley, *Job*, 463. He comments that Elihu formulates Job's complaint to make it sound as scandalous as possible so that his answer will sound more reasonable than Job's questioning.

4. The pronouns in this chapter are singular pronouns showing that Job is the one Elihu is primarily addressing.

to God. Therefore, Job's attempts at forcing God to descend in person and to vindicate his innocence are preposterous.[5]

God Does Not Respond to an Empty Cry (Job 34:9-16)
Elihu explains why God does not respond to people who cry to Him for help. He first deals with people in general (vv. 9-13) and then he applies what he has said to Job's situation (vv. 14-16). People call to God for help when they experience hardship and oppression because God has the power to deliver them. The problem is that people look to God only when they are in trouble. They do not have a relationship with God as a basis for their appeal for His help. They do not see God as their Maker and they do not look to God in worship[6] or for teaching on how to live (vv. 10–11). Their cry for help is seen by God to come from a heart of pride. It is an empty cry that God does not hear (vv. 12-13).

Elihu puts Job in the same category as one who cries out to God with an empty cry (vv. 14-16). In fact, Job has declared that although his case is before God, He has not responded to Job, even though Job has been eagerly waiting for Him. Job has drawn the conclusion from God's lack of response that He overlooks human transgression and does not punish evildoers. Elihu categorizes such assertions by Job as empty talk which multiplies words without knowledge. In other words, Job has no idea what he is talking about and has mischaracterized God's relationship to the world.

Evaluation of Elihu's Third Speech
Several issues are raised by Elihu's third speech. Some accuse him of presenting a God who is so transcendent that He is disinterested and has no concern for what human beings do (35:5-8).[7] The conclusion that justice means nothing to God is taking the words of Elihu too far.[8] His point seems to be that

---

5. Habel, *Job*, 491.

6. The phrase 'songs in the night' is a beautiful expression that emphasizes the praise of God even in the most difficult circumstances, represented by the night. These songs are given by God when least expected in the middle of the difficult circumstances a person is facing.

7. Longman, *Job*, 398.

8. Andersen, *Job*, 256.

human righteousness or wickedness does not benefit God or negatively impact Him so that Job is wrong in his statements that he is right before God and that it does not matter how he lives his life. Human behavior does matter because it impacts the one doing the behavior and it impacts others (v. 8). It also becomes clear that human behavior has some effect on God because He does not respond to the cry of one who only looks to Him when in trouble (vv. 10-12). The implication for Job is that Elihu has placed him in the category of persons who only cry out to God when in trouble. If God does not listen to an empty cry, and if God has not answered the cry of Job, then Job must be a person who offers an empty cry. Such a person does not have a relationship with God, does not worship God, and does not look to God for instruction (vv. 10-11). This description would place Job in the category of the wicked and does not fit the picture of him in Job 1–2 where he does have a relationship with God and does worship Him. Although it is possible in this speech to limit Elihu's concerns to how Job has responded verbally to his suffering, Elihu is not completely accurate in his view of God because he does eventually respond to Job. Therefore, Job's cries do not fit the definition of an empty cry. This also means the picture of the wicked in verses 10-12 does not accurately depict Job. Elihu gets some things right but he does not get everything right about Job and his relationship with God. Elihu anticipates some things that God will say to Job ('words without knowledge' in 35:16 and 38:2), but the very fact that God answers Job goes against Elihu's expectations. Elihu falls short of offering a true solution to Job.

God Needs No Defense

Pierce is doing better today and we are still praying that he can come home on or before his original due date of August 4th. Pierce is stable, but stable is a relative term. Just because Pierce is bigger does not mean he is on the same level vitality-wise as a baby his size that was born at full gestation. Even in the preemie world, those born at 23–25 weeks are in a whole different category from those that are born at 27–30 weeks and even further from those born at 31–40 weeks. The lungs aren't even fully developed at twenty-three weeks. That means that for the first 2–3 years of Pierce's life, RSV, which is a virus that causes the common cold in adults, can kill him. From October–April he will literally have to be quarantined. Just from the 'minor' set-backs of the past week, Pierce has had several spells where he turned blue and his heart rate dropped into the 30s.

So, the journey is long and is far from over. In addition to the above concerns, only time will tell if Pierce has incurred Cerebral Palsy. I say all this to put things into perspective. Nevertheless, we have great confidence in our God. Look at what He has done so far! Pierce isn't supposed to be here. Just this week, several medical professionals told us that they have never seen anyone survive who had a potassium level of 9 or higher; Pierce's was 10.3 for some time with no hope of reversing itself.

Let's keep moving forward and let's keep witnessing God display His glory. That is what He is doing. I recently heard the statement, 'Trying to prove God exists is like trying to defend a lion. It's unnecessary, just open up the cage.' We cut ourselves off from the very meaning of life when we say God doesn't exist or that He is impotent to save.

I ask you to continue to pray. Pray that Pierce would not need eye surgery and that his brain would fully heal, that he would not develop Cerebral Palsy, that his lungs will grow strong, and that he would not incur any infections. Due to Pierce's prognosis, Lindsay will not be working in order to stay home with him. I am looking for a stable job to provide for my family. We are praying that God would open up a ministry position that will have the most impact for His Kingdom.

With hands lifted and open,
Nik Franks (7/11/11)

Study Questions

1) What claim that Job makes does Elihu address in this speech? If the righteous suffer, what is the point of living a moral life?

2) How does Elihu answer Job's claim? What are the implications for Job (and other human beings) in Elihu's answer?

3) Does Elihu offer a true solution to Job?

28

The Fourth Speech of Elihu
(Job 36:1–37:24)

The Nature of God's Relationship to the World

The fourth and final speech of Elihu takes up two chapters. The typical introduction, 'And Elihu continued, and said,' begins chapter 36 and includes chapter 37. He returns to the theme of God's use of suffering to discipline people. He ends this speech with a focus on the glory and greatness of God as displayed in a thunderstorm. The goal of this speech is to remind Job of the wonders of God's ways in the world in order to persuade Job to seek God.[1]

Introduction to the Speech (Job 36:1-4)

Elihu begins his final speech with a request that Job would be patient with him and hear what he will say. He has something to say to Job on behalf of God. He speaks for God and in defense of God.[2] This means that his knowledge does not come from himself but from an outside source. The source of his knowledge is none other than the God who has created him and this God acts in righteous ways. If God is the source of Elihu's knowledge, then it is certain that the knowledge that Elihu is going to communicate to Job is not false. In fact, he even states, 'one who is perfect in knowledge is with

---

1. Hartley, *Job*, 467-68.
2. Hartley, *Job*, 468.

you.' The plural form of the word 'knowledge' means 'full knowledge' or knowledge that is complete and so beyond rebuttal.[3]

The meaning of 'one who is perfect in knowledge' is at the heart of how one views the character of Elihu. If one has a positive view of Elihu, then these words are not seen as a problem. Elihu is only claiming a fuller knowledge of God's ways than Job and his friends,[4] or he is claiming to be an accurate communicator of divine truth,[5] or he speaks as a prophet with the voice of one perfect in knowledge because he speaks God's words (33:23).[6] Those who take a negative view of Elihu argue that he is arrogant and condescending,[7] or that he is self-conceited, even blasphemous,[8] or that he is presumptuous,[9] or that he falls into the trap of playing God.[10] Even if one gives Elihu the benefit of the doubt, it seems strange that he would use terminology that he uses of God elsewhere to refer to himself. It certainly raises questions about Elihu and his role in the book (see the discussion at the end of this chapter).

God's Fair Treatment of the Wicked and the Righteous (Job 36:5-25)

The Basic Doctrine (Job 36:5-15)
Elihu does not quote Job in this speech but instead presents the core teaching about the subject of retribution. He sets forth the doctrine in verses 5-6, then elaborates on it in verses 7-15, before he makes application of the doctrine to Job in verses 16-21. Elihu focuses on God's actions in the world to show that His actions are just. The core of the doctrine is that although God is powerful He does not despise anyone. This

---

3. Ibid.

4. Jones, *Job*, 253.

5. Talbert, *Beyond Suffering*, 187. He specifically states that this is not a claim to omniscience.

6. Ash, *Job*, 361.

7. L. Wilson, *Job*, 173.

8. Whybray, *Job*, 151.

9. Andersen, *Job*, 284.

10. Habel, *Job*, 506.

means that God treats everyone fairly. This is strengthened by the statement that 'he is mighty in strength of understanding'. God knows the actions of people and how to respond appropriately to their actions. A summary of the doctrine is given in verse 6: 'He does not keep the wicked alive, but gives the afflicted their right.' God has the wisdom and the power to execute justice on the earth. He will give to the wicked and to the afflicted righteous[11] what they deserve.[12]

Elihu elaborates on the doctrine of divine retribution in verses 7-15. He first deals with God's treatment of the righteous (vv. 7-12) and then examines His treatment of the wicked (vv. 13-14), before ending this section with a concluding comment on the afflicted (v. 15). God keeps His eye on the righteous to protect them and bless them. He even exalts them by setting them with kings on a throne.[13] But the righteous do not only experience blessings from God because He also uses affliction to instruct them (vv. 7-8). He exposes their transgression and shows how they are acting arrogantly so that they can turn away from their iniquity (vv. 9-10). The righteous have a choice at this point (vv. 11-12): they can listen to God's discipline[14] and experience blessings from God or they can refuse to listen and perish in a violent manner ('by the sword') without learning the lessons God wants to teach them ('without knowledge').

Elihu briefly comments on the godless in verses 13-14. They are angry at God and so do not cry out to Him when He afflicts them. They die prematurely in their youth and their life ends in disgrace because they worship a false god when they go to temple prostitutes.[15] Thus adversity makes the situation much worse for the wicked. The afflicted

---

11. The afflicted are identified as the righteous in v. 7 and in the psalms (Pss. 10; 14:6) the wicked and the afflicted are often used as contrasting types (Newsom, 'Job', 4:585).

12. Although Elihu does not quote Job directly in this speech, he could be responding to Job's rhetorical question in 21:7, 'Why do the wicked live?' (Hartley, Job, 470).

13. Hartley, Job, 470.

14. The word for 'instruction' in v. 10 is $m\hat{u}s\bar{a}r$, a word that emphasizes instruction that shapes character and corrects moral faults.

15. Konkel ('Job', 6:212) takes the reference to prostitution to refer to 'immoral living'.

righteous, on the other hand, have a different relationship to God and to adversity. God uses hardship to teach them valuable lessons and He uses affliction as a means of deliverance for them.

A Warning to Job (Job 36:16-21)

Elihu addresses Job directly[16] and takes what he has said in the earlier part of the speech and applies it to Job. He begins by exhorting Job to choose how he is going to respond to his suffering. Just as God judges the wicked but delivers the afflicted by their affliction and opens their ear by adversity (v. 15), so God has also placed Job in a situation where it is important that he responds in the right way to his suffering. So verse 16 states: 'He also allured you out of distress into a broad place where there was no cramping, and what was set on your table was full of fatness.' It is not easy to pin down the part of Job's life to which this verse refers. The 'distress' highlights a difficult aspect of his life. The broad place without cramping[17] and the abundance of food is a picture of a life blessed overall. Is this a picture of the great blessings of Job's life before his current suffering overtook him (Job 1–2), or is the distress a reference to his current suffering with the hope that if he responds correctly to it he will experience freedom from the constraint of his suffering ('a broad place') and further blessings of abundance? Although the verbs would lead more to the idea that the distress is a past situation out of which God allured Job, many commentators understand the distress to be referring to what Job is currently experiencing,[18] with the hope of relief from his suffering if he responds in the right way. This focus certainly fits the context of Elihu's speech and his emphasis on how Job should respond to his suffering.

Job, says Elihu, has experienced the judgment that falls on the wicked. He has experienced God's justice (v. 17) and must be careful how he responds to his suffering (vv. 18-

---

16. In 36:16 Elihu moves from third person plural forms to second person singular forms.

17. Hartley (*Job*, 473) describes a broad place as an open space symbolizing deliverance whereas a cramped, narrow space connotes oppression.

18. See Hartley, Longman, and G. Wilson.

21). Elihu warns Job ('Beware') of several ways he could respond that would not be beneficial to him. He must not allow anger to entice him into scoffing. The word scoffing (*sepeq*) is understood by some to refer to riches, so that the warning is that Job should not be blinded by wealth.[19] The idea of wealth fits well with the next clause that Job must not allow the greatness of the ransom to turn him aside from responding with repentance to God's discipline (v. 18). It is hard to know exactly what Elihu has in mind.[20] Perhaps Elihu is urging Job to respond to the lure of God and not the lure of riches as a way to encourage him to seek God from pure motives.[21]

Elihu also raises the question whether Job's cry for help, no matter how strong it is, can keep him from distress (v. 19). The implied answer is no; a mere cry for help will not benefit Job without repentance. Job also should not long for the night when people vanish in their place. In other words, Job needs to move away from his response to suffering, as expressed in chapter 3, where he cursed the day of his birth and desired for darkness to overtake that day as a way of expressing his wish of never having being born. Job also ended several of his speeches by longing for darkness (7:21; 10:18-22; 17:13-16).[22] Instead of longing for death Job should seek to learn what God is trying to teach him in his suffering. Job should also be careful not to turn to iniquity because he has already chosen that path rather than the path of affliction. The idea is that Job has chosen iniquity over the disciplinary nature of affliction. Job charges God with wrongdoing rather than examining his life to recognize his sin and repent of it.[23] These warnings are meant to help Job respond in the right way to his suffering and to divert him from the rebellious response that Elihu has seen in Job.

---

19. Hartley, *Job*, 474.

20. Hartley (*Job*, 474) comments that the meaning of v. 18 is far from clear and that vv. 19–20 are so obscure that it is difficult to establish their meaning. Jones (*Job*, 257) sees the ransom as referring to the costliness of the repentance that is a prelude to restoration.

21. Hartley, *Job*, 474.

22. Hartley, *Job*, 474.

23. Longman, *Job*, 402.

Proper Response to God's Greatness (Job 36:22-25)

There is a difference of opinion whether the next part of Elihu's speech begins in verse 22 or in verse 26. Both verses begin with 'Behold' followed by a statement of God's greatness. Some begin the final part of Elihu's speech on God's greatness with 36:22. On the other hand, there is in verses 22-25 a call for Job to respond in the proper way to God's greatness. This call for response parallels a section in 37:14-24, so that each section of Elihu's final speech has a direct exhortation to Job on how to respond to God's greatness. So it is possible to understand these verses as concluding the first part of Elihu's speech.[24] The second part of Elihu's speech has the following outline: God's Greatness in the Storm (36:26–37:13) and The Proper Response to God's Greatness in the Storm (37:14-24).

This section begins with a statement of the greatness of God's power followed by three rhetorical questions. The first rhetorical question is, 'who is a teacher like him?' One wonders what the connection is between being exalted in power and being able to teach, but part of God's power includes His knowledge of the ways of the wicked and how the world works (see the next section on God's greatness in the storm). The implication for Job is that he has nothing to teach God and that he cannot change God's course of action by trying to take Him to court.[25] The second rhetorical question also touches this idea: 'Who has prescribed for him his way?' No human being can tell God what He should do or the path He should take. The third rhetorical question carries this idea further: 'who can say, "You have done wrong"?' No one can legitimately accuse God of doing wrong. This question is a direct response to some of the things that Job has said about God, specifically concerning how God has been treating him and that He allows the wicked to prosper. Rather than questioning God's justice and the exercise of His power, Job should join others and praise God for His great

24. It is also possible that 36:22–25 acts as a Janus that looks backward and forward to unite the units before and after (Bruce Waltke, *Old Testament Theology* [Grand Rapids: Zondervan, 2007], 121). Smick calls vv. 22–26 as both the climax of the preceding section and the first stanza of a hymn of praise ('Job,' 4:880).

25. Hartley, *Job*, 474.

work. Everyone has seen the work of God, even if from afar, so that praising God for His greatness is the right response.

God's Majesty in Creation (Job 36:26–37:24)

God's Greatness in the Storm (Job 36:26–37:13)
The final section of Elihu's speech focuses on the greatness of God in creation. This section also begins with the phrase 'Behold, God is great' followed by two implications for human beings. The first implication is that 'we know him not' (v. 26). God is so far above the world of human beings that it is difficult for humans to know God. The second implication is that 'the number of his years is unsearchable'. God is so exalted that He is not bound to time and the counting of years as human beings are. No one can search out the years of God because there is no end to His years. Of course, God is not subject to time and to years as human beings are subject to them, so this is a way of expressing the eternal nature of God.[26]

Elihu gives reasons for his statements in verse 26 (*kî*) by describing God's power in the weather. God is in control of the rain. He is in control of how the rain forms and where it falls (vv. 27-28). God is in control of the clouds and the thunder (v. 29). There is mystery and a lack of human understanding of how the clouds spread across the sky and of how the thunder makes its noise.[27] God is also in charge of the lightning and where it makes its marvelous display of power (vv. 30-33).[28] The lightning manifests His majestic presence. The power of God in a storm is a part of His work in the world to judge people and to provide food for people in abundance (v. 31).

---

26. Hartley, *Job*, 479.

27. The pavilion (*sukkāh*) in the phrase 'thunderings of his pavilion' probably refers to the surrounding dark rain clouds overarching the presence of God like a tent or temporary dwelling (G. Wilson, *Job*, 410; Smick, 'Job', 4:881).

28. The phrase 'covers the roots of the sea' (v. 30) is difficult if the roots of the sea refer to the depths of the sea (Hartley, *Job*, 479) or the base of the suboceanic mountains under the sea (G. Wilson, *Job*, 410), because it is not clear how lightning uncovers that part of the sea. One option is to understand this as referring to the lightning illuminating the surface of the sea (Hartley) or to render the verb 'uncover' (*kāssāh*) as 'his throne' (*kissô*): the roots of the sea are his throne (see G. Wilson). Alden (*Job*, 358) suggests a merism with the opposites of the sea and sky juxtaposed so that the verse refers to the all-encompassing effect of the storm.

While a storm can be very beneficial to human beings, it also can be very harmful. A storm can manifest the goodness of God but it can also manifest His judgment.

In 37:1-13 Elihu continues to reflect on God's work in a storm. He begins with the impact on his own life. It causes his heart to tremble and leap out of its place. Perhaps he has experienced what many people have experienced when the lightning flashes and the thunder roars. Their hearts seem to jump out of their chests. He exhorts people to keep listening to the thunder of God's voice in the storm (v. 2) because it will be beneficial to be reminded of God and His power. There is an emphasis in verses 2-5 on God's voice as a manifestation of His majestic power unleashed in the lightning and thunder (see Ps. 29:3-9). It is magnificent and reminds the earth of His majesty. It is also an indication of the great things God accomplishes that are beyond our comprehension.

Some of those great things are laid out in verses 6-13. The way God sends snow and the mighty downpours of rain are marvelous. His magnificent work in the storm also has an impact on human beings who are stopped in their tracks by the demonstration of His power in the storm (v. 7). The same thing happens among the beasts which remain in their dens (v. 8). Such restrictions of human activity keep humans from doing what they would like to do and remind them of a higher ruler who governs their destiny.[29] God commands the wind, the ice, and the storm to accomplish His purposes in the world (vv. 9-12). The various purposes that God can accomplish with the storm include correction,[30] benefit to the land, or a demonstration of His love (v. 13).[31] In other words, God causes

---

29. Hartley, *Job*, 481. This view understands the phrase 'He seals up the hand of every man' in v. 7 as describing the restriction of human activity. A seal can prevent action (by preventing unauthorized access) and it may also act as a reminder of God's great power displayed in nature (G. Wilson, *Job*, 413).

30. See 1 Sam. 12:18–19 for an example of the storm as judgment in response to the people's sinful request for a king (Longman, *Job*, 406). God also used destructive storms to give His people victory (Joshua 10; Judges 5; 1 Sam 7:10) promised in the covenant (Andersen, *Job*, 266).

31. It seems a bit strange that 'for his land' is mentioned between 'for correction' and 'for love' because the first and last items cover the blessing and judgment aspects of God's activity in the world. Some try to explain the middle phrase as God acts for His own divine program exclusive of human considerations (Estes, *Handbook*, 112). Others suggest a variety of emendations (see Hartley, *Job*, 479,

things to happen on this earth that benefits His creation, that corrects those who need correcting, and that demonstrates His love for people. God's wonders in creation are not purposeless but are sent to accomplish what He has ordained.

Proper response to God's Greatness in the Storm
(Job 37:14-24)

Elihu now addresses Job directly to drive home the point he is making about the greatness of God seen in the storm. He exhorts Job to hear what he is saying ('Hear this, O Job') and to contemplate the wondrous works of God (v. 14). He wants Job to pay close attention to his words so that he will come to understand God's superior wisdom and the limited knowledge of human beings, including lack of understanding.[32] Elihu asks Job a series of rhetorical questions to drive the point home (vv. 15-20). These questions expect a 'no' answer and show Job how little he knows about the way God works in the world. The following is a summary of the questions that Elihu asks Job. Do you know how God commands His wondrous works, the elements of the storm, so that they do what He desires? Do you know how God causes the lightning to strike (v. 15)? Do you know how clouds stay in the sky (v. 16)? Elihu also refers in this verse to God as the one who is perfect in knowledge. The point of verse 17 is to put Job in his place in light of the wondrous works of God in the world. Job is negatively impacted by the south wind that blows hot air and makes people feel like they are suffocating. Garments become unbearably hot and people are inactive due to the heat. In the next verse the question shifts from what Job knows to what he can do. Can you spread out the skies, 'hard as a cast metal mirror' (v. 18)?[33] Elihu exhorts

---

n. 38), but the best suggestion for emendation does not require changing the text but requires a different division of the consonants of the text (from *lĕʾarṣô* to *lōʾ rāṣû*), leading to the meaning 'they are unwilling'. Hartley translates the phrase 'Whether for discipline–if they are not obedient–or for mercy'.

32. Hartley, *Job*, 482 and G. Wilson, *Job*, 416.

33. Hartley (*Job*, 482, n. 8) notes that ancient mirrors were made of bronze and so were hard and unbreakable. In Deuteronomy 28:23 the sky is said to be bronze when it gives no rain. There is no need to argue that Scripture presents the sky as a hard, metal dome (see Paul H. Seely, 'The Firmament and the Water Above, Part 1: the Meaning of *rāqîaʿ* in Gen 1:6-8,' *WTJ* 53 [1991]: 228-41). The Bible uses

Job to teach them by answering these questions so that they can present a case before God; otherwise, they will remain in darkness (v. 19). Finally, Elihu raises the question of the appropriateness of a human being addressing God in the way Job has done. Human beings do not tell God when they want to speak. This approach to God only leads to a death wish of being swallowed up (v. 20).

Elihu brings his speech to a close by emphasizing the divine splendor and the way human beings should respond to God (vv. 21-24). He compares God's splendor to the light of the sun after the clouds have cleared and it shines with full brightness (v. 21). It is impossible to look at the sun without shading the eyes or squinting. If that is true of the sun, it is more true of the God who is clothed with awesome majesty. He is the Almighty God, who cannot be found by human beings because He is far beyond human reach.[34] He is great in power and operates in the world with justice and abundant righteousness that He will not violate. Everything that God does is right (v. 23). Therefore, the proper response is to fear Him because He will not regard any who are wise in their own conceit (v. 24).[35]

Evaluation of Elihu's Fourth Speech

Elihu offers a defense of divine retribution by analyzing the way God treats the wicked and the righteous. God gives

---

phenomenological language and this is a poetic description. Plus, there are negative implications for arguing that the Scriptural writers present a mistaken cosmology (see James W. Scott, 'The Inspiration and Interpretation of God's Word, with Special Reference to Peter Enns; Part I: Inspiration and its Implications,' *WTJ* 71 [2009]: 129–83, and 'The Inspiration and Interpretation of God's Word, with Special Reference to Peter Enns; Part II: The Interpretation of Representative Passages,' *WTJ* 71 [2009]: 247-79; Noel K. Weeks, 'Cosmology in Historical Context,' *WTJ* 68 [2006]: 283-93; and Vern S. Poythress, 'A Misunderstanding of Calvin's Interpretation of Genesis 1:6-8 and 1:5 and its Implications for Ideas of Accommodation,' *WTJ* 76 [2014]: 157-66 and 'Three Modern Myths in Interpreting Genesis 1,' *WTJ* 76 [2014]: 321-50).

34. Hartley, *Job*, 484.

35. The meaning of the phrase 'wise in heart' is debated. Hartley (*Job*, 483) argues that this phrase is never used in a negative way in Scripture and so he takes its meaning to be positive in parallel with the previous clause ('the wise of heart will see him'). This view requires taking the negative 'no' (*lō*') as the asseverative 'surely' (*lû*'). Others take it as a negative phrase, 'wise in their own conceit' (as in the ESV), or as referring to the wisdom of the truly wise which is not regarded by God who alone is wise (Whybray, *Job*, 156).

everyone what they deserve because He has the wisdom and power to execute justice on the earth. He does not keep the wicked alive, but He does act on behalf of the righteous. God can use suffering in the life of the righteous to instruct them, to expose their arrogance, and to show them their transgressions so that they turn away from iniquity. If the righteous will listen to God's discipline, they will experience blessings from God; but if they refuse to listen, they will perish in a violent manner (36:7-15). The disciplinary nature of suffering is the feature of Elihu's teaching that many see as his distinctive contribution.

Elihu then applies this teaching to Job (36:16-21). God has placed Job in a situation where it is important that he respond in the right way to his suffering (vv. 18-21). It is unclear whether the 'distress' in verse 16 from which God has allured Job is a past distress or a current distress. The Hebrew uses the perfect aspect which generally refers to what has taken place in the past, but it can also stress implications for the present and the future. This makes the description in verse 16 ambiguous. What is not ambiguous is Elihu's analysis of the reason for Job's suffering. He clearly states that Job is experiencing the judgment that falls on the wicked (v. 17). Part of Elihu's concern is that Job would respond in the right way so that he could be restored through repentance.

Elihu has already set forth the two sides of divine retribution concerning the wicked and the afflicted righteous (vv. 5-15). If Job's suffering is viewed as judgement on the wicked, instead of the experience of the afflicted righteous, then it is difficult to restrict Elihu's words to Job's response to his suffering. Job must be suffering because of his wickedness, a view that contradicts God's verdict concerning Job's righteous character in chapters 1–2. It is possible to conclude from 36:5-21 that Elihu is focusing on how Job should respond to his suffering. But it is not possible to restrict what Elihu says to Job's response to his suffering.[36] Elihu is at best ambiguous whether Job's situation before his suffering is in view, but

---

36. Several commentators argue that Elihu only focuses on Job's response to suffering. Talbert (*Beyond Suffering*, 188) states that Elihu refuses to focus on Job's supposed past wickedness and zeroes in on his present iniquity (see also Jones, *Job*, 255 and Ash, *Job*, 362).

more likely he agrees with the friends that Job is suffering because of some wickedness he has committed.[37]

Both Elihu and the friends also agree that Job must repent. Elihu's difference with the friends is that he does not try to manufacture a list of sins of which Job must repent. He also highlights that God uses suffering to discipline people and to instruct them how they should respond to God's chastening hand. Times of affliction are an occasion for God to disclose to people their sins and to provide them with an opportunity for repentance.[38]

The Function of the Elihu Speeches in the Book of Job
There are various views concerning the character of Elihu and his function in the book of Job. At the beginning of our discussion of the speeches of Elihu, the main views concerning Elihu were examined (see chapter 24). The positive view of Elihu understands him as arguing differently from the friends' narrow view of retribution by emphasizing the disciplinary nature of suffering. What he says to Job is right and he anticipates the divine speeches in his fourth speech which exalts the glory of God in creation. The negative view of Elihu understands him to be brash, opinionated, and full of himself. He adds very little to the debate and has the same view as the friends concerning divine retribution. The mixed view of Elihu understands him to add to the debate by emphasizing the disciplinary nature of suffering, but also sees evidence that Elihu has the same view of divine retribution as the friends. Elihu anticipates the speeches of God, but he is also wrong in some of his assessments of Job and what Job should expect from God.

One of the main issues to help answer this question is whether he holds to the same view of divine retribution as the friends (that Job is suffering because of sin he has committed), or whether he only focuses on what Job says in response to his suffering. If one can clearly argue that Elihu only deals

---

37. Other commentators do not restrict what Elihu says to Job's response to his suffering. Hartley (*Job*, 474) comments that Elihu believes that God has devastated Job's former tranquil life for his own good. Rowley (*Job*, 229, 232) argues that the afflictions of Job can be traced back to his own iniquity.

38. Newsom, 'Job,' 4:586.

with Job's response to his suffering, then a more positive view
of Elihu is warranted. It is not clear, however, that Elihu limits
his remarks to Job's response to his suffering. At best, his
argument is ambiguous even when he does have in view Job's
response (36:16-21). In 33:9-11 Elihu's argument reflects the
same argument of Zophar in 11:4 which makes it difficult
to avoid the conclusion that the starting point for Elihu is
the same as the friends' starting point (see the evaluation
of Elihu's speech in chapter 25). In Elihu's second speech
he condemns Job not just for what he has said but also for
what he has done (34:11). He offers him a possible confession
based on his deeds (34:32). Thus when Elihu states that Job
adds rebellion to his sin (34:37), it is difficult to limit this to
his response to suffering. In the third and fourth speeches of
Elihu there is an emphasis on how Job should respond to his
suffering, but it is unclear if his words should be limited to his
response. In the third speech Elihu places Job in the category
of the wicked person who cries out to God only when he is in
trouble (35:10-12), but this is not an accurate picture according
to chapters 1–2. In the fourth speech it is also unclear whether
Elihu restricts his words to Job's response to suffering (36:18-
21). He places Job in the category of the wicked rather than
of the afflicted righteous, which makes it difficult to limit
his suffering to what he has said. The ambiguity in Elihu's
speeches concerning what he says about Job's situation and
how he describes him makes it impossible to argue that he
limits his remarks to how Job has responded to his suffering.

The best view of Elihu is the mixed view. He says some
positive things concerning the nature of suffering and he seeks
to uphold God's honor in response to some of the assertions
of Job that have questioned God's justice.[39] In several ways
Elihu anticipates what God is going to say, but in other ways
he falls short of accurately describing Job's situation.

There are positive ways that the Elihu speeches function in
the book of Job. Job ends his speeches with a strong assertion of
his innocence that calls his accuser to present his case against
him (Job 29–31). If God would have responded right away to

---

39. Hartley (*Job*, 485) argues that Elihu does not completely agree with the
friends' view of divine retribution because he affirms that the righteous may indeed
suffer.

Job, it would have appeared that God was at his beck-and-call.[40] Elihu provides space between Job's summons and God's appearance. Elihu also reminds the readers of Job's arguments by summarizing what Job has said in the debate with the friends that keeps before the reader the main issue of the book: Job's innocence versus God's justice.[41] In the fourth speech Elihu shifts from a defense of God's justice to a description of God's power and wisdom in controlling the elements of nature (36:26–37:24). This shift anticipates the speeches of God who will also assert His control over His creation. The rhetorical questions that Elihu uses to stress Job's limited knowledge (37:15-20) anticipate God's speeches which will also use rhetorical questions to expose Job's limited knowledge.[42]

Some argue that Elihu must be understood in a positive way as providing a partial answer to Job's dilemma because so much space is given to his speeches.[43] But this argument is weak in light of the amount of space given to the friends of Job whose views are wrong. The friends take up nine chapters in the book versus Elihu who has six chapters. Wisdom literature is concerned about the right answer, but it is also concerned about how one gets to the right answer. The application of wisdom to life's situations is not always easy and there are difficulties as people try to comprehend them. The process of how one responds to life is also important. Wisdom is not always able to give a quick answer because life can be complex. So the amount of space given to Elihu in the book of Job is irrelevant to whether his teaching should be understood as offering wisdom to Job.

There are also negative ways that the Elihu speeches function in the book of Job. Elihu's views do not always match up with the presentation of Job in chapters 1–2 and with the

---

40. Robert V. McCabe, 'Elihu's Contribution to the Thought of the Book of Job,' *DBSJ* 2 (Fall 1997): 77–78.

41. McCabe, 'Elihu's Contribution,' 73-75.

42. McCabe, 'Elihu's Contribution,' 79.

43. Green, *Conflict and Triumph*, 124 and Talbert, *Beyond Suffering*, 191. Whybray (*Job*, 23) argues that the fact that Elihu is the only human speaker who speaks at great length with no interruptions suggests that he makes a substantial contribution to the debate. A more important question is how Elihu lines up with God's evaluation when God finally speaks (a point discussed in that section).

evaluation by God in 42:7. Job is presented at the beginning of
the book as a blameless man who fears God and turns away
from evil. Elihu places Job in the category of the wicked in
his discussion of divine retribution (36:17).[44] The fact that it
is impossible to restrict Elihu's arguments to Job's response
to suffering means that Elihu does not completely agree with
God's later verdict of Job in 42:7. When Elihu emphasizes the
words of Job he does agree with God's later assessment that
Job speaks in ignorance with words without knowledge (34:35;
35:16; 38:1). When Job repents, he repents of the words he
has spoken (42:3). But God is also able to declare that Job has
spoken of Him what is right in contrast to the arguments of the
friends (42:7). Thus God distinguishes between Job's situation
before his suffering (blameless and righteous) and his situation
after his suffering (where his response is characterized as
words without knowledge). This key distinction is not clear
in Elihu, which makes some of his statements about Job wrong
and leads to an evaluation of Elihu as a rival explanation to the
explanation of Yahweh. Elihu, the last representative of human
wisdom, gives a final demonstration of the failure of human
wisdom in dealing with Job's suffering.[45] This evaluation leads
to a mixed view of Elihu's role.[46]

Elihu also anticipates God's response in a negative way.
Job has pushed for a divine response (31:35) but Elihu clearly
affirms that God has no need to answer Job. First, Elihu wants
to show that God speaks to people in a variety of ways even
if they do not perceive it (33:14-18). He speaks to people in
dreams or visions of the night while they are sleeping; He
also may speak to a person through the pain of illness to
rebuke a person (33:19-22).

Second, Elihu argues that God has no compelling need
to enter litigation with human beings (34:23). God does not

44. McCabe, 'Elihu's Contribution', 65-66.

45. Some call Elihu a 'theological foil' for God (McCabe, 'Elihu's Contribution,' 71).

46. McCabe ('Elihu's Contribution,', 67-71) contends that Elihu's arguments
should not be seen as normative, including his statements on the disciplinary nature
of suffering because God does not give this as a reason why Job is suffering and it
does not fit the picture of Job in chapters 1–2. The reason for Job's suffering remains
a mystery. McCabe also does not make a clear distinction between the situations
before Job's suffering and after his suffering.

need to convene a court to find out the evidence in a case because He already knows all about it. Thus, God can shatter the mighty without an investigation. He can put people in their place, crush them in the night by overturning them, and strike them for their wickedness because they turned aside from following Him (34:24-27).

Third, Elihu argues that God does not respond to an empty cry (35:9-13). People call to God for help when they experience hardship because He has the power to deliver them. The problem is that people look to God only when they are in trouble. Elihu sees Job's cry to God as an empty cry (35:14-16). Job has drawn the conclusion from God's lack of response that He overlooks human transgression and does not punish evil doers. Elihu categorizes such assertions by Job as empty talk which multiplies words without knowledge. The implication one can draw from these words of Elihu is that God will not answer Job. In fact, he ends his speeches with the words, 'he does not regard any who are wise in their own conceit' (37:24). But Elihu is mistaken because God does answer Job (38:1).

Another important issue is what conclusion should be drawn from the fact that neither God nor Job responds to Elihu's speeches. Those who have a positive view of Elihu offer positive reasons for the lack of response. Job does not respond to Elihu because he has nothing to say in opposition to what he has heard. Job has been convicted by the truth of what Elihu has said and he has come to understand God's inexplicable providence.[47] God does not respond to Elihu because Elihu was not one of the original parties to the debate but acts as an arbiter whose decision the Lord assumes as preliminary to His own.[48]

Those who have a negative view of Elihu offer negative reasons for the lack of response. Job does not respond to Elihu because his views are the same as the friends which Job has already rejected.[49] The very fact that God responds to Job when Elihu has told him that God would not respond,

---

47. Green, *Conflict and Triumph*, 125, 133–34.

48. Green, *Conflict and Triumph*, 125. Smick ('Job,' 4:851) argues that there is no response to Elihu by God because Elihu is not guilty of false accusations against Job.

49. Longman, *Job*, 409.

marginalizes the role of Elihu in the book.[50] God ignores Elihu and the very silence of God pronounces a negative verdict on Elihu's position.[51]

The fact that God answers Job even though Elihu argues that God would not answer him, puts Elihu in a negative light. But not everything about Elihu's speeches are negative. He plays both a positive and a negative function in the book of Job. On the positive side Elihu delays God's response so it does not seem like God is forced to respond to Job. He also summarizes the view of Job to remind the reader of the main issues from Job's perspective. He highlights the disciplinary nature of suffering and how God can use suffering to instruct people. He prepares the reader for God's response by ending his last speech with the greatness of God displayed in His works of creation. On the negative side, he misunderstands Job's character by placing him in the category of the wicked. He basically operates with the view of divine retribution argued by the friends, even if at times he emphasizes Job's response to his suffering. Thus he does not provide clarity concerning Job's situation and so falls short of speaking wisdom to Job. Elihu is another example of the failure of human wisdom to provide an answer. Wisdom only resides with God (Job 28) and the reader longs to hear from Him. The fact that God speaks is a welcome surprise giving hope that this issue can be resolved.

Home at Last

After 118 LONG days in the NICU at Levine Children's Hospital, Pierce came home!!! In fact, he's sleeping right beside me as I type. It happened exactly like they said it would. One moment we were thinking we'd never leave that place, the next moment we were walking out, baby in tow. Literally, here's what happened: we roomed in on Friday night (8/5) but things did not go well. Pierce did not eat very well and our confidence was shattered. We felt for sure he wouldn't be going home anytime soon. Then, on Sunday night (8/7), we

---

50. Fyall, *How Does God Treat His Friends?*, 100–01.
51. G. Wilson, *Job*, 368 and Habel, *Job*, 516.

gave rooming in a second go. This time, they put us in a different room (we had suspicions that something was wrong with the oxygen meter in the first room). Things went SO much better. Pierce took his bottles like a champ, and Nik and I began to regain the level of confidence that we had developed throughout our four-month NICU stay. So, on Monday morning the doctor came in and asked us if we wanted to take him home with us! We were thrilled. Then we immediately realized that NOTHING was ready for him at home. (Over the past four months, our time has been consumed with the back and forth trips to the hospital). SO, being the good parents we are, we took advantage of the free babysitting and asked if we could leave P with the nurses while we ran to the store to get a few things. The staff laughingly agreed.

And oh what a funny sight we were at the store, bassinet-check, stroller-check, sheets-check. When I said we had nothing ready, I really meant it! My baby shower was on Sunday and everything was (and is) still sitting in the garage. BUT nothing was going to stop us from bringing P home yesterday.

And so, we returned to the hospital to pick up our boy. We had lots of tearful goodbyes. I underestimated how close I've become to the staff and fellow parents at Levine Children's Hospital. They've been our life for four months. We are forever grateful for all they've done to help our son (many stepped in and literally saved his life) throughout these past few months.

As we stepped out of the hospital with our almost four-month-old baby, I don't think I've ever been more scared in my life: walking out the door, knowing that P was now our responsibility. Of course, it probably doesn't help that he comes with a load of gear – oxygen tank, apnea monitor, pulse ox monitor, car seat, diaper bag.... But nonetheless, God granted us peace. And once again, I was reminded that He is the one who is in control. He is the one who graciously allowed us this opportunity. And we are so grateful. We know all too well how quickly we could've lost this experience.

Last night and today was a lot calmer than I expected. Pierce has done remarkable. One benefit of having a chronic NICU baby is that they are used to a routine and they're used to waiting their turn. How does this play out at home? It means that P sleeps peacefully and entertains himself until we step in to feed him. It's marvelous! And even though he comes with an assortment of medical gear, I can honestly say I've never met a more low-maintenance newborn. It's nice!

How you can pray? First, please join us in rejoicing that God has brought us to this point. It still seems surreal to have our little boy at home with us! Secondly, remember to pray for Pierce's ventricles. We will go to P's neurosurgeon next week for an outpatient ultrasound and to discuss what our course of action will be. Please pray that the next ultrasound will be stable or smaller and continue praying with us that P can avoid a permanent shunt. Before P left the NICU, he had a hearing screen. Unfortunately, he did not pass. While it's a little too early to tell (many preemies fail the first test and go on to have perfect hearing), it's something we're definitely praying about. Please pray that when we go for our follow-up appointment next month, that P will pass this test. Finally, pray for wisdom and guidance as Nik and I begin caring round-the-clock for P. His medical needs are far from over. We have seven different doctor's appointments in the next two weeks – and we still have a LONG road as we deal with the effects of his extreme prematurity. Pray for continued endurance as walk this journey.

Thanks for sharing in our journey.

Christ is All,
Lindsay Franks (8/10/11)

Study Questions

1) What are the various ways that the phrase 'one who is perfect in knowledge is with you' is understood?

2) Why does God send suffering to the righteous?

3) How should Job respond to his suffering? How would that be different from how he has responded in the speeches?

4) How does the storm demonstrate God's greatness? How should Job respond to God's greatness?

5) How does both Elihu and the friends agree that Job should respond a certain way? What is distinctive about Elihu's teaching?

6) What is the final verdict on whether Elihu agrees with the friends' view of retribution or not?

7) How do the speeches of Elihu function in positive ways in the book of Job? How would you explain the amount of space given to the Elihu speeches? What do we learn about life from this?

8) How do the speeches of Elihu function in negative ways in the book of Job? How do his speeches anticipate God's response in a negative way?

9) How do people explain the significance that God does not respond to Elihu? What does Elihu teach about human wisdom?

29

God's First Speech and Job's Response
(Job 38:1–40:5)

Introduction to God's Speeches

In light of Elihu's assertions that it is impossible to find God (37:23), it is rather shocking to the reader that Yahweh suddenly appears to address Job.[1] The surprise is not just that God addresses Job, but also how He addresses Job. He does not directly answer Job's complaint, He does not respond to his avowal of innocence in chapter 31, and He does not reprove Job for wrongdoing. He does confront Job on what he has said about God's justice and His governing of the world.[2]

The way God addresses Job is also important. He bombards Job with a list of rhetorical questions that show his ignorance and powerlessness in the face of the vastness of God's creation. This form of address allows Job to accept what God says of his own accord without it being imposed on him from the outside.[3] The dramatic way in which God approaches Job[4] and the undeniable recognition of Job's inability and ignorance in response to the rhetorical questions

---

1. Whybray, *Job*, 156.

2. Hartley, *Job*, 487. Longman (*Job*, 425) notes that instead of Job confronting God on the unjust way he has been treated, God confronts Job.

3. Hartley, *Job*, 489. He calls this a disputation speech that challenges Job without filing a formal complaint against him.

4. Hartley (*Job*, 487) lists the following as dramatic actions: Yahweh Himself speaks, a tempest attends His appearing, and the special name Yahweh is used.

will cause Job to acknowledge the futility of much of what he has said about God in his previous speeches.[5] Part of the purpose of this approach is to persuade Job to surrender his complaint against God so that Job can trust his own destiny to the sovereign rule of Yahweh.[6]

The first speech focuses on the world of God's creation and how little Job understands concerning the way the world works (38:1–40:2). This includes an exhortation for Job to answer God (40:1-2), which he does by acknowledging that he cannot answer God's questions because he is insignificant in the vastness of God's work in creation (40:3-5). The second speech raises the question of God's justice (40:6–41:34), followed by Job's response of contrition (42:1-6).

What Do You Know about God's Design of the World? (Job 38:1–40:2)

The Opening Challenge to Job (Job 38:1-3)
The LORD answers Job in a dramatic way out of a whirlwind. Elements associated with a storm are used to describe theophanies of God in the Old Testament (Exod. 19:16-20; Ezek. 1:2-4; Isa. 29:5-6).[7] The storm enhances the majesty and grandeur of God as He addresses Job concerning His power in the works of creation. Such a display of power would strike awe in the one who beholds it. The storm also represents God's personal presence demonstrating His control in the midst of chaos.[8]

God begins by asking Job a question: 'Who is this that darkens counsel by words without knowledge' (v. 2)? The

---

5. It is important that a distinction is made between the original point of debate that Job is suffering because of his sin and the response of Job to his suffering. The speeches of God focus on the inappropriate things that Job has said about God's justice, and Job will repent concerning what he has said. God will declare Job to be right over against the friends concerning whether Job is suffering because of sin (42:7). Mistakes can be made in understanding the divine speeches and Job's responses if the two situations are not differentiated (see G. Wilson, *Job*, 421 who does not operate with this distinction).

6. Hartley, *Job*, 489.

7. Hartley, *Job*, 490, n. 3. He summarizes the texts that use the storm for a theophany. The name 'Yahweh' is normally used in theophanies and this name of God reappears here for the first time since the prologue (p. 491). Job has also mentioned the possibility of God appearing in a storm to crush him (9:17). God does not crush him but puts him in his place (Longman, *Job*, 427).

8. Talbert, *Beyond Suffering*, 198.

word 'counsel' ('$\bar{e}\bar{s}\bar{a}h$) refers to the plan or design of Yahweh by which He governs the world.[9] This question highlights a problem concerning the words of Job in his debate with the friends. Job has spoken about matters of which he has no knowledge, with the result that his words have not always brought clarity to the debate. God has a design for the world, but Job's anxious fears about his suffering have clouded his thinking about the plan of Yahweh. He does not have the insight to understand the way God governs the universe.[10] Thus God tells Job to get ready for His questions to see if he can answer them. Job is told to 'Dress for action' (from a Hebrew phrase that means 'to gird up the loins'), an action that symbolizes using one's strength to meet a difficult task.[11]

Divine Interrogation about the Created Order (Job 38:4–39:30)
God peppers Job with an overwhelming series of questions concerning the way the world operates. He aims to show Job that he has spoken 'words without knowledge' concerning the plan of God. The questions that God asks Job are meant to show his ignorance of the way the world works. The purposes of God in His universe are so vast that a human being is not able to comprehend the wonder and complexity of God's design. These questions are meant to get Job to see beyond the narrow view of his own suffering to the vast panorama of creation.[12] These questions also serve to rebuke Job concerning his lack of understanding of God's governing the world. God's rebuke, however, is not meant to destroy Job but to teach him a valuable lesson concerning the relationship of his own life to God's government of the world.[13] Although Job's suffering is important to God, evidenced in the fact that

---

9. Habel, *Job*, 536.

10. Hartley, *Job*, 491.

11. Hartley, *Job*, 492. The action of girding up the loins refers to drawing up the flowing robes into a belt to free the legs for action (G. Wilson, *Job*, 424).

12. Brown, *Wisdom's Wonder*, 110. He notes that the questions are meant to challenge Job in his creaturely status as well as broaden the perceptual horizons of his worldview.

13. There is more going on in the questions God asks Job than a father inviting a son to see the wonders of creation to teach him valuable lessons (Estes, *Handbook*, 114). There is also an element of rebuke as God confronts Job with his view of the world expressed in his speeches that is contrary to God's ways in the world.

God answers Job, there is mystery concerning the way God governs the world, which means there is mystery from a human standpoint concerning Job's suffering.

Questions concerning the Structure of the World (Job 38:4-21)
The questions in this section deal with God's creation of the world and how He structured it. God's initial creation of the world is in view in verses 4-7. Poetic language is used to describe the creation of the world under the image of constructing a building.[14] God asks Job where he was when God laid the foundation of the earth like a master builder. Of course, the obvious answer is that Job was not present when God created the world and so Job is not able to answer the questions that God asks him. Job cannot answer who determined its measurements or who laid its cornerstone or how God firmly established the earth on its base. Job was not present at this glorious event when the angels (the morning stars and the sons of God) sang and shouted for joy at the magnificent act of creation. Job must admit both his lack of knowledge and that God is the one with the power to create the universe.[15]

The next several sections continue the theme of Job's ignorance of the way the creation operates. The creation of the sea is described in verses 8-11, 'when it burst out from the womb' and God set limits to the waves.[16] The function of the morning light of dawn is described in verses 12-15. God specifically asks Job whether he has ever commanded the morning to shine or caused the dawn to know its place. The significant aspect of the dawn is its relationship to the wicked. The light of the morning exposes their deeds (v. 13). The dawn light etches multiple designs on the horizon in an array of colors under the beauty of the sun's first rays. The beauty of the morning light on the earth is like a lump of clay that is turned into a beautiful design beneath a seal or like a beautiful garment covering the earth (v. 14). The light of the sun deprives the wicked of the protection of the

---

14. Hartley, *Job*, 494.

15. G. Wilson, *Job*, 429.

16. The origin of the sea is described as a birth. There is no hint of conflict between Yahweh and the sea, as is common in ancient Near Eastern texts (Longman, *Job*, 429).

night and prevents them from carrying out their evil designs, represented in the statement that their uplifted arm is broken (v. 15).[17] The light confines the work of the wicked to certain limits. So the wicked are under the control of God.[18]

God asks Job in verses 16-18 whether he has seen the gates of death. Of course, the answer is again 'no' because Job would have had to have walked in the recesses of the sea. The gates of death are hidden in an inaccessible place and there is no way Job would have had access to them, just as he is not able to traverse the outer limits of the earth. The origins of light and darkness are mentioned in verses 19-21. God asks Job if he knows the way to where light dwells or to the place of darkness. With some sarcasm, God tells Job that he must know the answer to these questions because he was born then and so the number of his days must be great. It is impossible for Job to answer any of those questions. He does not have the knowledge or the experience to answer them because he was not present when God created the world.

Questions concerning the Maintenance of the World
(Job 38:22–39:30)
Hartley begins this section at verse 22 because he contends that verses 22-25 deal with the question of the structure of the world and that verse 25 begins to explore God's maintenance of the world.[19] Most commentators understand verse 22 to go with the following verses that also mention rain, snow, wind, and lightning. Plus, verse 23 deals with how God governs the world through His use of snow and hail in the day of battle and war. This section can be divided into God's government of the inanimate world (38:22-38) and His government of the animate world (38:39–39:30).

God's Government of the Inanimate World (Job 38:22-38)
God asks Job whether he understands how the snow and hail operate (vv. 22-24) and how God uses them for His providential

---

17. Hartley, *Job*, 497. Longman (*Job*, 430) notes that the earth is flat and featureless in the darkness but the morning light reveals the hills and valleys.

18. Hartley, *Job*, 497.

19. Hartley, *Job*, 500. G. Wilson (*Job*, 435) argues that a new style of question involving verbs of action begins in v. 31 to show the powerlessness of Job, and all other human beings, to order creation.

purposes 'for the day of battle and war'. God can use the elements of weather to fight for His people (Josh. 10:11; Ps. 78:47-48). God asks if Job knows how the storm originates by knowing the place where the light is distributed or where the east wind is scattered upon the earth. God asks Job if he knows how God uses the storm (torrents of rain and the thunderbolt) to water the ground in places where no human being dwells (vv. 25-30). Can Job explain how the dew forms or how the waters become frost? The fact that God satisfies desolate land with water, makes grass grow where human beings do not live, and gives birth to the dew and the frost shows that His purposes are broader than the needs of human beings. In other words, to focus only on God's purposes for human beings is narrow and presents a distorted view of His work in the world.[20] The ways of God cannot be understood solely from the human vantage point and surely not from the perspective of one human being.[21]

Next, God asks Job whether he understands the heavenly constellations and their relationship to the earth (vv. 31-33). Can Job control the Pleiades and the Orion? Can he give direction to the Mazzaroth or the Bear?[22] Does Job know how these constellations are governed and how they impact things that happen on the earth? The stars were created by God to rule the night (Gen. 1:14-19). They indicate time, announce the seasons, and chart directions.[23] The starry heavens are so far away from the existence of human beings that it is impossible for any human being to answer those questions. Job is not able to offer a decree the heavenly bodies must obey or to establish their dominion over the earth. Finally, God asks Job whether he can direct the storm where to go so that the lightning answers to the voice of a human being (vv. 34-36). God also asks whether Job has the wisdom to number the clouds or to direct the rain where to fall in order to loosen up the hard ground[24] (vv. 37-38).

---

20. Smick, 'Job', 4:896. He notes that people are not the measure of all things.

21. Robert Gordis, The Book of God and Man: A Study of Job (Chicago: University of Chicago Press, 1965), 118.

22. Longman (Job, 433) gives a description of each of these constellations. The meaning of 'Mazzaroth' is uncertain. Hartley (Job, 500) translates it as 'the planets' and Longman transliterates the term from the Hebrew, as in the ESV.

23. Hartley, Job, 502.

24. Longman, Job, 434. The rain turns dry dust into muddy clods.

God's Government of the Animate World (Job 38:39–39:30)
God not only governs the heavenly world, but He governs the
animal world as well. The animals described here typically
live in desolate places and, except for the horse, they are wild
beasts that are a threat to the existence of human beings.
There is also a beauty and wonder associated with some
of the animals that act in strange or humorous ways. These
animals show that God takes great pleasure in what He has
created and that no part of the world is outside of His control.
The animals and birds described include the lion, the raven,
the mountain goat, the hind, the wild ass, the wild ox, the
ostrich, the horse, and birds of prey.[25]

The description of the lion and the raven (38:39–41) focuses
on how they obtain food. Both the lion and the raven must
find food for their young. God asks Job if he can hunt prey
for the lion so that the young lions can be fed. He also asks
Job who provides prey for the raven when their 'young ones
cry out to God for help, and wander about for lack of food'?
The answers to these questions are obvious as Job cannot find
food for the lions because they terrify human beings. The
young of the raven even cry out to God for their food, so He
must be the one who provides it for them. Those creatures
are aware of the ultimate source of their food. Human beings,
like Job, must learn to live in dependence on God.

The description of the mountain goats (39:1-4) highlights
the birth and maturation of the young. God asks Job whether
he knows when the mountain goats give birth or whether he
observes the calving of the does. The timing of birth for any
animal is not an exact science and there are many factors that
impact when birth occurs. Job is not able to pinpoint when a
goat will give birth because such knowledge is beyond him.
The newly born goats grow strong and make it on their own.
The whole process is part of the wonder of God's creation.
The mountain goat gives birth apart from human help.[26]

The descriptions of the rest of the creatures in chapter
39 focus on a particular characteristic of the one described.
God asks Job who has determined the free nature of the wild

---

25. Hartley, *Job*, 504.

26. Hartley, *Job*, 506.

donkey (39:5–8). The wild donkey roams free over desolate lands and makes his home in places not inhabited by human beings. The donkey scorns the tumult of the city and freely roams the mountains searching for food. Clearly Job has had nothing to do with the free spirit of the wild donkey. Job is also not able to force the wild ox to submit to him (39:9–12). The wild ox (*rêm*) cannot be made to settle down overnight as a domestic ox (*bāqār*) and he cannot be used to plow land because of his stubborn character. Although the wild ox is very strong, he cannot be depended on to help human beings in their labors. Job has no power to tame such an animal.

The description of the ostrich (39:13-18) demonstrates that this creature has great ability but also demonstrates strange behavior. The ostrich is a large bird with short, stubby wings,[27] but those wings are not used to fly or to beneficially protect her young.[28] The ostrich treats her young cruelly as if they are not hers. She leaves the eggs in the earth to be warmed and so exposes them to being crushed by the feet of humans or beasts. The ostrich does not protect her eggs by sitting on them herself. The reason for this behavior is that God has made the ostrich this way. He has not given this bird wisdom or understanding. God has endowed the ostrich with a fearless attitude and she can outrun a horse. Her carefree attitude is seen when she laughs at the horse as she flees.[29] Who would ever make a creature like the ostrich? God did, and it shows the mysterious wonder of His creation that cannot be comprehended by human understanding. It becomes clear that God gives wisdom to some animals but not to others, an observation that supports the view that wisdom only comes from God.[30]

The character of the horse is described as it fearlessly faces battle (39:19-25).[31] God asks Job who has given the horse his

---

27. Longman, *Job*, 436.

28. Hartley, *Job*, 510. He notes that the ostrich is a huge, peculiar looking bird that makes one chuckle because of its small head attached to a large body by a long, skinny neck. The Hebrew word for ostrich (*rĕnān'm*) means 'the screamer, or the one of piercing cries'.

29. G. Wilson (*Job*, 444) notes that the ostrich has been clocked at speeds reaching 80 kph (50 mph).

30. Longman, *Job*, 437.

31. Longman (*Job*, 437) comments that although the horse is domesticated, it is a dangerous animal.

might or clothed his neck with a mane. The horse is made for battle because he is fearless as the battle approaches. His snorting is terrifying and he paws the ground exulting in his strength as he goes out to meet the weapons of warfare. The horse leaps like a locust and with fierce rage swiftly moves toward the fight when the trumpet sounds. Such a magnificent animal is made by God and humans stand amazed at the fearless, majestic strength of the horse.[32]

The description of the hawk and the eagle (39:26-30) emphasizes the mystery of their flight. God asks Job if he has wisdom concerning how the hawk soars in the sky or how he makes his nest among the rocky areas high above the rest of the world. The eagle effortlessly rides the wind and can see prey down on the earth as he seeks food for his young. The use of the word 'understanding' (*b'nāh*) forms an *inclusio* with 38:4 where the same word is used. This highlights the key question of this speech concerning Job's capacity to understand how the works of God in creation operate and His ability to control their movements.

An Invitation for Job to Respond (Job 40:1-2)
God first asks Job another question and then He exhorts him to respond to what He has said. The question is, 'Shall a faultfinder contend with the Almighty?' Several things are important about this question. First, God calls Job a 'faultfinder'. The Hebrew term (*yissôr*) refers to one who reproves or corrects. Job has made statements that have called into question the way God governs the world (10:3). God has understood these statements as reproving Him or correcting Him for His governance of the world, or more specifically, for the way He has treated Job. Job has sought to 'contend' (*r'b*) with God. This word means 'quarrel' or 'dispute' and it is also the word used in the prophets for the covenant lawsuit God brings against His people because of their disobedience.[33] Job has disputed with God over how God has treated him and he has sought a hearing before God to lay his charges before

---

32. Hartley, *Job*, 513.

33. For discussion of the covenant lawsuit, see Herbert B. Huffmon, 'The Covenant Lawsuit in the Prophets,' *JBL* 78 (1959):286-95 and James Limburg, 'The Root רִיב and the Prophetic Lawsuit Speeches,' *JBL* 88 (1969):291-304.

God. The name used for God is 'the Almighty' (Shaddai). This name fits the character of God in the first speech who is powerful enough to govern the world and reinforces with Job his own lowly place as a creature of God.

The exhortation to Job is, 'He who argues with God, let him answer it.' Job has been arguing (*yākāḥ*) with God, a word that means 'to set someone right' or 'to reproach someone for something'. Job has sought to reproach God for the way he has been treated and by arguing his case has sought to set God right in relationship to how he has been treated. The Almighty has now spoken and so God exhorts Job to give an answer.

Job's First Response (Job 40:3–5)
Job answers the LORD by declaring that he does not know what he should answer. If Job remains silent he would void his oath of innocence (Job 31), but if he continues to argue he leaves himself open to further divine rebuke.[34] He calls attention to the fact that he is 'of small account' (*qālāl*). In light of the majesty of the Almighty and His power to govern the world, Job recognizes his insignificance before God and the panorama of creation. He has been left speechless, so that he does not know what he should answer. Job does not renounce anything he has said,[35] including his avowal of innocence, but he also does not want to continue the discussion. He feels the impact of Yahweh's speech and is reduced to silence. He places his hand over his mouth, a gesture of deference and respect that others had shown to Job by not speaking in his presence (Job 29:9-10).[36] Job had feared that if granted a meeting with God he would not find words to dispute with him (9:3, 14).[37] His silence is not because God has beaten him down with His power but is due to the grandeur of God's power in governing the world. In fact, he acknowledges that

---

34. Hartley, *Job*, 515.

35. Although Job is humbled into silence, there is no clear statement of repentance in his first response concerning what he has said (contra Alden, *Job*, 392). Job's response, however, is not ambiguous. He is not offering words behind which he may keep his own counsel so that God is not sure what he is affirming (J. Gerald Janzen, *Job* [Atlanta: John Knox Press, 1985], 243).

36. Newsom, 'Job,' 4:613.

37. Hartley, *Job*, 518.

he has already spoken too much and that he will not speak any more. The LORD's first speech leaves Job speechless.

The Function of God's First Speech
The barrage of questions that God asks Job is meant to overwhelm him with the mystery, wonder, beauty, and power of God's activity in governing the world. Part of the function of the questions is to show Job's inability to do the things that God can do in His awesome control of creation. Another function is to demonstrate Job's ignorance of the way the world operates. There are many things in the world that humans have little opportunity to see or to understand. Many of the questions are meant to evoke awe in Job (38:4), but this does not mean that Job's lack of knowledge is also not in view.[38] The first speech focuses on the wonderful way God governs the world over against the limited understanding of human beings, particularly Job, on how the world operates. Job has not spoken correctly about God's design of the world (38:2). The focus of the first speech is how God governs the world, but the emphasis is on the mysterious and wondrous way that the world works.

There are several results that God's first speech begins to produce in the viewpoint of Job. The curse-lament of Job in chapter 3 exposed the world of Job's inner torment. Job wanted darkness to win the day so that he would not have been born. He ended the curse-lament with a self-centered focus by using a series of personal pronouns in 3:24-26. Job's world became confined to his own suffering and he lost the broader horizon of life. God's first speech shows Job the panorama of creation to move him beyond his truncated view that the world revolves around him and his suffering.[39] Job's suffering is not unimportant, but the world is a vast and glorious world beyond his personal experience. If Job is not able to understand the way God governs the world, there is no way he can understand the mystery of his own suffering.

38. Michael Fox, 'Job the Pious,' *ZAW* 117 (2005), 354. Although Fox emphasizes divine power over human ignorance, he does acknowledge the aspect of human ignorance in the questions.

39. Robert Alter, *The Art of Biblical Poetry* (New York: Basic Books, 1985), 96-100. Alter develops extensively the connections between God's speeches and Job 3.

Several contrasts between what Job has said and the first divine speech highlights the mystery of the way God governs the world. Job had accused God of relentlessly hunting him down like a lion (Job 10:16), a negative picture of his relationship to God. God states that He does hunt down prey for the lion (38:39), a positive action of God. Job complained that God did not hear his cry for litigation (19:7), but God reminds Job that even the raven's cry is heard by God (38:41).[40] What Job perceives as negative actions of God toward him are positive actions that God takes toward His animal creatures. Job accuses God of afflicting him without reason while smiling on the design of the wicked (10:3), but contrary to Job's claim the design of God exposes the wicked each dawn (38:15). In 3:23 Job had felt 'hedged in' (*skk*) by God, trapped in his suffering, so that he had lost the purpose for life, but God shuts (*skk*) in the sea to limit and keep it under control (38:8). These parallels show that Job has a limited, negative view of God's actions toward him.

Job's response of silence recognizes that he cannot answer God because he is not able to explain how the world works. Job can answer many of the questions God asks because the answer is obvious – God is the only appropriate answer. So Job has a limited amount of wisdom, but the areas he does not understand are vast and significant.[41] This theme reinforces the point of Job 28 that wisdom is only found with God. He is the only one who knows its place because it originates with him (28:20-23). If God governs the world with wisdom, then Job must realize that even though he is suffering greatly, his suffering is not beyond the wisdom of God. This idea should lead Job to trust in the wise rule of God, even in his own life.

Constructing our Beliefs

My mom tells a story from when she and my dad were building their first home. The home was in one of those sprawling neighborhoods that could likely have

---

40. Habel, *Job*, 544.

41. Konkel ('Job,' 6:228) makes the point that there is great gain in knowing what one does not know.

its own zip code. Every section, a different builder was responsible for crafting the home of the buyer's dreams. Several years later, it became increasingly evident that one specific builder took numerous shortcuts. As houses in that particular section began to settle, the foundations cracked and the structures became unstable. Families were forced to abandon the homes of their dreams because they were deemed unsafe.

Without caution, our own worldviews (beliefs we hold which inform our thoughts, feelings and actions) can be like those unsteady, broken homes. We build them up with faulty materials, taking shortcuts and not investing much time into the careful studying of God's Word. This leaves us with disjointed, inconsistent and unbiblical worldviews. Our belief systems may give the appearance of being stable, but waves of pain and disappointment can cause them to crack, threatening the integrity of all we hold to be true.

Browse today's popular 'Christian' authors and it won't take you long to see that a common theme in American Christianity: God loves you and wants you to live a happy, healthy and fulfilled life. And while God certainly does love His people, the Bible paints a much different portrait of what He desires for us. We long for personal happiness in this present life; God wants us to long for His happiness in light of eternity. We want to get our needs met by created things; God wants us to see that our needs can only be met by Him. We desire for God to serve us; God serves His own glory.

As often happens, what we think God wants for us and what He actually wants for us are two totally different things. But the Bible allows us to make sense of what God is doing in the midst of our suffering. It's true we won't always understand His ways, but we will be able to take comfort in knowing His promises, His character and His overarching purposes. When we set the Bible as the ultimate standard for which we view everything, it becomes the filter for our thoughts and emotions, straining out the impurities.

And so I encourage you to let your worldview be shaped by what God has said about Himself instead

of what you currently think or feel about Him. When
you do this, you'll find that your foundation is solid and
unmovable, able to withstand whatever trials come your
way.

Lindsay Franks, www.lindsayfranks.com (3/4/16).

Study Questions

1) What impact does God's appearing in the storm have on
   Job? What is the focus of the first question that God asks
   Job?

2) What role do the rhetorical questions that God asks Job
   have in God's first speech?

3) How does the question of the morning light relate to
   the wicked and what does this teach concerning God's
   relationship to the wicked?

4) What is the point that God provides for desolate places
   of the earth where no human beings live?

5) What is the purpose of the questions concerning the
   animal world?

6) What lesson is learned from the description of the ostrich?

7) What does God charge Job with at the end of the first
   speech?

8) How does Job respond to God's first speech?

9) What impact does God's first speech have on Job's
   viewpoint? What contrasts are there between what Job
   has said in his speeches and what God says in the first
   speech? What do these contrasts show?

10) Is suffering beyond the wisdom of God?

30

God's Second Speech and Job's Response
(Job 40:6–42:6)

A Renewed Challenge: Do You Have the Power to Establish Justice? (Job 40:6-14)

God's second speech is introduced like the first speech (40:6-7). He addresses Job out of the whirlwind and asks a series of questions for Job to answer. The focus of the questions is different from the focus of the questions in God's first speech. The emphasis of the new questions is highlighted in verses 8-9. In verse 8 the issue is whether Job really wants to condemn God so that Job can be right. This question gets at the heart of the issue that has troubled Job. He has declared his innocence over against the accusations of his friends that his sin is the cause of his suffering. But if Job is innocent, then the conclusion is that he is suffering unjustly, which brings into play the character of God's justice. If Job is suffering unjustly, then God must be the blame. Job has made such a claim in 9:20, 24 and 27:1-6. Job and his friends are caught on the false dilemma that either his suffering is justified because of sin or that God is unjust in the way that He is treating Job. The friends argue that God is a just God and so Job must have sinned to bring about his suffering. Job argues that he has not sinned to cause his suffering, so God must be treating him unfairly. Although Job at times explores the mystery of God's ways in the world and utters statements of God's goodness, this false dilemma remains at the heart of the debate. In this second speech, God confronts Job with the accusation that He has treated Job unjustly. Will Job condemn God's justice to make the case that he is in the right?

The question in verse 9 relates to the issue of God's justice. God asks Job if he has an arm like God. The arm is a symbol of power and so this question raises the issue of whether Job is as powerful as God. Also, God many times uses the power of his voice to accomplish His purposes (Ps. 29). Can Job 'thunder with a voice like his'? In other words, can Job accomplish his purposes in the world through a mighty voice like God does? The questions in verses 8-9 set up the rest of God's speech that will focus on whether Job has the power to control the events in the world to accomplish his purposes. Power and justice go hand in hand. In order to establish justice in the world, power is needed. Does Job have the power to establish justice? What will this second speech of God say about God's own power and justice?

Instead of questions, God addresses Job with commands in verses 10-14 to highlight whether Job has the power to establish justice. God first tells Job to adorn himself with majesty and dignity and to clothe himself with glory and splendor. These are weighty characteristics, associated with God,[1] that are needed to accomplish justice in the world. Then God commands Job to deal with the proud and the wicked (vv. 11-14). Job should pour out his anger on the proud to bring him low from his exalted position; he should tread on the wicked and so stop them right where they stand; and he should bring them low to the dust and commit them to the world below. In other words, Job should demonstrate his power by stopping the proud and the wicked from accomplishing their purposes. He should be able to show God how the world should be governed justly.[2] If Job can do that, then God will acknowledge that Job has the power to save himself. This means that Job's righteousness will be established and God will be shown to be unjust.[3] If Job can

---

1. G. Wilson, *Job*, 455.

2. Rowley, *Job*, 254.

3. Walton (*Job*, 405) argues this point based on the parallel between vv. 8 and 14, which form an *inclusio*.

save himself, then he does not need God.[4] Of course, the implication is that Job does not have the power to establish justice on the earth and so he does not have the power to save himself. This means he is ultimately dependent on God's power and justice to save him.

The Identification of Behemoth and Leviathan (Job 40:15–41:34)

The challenge by God for Job to establish justice by governing the world is illustrated in the examples of Behemoth and Leviathan. There is a lack of agreement among scholars concerning the identification of these creatures. It is helpful to review the basic positions before the text is examined.

Literal Animals

God has already used literal animals to make a point in the first speech (39:1-30), so it is possible that He would use other animals to make His point in the second speech. There is not agreement, however, concerning which animals are in view. The Behemoth has been identified with an elephant or a hippo. Yet, the description of the tail as 'stiff like a cedar' does not fit the description of the tail of an elephant or a hippo. Some have suggested this might refer to the sexual organ of the animal because the loins are the seat of procreative powers.[5] There is also the suggestion that Behemoth is a description of a dinosaur.[6]

The evidence that these creatures are literal animals is seen in the way their habitat and their diet are described (40:15-16, 23), in the description of how one might try to capture the animal (40:24; 41:1-8, 25-32), and in the designation that they are creatures created by God (41:33) just as God created Job ('Behemoth, which I made as I made you' [40:15]).[7] Plus, Behemoth and Leviathan are used in the Old Testament

---

4. Hartley, *Job*, 521.

5. Konkel, 'Job,' 6:231.

6. Allan Steel, 'Could Behemoth Have Been a Dinosaur?' *TJ* 15. 2 (2001): 42-45.

7. Commentators on Job who take a literal view of the animals are Andersen (he calls it the majority view), Konkel, Alden, Rowley and Talbert; also see Michael Fox, 'Behemoth and Leviathan,' *Bib* 93 (2012): 261-67.

without any symbolic meaning (Pss. 8:8; 50:10; 73:22; 104:26; Joel 1:20; 2:22; and Hab. 2:17).

There are problems with identifying these creatures with literal animals. The descriptions do not always match an animal, so there is debate about which animals are in view. Also, part of the description of Leviathan seems to go beyond a description of a normal animal when it describes fire coming forth out of his mouth and smoke coming from his nostrils (41:18-21). A literal animal would not be described in this way. The answer to this objection is the poetic use of hyperbole to emphasize the fierce character of the animals.[8] Talbert has an appendix where he gives a naturalist's description of the crocodile lying in the water in the early morning with what looks like smoke coming out of his nostrils.[9] Another problem is whether these literal animals are really beyond the control of human beings. Perhaps the point is that Job could not capture these animals by himself, but there are examples of humans capturing the hippo or the crocodile. The question of whether Job can establish justice in the world seems larger than Job's ability to control these animals.[10]

Mythological Creatures
This view argues that Behemoth and Leviathan are mythic symbols of the forces of chaos used in ancient Near Eastern myths that describe the battles among the gods. These forces of chaos are overcome by Baal in the Canaanite tradition,[11] by Marduk in the Babylonian *Enuma Elish,* and by Horus in Egyptian mythology. Links with the hippopotamus and the crocodile arise from the use of these figures as symbols of chaos in Egypt where the god Seth assumes the form of a hippopotamus and a crocodile in the battle with Horus.[12] This approach finds

---

8. Robert Gordis, *The Book of Job* (New York: Jewish Theological Seminary of America, 1978), 571. Gordis argues that the animals are literal animals but he is willing to say that hyperbole utilizes traits from mythology to describe these animals.

9. Talbert, *Beyond Suffering*, 276-77.

10. Ash, *Job*, 418.

11. Marvin H. Pope, Job (Garden City, NY: Doubleday, 1965), 268-70.

12. This summary comes from Habel, *Job*, 557; see also Leo G. Perdue, *Wisdom Literature: A Theological History* (Louisville: Westminster John Knox Press, 2007), 124.

support in the fact that Leviathan is used in Scripture to refer to the chaos dragon of the sea (Isa. 27:1; 51:9; Ps. 74:14).[13]

There are several problems with the mythological view. The focus of God's second speech is not on the dim mythological past but is on the present vast universe as it is governed by its Maker. God includes Behemoth in the same category as a creature like Job (40:15). The description of Behemoth is not horrendous and predatory as in the creation myths, but he is described as a herbivore, peacefully lying in the river.[14] The description seems very much a part of the natural world.

Literal animals with Mythic Metaphors
This view argues that although features of these creatures are drawn from literal animals, like the hippopotamus and crocodile, the poetic language is also symbolic of something beyond the mere animal world. Both the world of creation and the world of mythological associations are used to make the point. This view is supported by several arguments. The discussion of these animals comes after God challenges Job to establish justice on the earth. These animals must refer to something more than a literal animal. Leviathan sometimes symbolizes evil powers (Isa. 27:1; 51:9; Ps. 74:14).[15] Mythological terminology is used to present graphic descriptions of the powers of evil.[16]

Fyall develops these connections further by associating Behemoth with death and Leviathan with the embodiment

---

13. John Day, *God's Conflict with the Dragon and the Sea* (Cambridge: Cambridge University Press, 1985). He argues for the mythological view but does not want to deny that the author thought these creatures existed (pp. 82-83). He also highlights the differences between the description of Behemoth and the hippopotamus and the description of Leviathan and the crocodile (pp. 76-77).

14. Gordis, *Job*, 571.

15. Smick ('Job,' 4:906-07) argues that Scripture historicizes the many-headed Leviathan and uses it metaphorically to describe the Lord's victory in history at the Red Sea (Ps. 74:12-14) and to represent the final evil power at the end time (Isa. 27:1).

16. Smick ('Job,' 4:697-706) has an extensive section on 'mythopoeic language' that is used to describe mythological concepts by Scriptural writers. He also connects the graphic pictures of the powers of evil in Behemoth and Leviathan to Satan in Job 1–2, but states that Satan cannot be openly mentioned here without revealing to Job information he must not know if he is to be a model to those who must suffer in ignorance of God's explicit purpose for their suffering ('Job,' 4:907).

of evil, even Satan himself. The description of Behemoth's habitat in 40:20-22 has a dual purpose. On the one hand, the details are vivid and realistic and evoke a marshy scene which roots the creature in the natural world. On the other hand, the words resonate with deeper meanings which point with increasing clarity to the creature's identity and the true location of his haunts as the underworld. Fyall believes that such associations make the identification of Behemoth with Mot, the god of death, a very strong possibility. Leviathan is described in terms drawn from the world of nature of which he is a part and to which he is a threat. Leviathan is introduced deliberately as the climax of the supernatural imagery of the poetic dialogue. He is a supernatural creature which manifests itself in physical violence and awesome force in the natural world. Supernatural elements begin to proliferate, with an emphasis on fire with its theophanic elements. Leviathan is a guise of Satan, the more sinister power behind death. The Satan/Leviathan figure is unmasked as the climax of the imagery and theology of the book.[17] Job is challenged by God to contain and control death, and even Satan himself.[18]

Behemoth (Job 40:15-24)

God first presents Behemoth to Job. Behemoth is a creature created by God just as Job is a creature created by God (as stated in v. 15: 'which I made as I made you'). The identification of Behemoth with an animal has been difficult because of the way the tail is described in verse 17. If the 'tail' refers to the sexual organ, then the description fits well the hippopotamus.[19] These verses focus on this animal as a living creature with descriptions of his bodily strength (vv. 15-18), his prominence (vv. 19-20), and his habitat (vv. 21-23). The section closes with a question that highlights the power of Behemoth.

Behemoth is a living creature who eats grass like an ox (v. 15), but he is also a very powerful animal. His strength

---

17. Fyall, *Now My Eyes Have Seen You*, 135, 137, 157, and 165.

18. Ash, *Job*, 421.

19. Konkel, 'Job,' 6:231-32. He gives a detailed description of the hippopotamus. Those who favor an identification with the elephant translate 'tail' as 'trunk' (Alden, *Job*, 396).

lies in the power of his muscles, the sinews of his thighs that are firmly knit together, and his bones that are like bars of iron. This is a mighty animal that few other living creatures could match. The prominence of Behemoth is highlighted in the statement that 'he is the first of the works of God' (v. 19). The word 'works' is the Hebrew word that can also mean 'ways' (*derek̲*) and seems to be saying that he is the crown of the animal creation.[20] The first of the land beasts created in Genesis 1 was the cattle (*běhēmāh*, singular of *běhēmôt̲*).[21] The fact that he is the first of the animal creation establishes his prominence. Since God created Behemoth, God also has mastery over this creature (v. 19b).[22] The habitat of Behemoth is described in verses 20-23. He lies under the water in the shelter of the marsh with only his eyes above the surface of the water. He leaves the river to find food on the mountains and because he is an herbivore, animals do not fear him. He is so powerful that even a turbulent river does not frighten him. He is confident that in his strength he can withstand the power of its currents. The section ends with a question concerning whether anyone can capture this animal by piercing his nose with a snare. In popular lore, it was considered impossible to capture this great creature and in Egypt only the divine Pharaohs or the ruling god Horus could hunt this powerful animal.[23] Job is not able to capture or control this animal. He is powerless before a living creature of God. If Job cannot control Behemoth, how will he control the proud (40:12a)?[24] Only God has sufficient wisdom and power to rule the world.[25]

---

20. Hartley, *Job*, 525.

21. G. Wilson, *Job*, 457.

22. The translation of v. 19b is difficult. The fact that God can master Behemoth with a sword has led many to see conflict in this passage. Another translation is possible without changing the consonantal text of the Hebrew that fits better the context: 'He is the first of the ways of God, made to dominate his companions' (Newsom, 'Job,' 4:619). This translation fits well with the verses that follow where the evidence is given to show his dominant position, 'For the mountains yield food for him.'

23. Hartley, *Job*, 524, 526. A favorite tactic in hunting a hippopotamus was to pierce its nose to make it breathe through the mouth so that a fatal blow could be inflicted through the open mouth.

24. Talbert, *Beyond Suffering*, 212.

25. Estes, *Handbook*, 122.

The description of Behemoth seems to stay within the boundaries of the animal world. There is little evidence of mythological terminology used to describe this creature (unlike Leviathan in the next section). There are views that go beyond the mere description of an animal. If Behemoth and Leviathan are understood together and are not considered real creatures, they could represent the ultimate in land and sea creatures.[26] The plural form Behemoth could be an intensive plural meaning that Behemoth is the beast par excellence; that is, the beast becomes a monster.[27] If the two animals are lumped together,[28] then mythological associates come into play because they are part of the description of Leviathan. Fyall finds mythological associations in the description of Behemoth's habitat in verses 20-22 that serves a dual purpose of describing the natural world and the underworld. Thus he concludes that the identification of Behemoth with Mot, the god of death, is a very strong possibility.[29] These associations, however, are not as clear as they are in the description of Leviathan. Is it possible that there is a progression from Behemoth to Leviathan? Behemoth describes a land animal to make the point that even with a land animal Job has no power to capture or control this animal. If that is the case there is no possibility that Job could control Leviathan, who symbolizes the powers of evil.

Leviathan (Job 41:1-34)

The section on Behemoth did not utilize rhetorical questions as in God's first speech, but was an invitation to observe Behemoth, with a question at the end.[30] The section on Leviathan again uses the interrogation format with questions

---

26. Longman, *Job*, 441.

27. Smick, 'Job,' 4:911.

28. Kline takes the two terms Behemoth and Leviathan as referring to the same creature, which he thinks may be the crocodile (Meredith G. Kline, 'Trial by Ordeal,' in *Through Christ's Word: A Festschrift for Dr. Philip E. Hughes*, eds. W. Robert Godfrey and Jesse L. Boyd III [Phillipsburg, NJ: Presbyterian and Reformed, 1985], 81-93). Although Kline lumps the two together, he views them as literal animals. If there are clear mythological associations in the description of Leviathan, then lumping the two together could bring mythological associations into play with Behemoth.

29. Fyall, *Now My Eyes Have Seen You*, 135, 137.

30. Alden, *Job*, 396.

interspersed with comments.[31] Leviathan is either a crocodile or a sea creature (Ps. 104:26), but the description of this animal will clearly go beyond the description of a normal animal as an embodiment of the forces of evil.[32] The terrifying nature of Leviathan is described in 41:1-11 (40:25–41:3 in Hebrew) and the physical characteristics are given in 41:12-34 (41:4-26 in Hebrew).[33]

The section on Behemoth ended up with a question on the impossibility of capturing it (40:24). This theme continues at the beginning of the section on Leviathan where the impossibility of capturing or negotiating with Leviathan to control him is explored (41:1–11). Leviathan cannot be captured with a fishhook[34] or with a rope in his nose. He is not an animal that a human being should bother. He does not speak soft words nor will he plead with anyone who is trying to capture him. It is impossible to subdue him by figuratively entering into a covenant with him so he becomes a servant who is submissive to human demands. It is dangerous to play with him as a pet and you would not want a little girl to have him on a leash. Traders will not bargain over Leviathan because no one can capture him. Harpoons and spears are not effective to bring him down. If Job would lay a hand on him, the experience would be so terrifying that he would never try it again.

The implication of the fierceness of Leviathan is brought out in verses 9-11 in a series of statements followed by questions that bring out the point that is being made. The hope of a man to capture him is destroyed just at the sight of him. He is so fierce that no one dares to stir him up. The implication is brought out in two questions. The first question is (v. 10): 'Who then is he who can stand before me?' If Job cannot

---

31. Talbert, *Beyond Suffering*, 212. He states that there are sixteen questions in this section.

32. Hartley, *Job*, 530.

33. The English and the Hebrew chapter and verses do not match. The English is given first followed by the Hebrew in parentheses.

34. If a crocodile is in view, they were often hunted with a baited hook. When the bait was swallowed and the hook lodged inside the mouth, the tongue was pressed down by the rope tied to the hook (Hartley, *Job*, 530). Although it is possible for those who are skilled to capture a crocodile, it would be disastrous for Job to try it. Most humans would not dare attempt such a feat. This becomes even more evident when Leviathan takes on greater symbolic connotations.

control Leviathan, how can he ever hope to stand before God and question Him? If Job cannot negotiate with Leviathan to bring him under control, what makes him think that he can haul God into court and question His justice? These issues are beyond Job's understanding or power to accomplish.

The second question God asks Job is (v. 11), 'Who has first given to me, that I should repay him?' God is not under any obligation to repay anyone anything because He owes no one anything. He is not under obligation to anyone because He owns everything in the universe. This question, and the statement that follows, hit at the heart of the friends' view of the principle of retribution. They believed that God must repay obedience with blessing and disobedience with judgment. It also begins to challenge Job's assumption that God has not treated him fairly. God is free from such a cause-and-effect relationship between human action and divine response.[35] In reality, what God states here is in agreement with Job's first response to suffering that we are born with nothing and that all that we have is a gift from God because He does not owe us anything (Job 1:21).

The physical characteristics of Leviathan, and their impact, are laid out in verses 12-34. This section begins with a statement that God will not keep silent concerning the mighty strength of Leviathan in his limbs or his frame. The next several verses describe how much Leviathan is impregnable,[36] protected from any danger in his 'outer garment' (vv. 13–17). The face of Leviathan strikes terror into people who might come near him with a bridle. It is impossible to pry open his mouth, and even if one could accomplish this feat, his teeth are frightening. His back is like a row of shields so closely tied together that no air can come between them and they cannot be separated. No weapon can penetrate the armor of this creature.

The description of what comes out of Leviathan's mouth in verses 18-21 shows that this creature is more than a normal animal.[37] His eyes shine with a light 'like the eyelids of the

---

35. G. Wilson, *Job*, 462.

36. Hartley, *Job*, 532.

37. Hartley (*Job*, 532) calls this creature a mythical dragon. He is described as a fire-breathing sea dragon.

dawn'.[38] Sparks of fire leap from his mouth like flaming torches. His sneezes flash forth light and smoke comes out of his nostrils as from a boiling pot. His breath is hot enough to kindle coals. Further descriptions of his physical characteristics are given in verses 22-24. His neck is strong and the raising of the neck strikes terror in people. The folds of his flesh are invincible[39] and his heart, or breast, is as hard as stone.[40]

The impact of such a creature is given in verses 25-34. When he raises himself up the mighty ones are afraid.[41] He crashes around in a terrifying way (v. 25b).[42] Neither the sword, nor the spear, nor the javelin has any effect on him because iron is to him as straw and bronze is to him as rotten wood. Arrows do not make him afraid because sling stones and clubs are turned to stubble. Even the underparts of this animal, usually considered to be vulnerable, are like sharp potsherds. To be run over by Leviathan would be like being run over by a threshing sledge.[43] His movements make the sea boil like a pot.[44] When he moves he leaves behind such a shining wake that one might conclude the deep to have white hair. There is no other creature on earth like Leviathan. He has no fear of anything and cannot be intimidated. He is the king over all the sons of pride. No creature on earth is greater than him.

The Purpose of God's Second Speech

The second speech specifically focuses on the matter of justice (40:8). Job has condemned God in order to declare his own

---

38. Habel (*Job*, 572) comments that the intensity of heat is such that his eyes light up red like the dawn.

39. The verb 'firmly cast' (*yṣq*) can refer to the hardness of cast metal (Longman, *Job*, 447, n. 67).

40. Hartley (*Job*, 533) states that the lower millstone is harder than the upper millstone because it must bear the weight of the upper millstone and the brunt of the grinding.

41. The word 'mighty' (*ʾēl'm*) is the word for 'gods', but it can also mean 'chiefs' (Ezek. 31:11; 32:21). Some take the word to refer to the mighty among humans (Hartley, Alden). The meaning 'gods' supports the view that Leviathan is more than a creature but that it is symbolic of evil. Even the gods are afraid of him (Newsom, 'Job,' 4:624).

42. Ash, *Job*, 414.

43. Longman, *Job*, 448.

44. The pot of anointment was used to mix perfumes. Just as small quantities were thoroughly mixed together, so Leviathan agitates the entire sea (Alden, *Job*, 406).

righteousness. He has called into question the justice of God in his earlier speeches (9:22–24). It is important, however, to define the word 'justice' (mišpāṭ) to help clarify the matter between Job and God. Job is using the term justice with the forensic meaning of a lawsuit. He wants to take God to court to declare his innocence (13:3, 18). Job charges God with wrongdoing (ḥāmās, 19:7). The friends of Job also use justice with this meaning, so they see Job's suffering as moral recompense for Job's sin (4:7-8; 8:3-4).[45] They operate with the dilemma that Job's suffering must mean that he is being punished by God for sin.

God uses justice with a different meaning. God understands justice as executive sovereignty, the prerogative of the ruler to govern the universe and his subjects as he sees fit. This usage occurs in 1 Samuel 8 where the king may use his sovereign authority to remove the property of a subject as he deems necessary for the smooth operation of his kingdom. God does not use the term justice in the legal sense of the courtroom but in the sense of His authority to rule the universe.[46] The first speech of God focused on His design for the world as seen in His power and authority to govern the world. This speech reduces Job to silence. The second speech of God focuses on His justice as the ruler of the world. God challenges Job to rule the world as a sovereign king by bringing low the proud and by treading down the wicked (40:10-14).

God uses two examples to confront Job with his inability to govern the world. The first is Behemoth and the second is Leviathan. Both examples are living creatures who are a part of the world that Job inhabits. The description of Behemoth hardly goes beyond a description of a literal animal. There are creatures made by God that Job is not able to control. The description of Leviathan goes beyond the description of a literal animal when it is described as a fire-breathing dragon with smoke coming out of its nostrils. Other ways that Leviathan is described shows that even though it is a creature made by God (41:33), it becomes symbolic of the chaotic and

---

45. Sylvia Huberman Scholnick, 'The Meaning of mišpāṭ (Justice) in the Book of Job', in Sitting with Job, ed. Roy B. Zuck (Grand Rapids: Baker, 1992), 350-51.

46. Scholnick, 'mišpāṭ (Justice) in Job,' 350.

evil forces in the world. This connection is also evident in the impact that Leviathan has in the sea (41:30-32). His abode is the primordial abyss where he churns up the ocean's depths as the symbol of chaos, the meaning of Leviathan in Psalm 74:14 and Isaiah 27:1 and 51:9.[47] This picture of Leviathan fits with Job's own demand that those who curse the day rouse up Leviathan to obliterate the day of his birth (3:8). When God confronts Job with Leviathan He confronts him with the impossibility of subduing evil and wickedness in the world. Job is not able to establish justice in the world because he is not able to control evil or subdue the wicked. Job is not able to execute the sovereign prerogative of a ruler by exercising dominion over evil.

The emphasis on God as the sovereign ruler who can run the universe according to His design takes the focus away from the issue of punishment for wrongdoing. Justice in the context of divine sovereignty means that the great loss that Job has experienced is not necessarily a punishment for sin but is related to God's prerogative as sovereign ruler of the universe. Divine justice includes the power to rule and the authority to control the well-being of His subjects. The power of evil is under the sovereign rule and control of God. God may have a purpose to Job's suffering that is not related to whether Job has sinned.[48] Job's claim that God is not a God of justice is answered by His control of Leviathan, a symbol of evil and wickedness in the world. The issue is much broader than Job's own suffering.

Job's Second Response (Job 42:1-6)
Job responds to God's second speech but exactly what he means is debated. There are several different ways that Job's answer is understood. There is a strong consensus among scholars that Job does not show contrition in his second response to God. Part of the issue is how the words Job uses in 42:6 are understood. The word *mā'as* (translated 'despise' in the ESV) can mean 'to refuse or reject' and it is used without a direct object. Therefore, there is debate concerning what Job

---

47. Habel, *Job*,573.
48. Scholnick, '*mišpāṭ* (Justice) in Job,' 356.

rejects. The word *nāḥam* can mean 'repent', 'change one's mind', or 'comfort', and the meaning of 'dust and ashes' is also debated. Perdue argues that Job protests (*mā'as*) against God and expresses his despondency over the human condition ('dust and ashes'). Job refuses to be intimated by God but remains defiant against God who is judged to be the guilty one.[49] God is also perceived as a divine bully. Job rejects God as unjust, unfeeling, and an irrelevant deity.[50] Of course, this view does not fit the picture of God in the rest of the Old Testament, much less the picture of God in the book of Job.

Some take an ironic view of Job's confession. In this view, it is impossible that Job would repent, so when he does repent, it must be understood ironically. Job prostrated himself before God as if he were a defeated antagonist, realizing that God was a being who could not be judged morally.[51] Job's confession was hypocritical, a 'tongue-in-cheek' response made to calm God in the whirlwind.[52] This does not fit the picture of Job earlier in the book. It is peculiar that Job, who was outspoken and honest about his situation in the speeches, would now become shifty and evasive.[53]

Others argue that Job does not repent but that he does change his viewpoint, attitude, or behavior in some way. One view is that Job understands from the content of God's speeches that justice is not an integral part of the universe and so a person should not expect anything from one's behavior. Job is prepared to live a pious life without false hopes or claims of reward or justice.[54] Another view is that Job did not

---

49. Perdue, *Wisdom Literature*, 126.

50. John B. Curtis, 'On Job's Response to Yahweh,' *JBL* 98 (1979), 510. He translates 42:6 as 'Therefore I feel loathing contempt and revulsion (toward you, O God); and I am sorry for frail man.' For extensive interaction with Curtis' views, see R. Lynne Newell, 'Job: Repentant or Rebellious?' in *Sitting with Job*, ed. Roy B. Zuck (Grand Rapids: Eerdmans, 1992).

51. C. G. Jung, '*Answer to Job*' (New York: Pastoral Psychology Book Club, 1955), 31.

52. David A. Robertson, 'The Book of Job: A Literary Study,' *Soundings* 56 (1973), 466.

53. Michael Fox, 'God's Answer and Job's Response,' *Bib* 94.1 (2013), 20.

54. Matitiahu Tsevat, 'The Meaning of the Book of Job,' in *Sitting with Job*, ed. Roy B. Zuck (Grand Rapids: Eerdmans, 1992), 216.

repent but he is willing to change his speech from lamentation and accusation of God to praise and rejoicing.[55] Another possibility is that Job retracts his desire for a lawsuit against God and recognizes his humble place in the universe.[56]

The best way to understand Job's response is that he acknowledges his limitations and repents of what he had said about God in the speeches. There are good exegetical reasons for this view. Job feels disgust (*māʾas*) at himself and his words, for he has spoken words without knowledge.[57] In rejecting his words he is withdrawing all charges against God and dropping his case.[58] The verb *nāḥam* in the nifal can mean 'repent' or 'relent'.[59] Although God is usually the subject of the verb, it is used with humans to indicate sorrow or regret because of wickedness (Jer. 8:6; 31:19).[60] The use of 'dust and ashes' could refer to the place where Job is sitting and it is used in other places of the Old Testament to signify humility or humiliation (Gen. 18:27; Job 30:19). Job has experienced humiliation by sitting among the dust and ashes.[61] He repents of what he has said about God in calling into question His justice. The fact that Job repents of what he has said fits into the flow of the argument of the book that recognizes the distinction between the point of the original debate concerning why Job is suffering and Job's response once he is in the middle of suffering.[62] Job has

---

55. Patrick, 'Job's Address,' 281.

56. Sylvia Huberman Scholnick, 'Poetry in the Courtroom: Job 38–41,' in *Sitting with Job*, ed. Roy B. Zuck (Grand Rapids: Eerdmans, 1992), 438–439, and William J. Dumbrell, 'The Purpose of the Book of Job,' in *The Way of Wisdom*, edited by J. I. Packer and Sven Soderlund (Grand Rapids: Zondervan, 2000), 91-105.

57. The verb *māʾas* can be used with or without a direct object but verbs of emotion many times will have a contextual object at which the emotion is directed (Fox, 'God's Answer and Job's Response,' 19).

58. Talbert, *Beyond Suffering*, 221.

59. Alden (*Job*, 409, n. 139) comments that usually *nāḥam* in the nifal means 'repent' and in the piel means 'comfort'.

60. Newell ('Job: Repentant or Rebellious?' 453-55) lays out the exegetical reasons for understanding Job's second response as repentance.

61. Whybray (*Job*, 170) denies that 'dust and ashes' refers to the place where Job is sitting because he associates that place with grief, but humiliation is also a part of Job's experience on the ash heap.

62. Newell ('Job: Repentant or Rebellious?' 443-55) argues that the ANE parallels of similar genres also support the view that Job repented.

asserted his own innocence at the expense of God's justice. Job is right that he is innocent because sin is not the cause of his suffering. Job is wrong in his statements that question God's justice.

A Response of Contrition

Job's second response begins with an affirmation that responds to God's first speech concerning Job's limited knowledge of God's design of the world. Job affirms that God can do all things and that none of His purposes can be thwarted (42:2). Job asks the same question in verse 3 that God had asked in 38:2: 'Who is this that hides counsel without knowledge?' Job recasts God's opening accusation into a self-judgment that shows he is responding to God's speeches.[63] By using God's words in his response it is clear that Job also views himself from God's perspective.[64] He answers this question by concluding that he has uttered things which he did not understand. There are things in the world that are too wonderful for Job to comprehend that take place within the framework of God's wisdom. He confesses his ignorance of these things and that he has spoken beyond his knowledge when he complained that God ruled unjustly.[65] He then quotes God in verse 4, 'Hear, and I will speak; I will question you, and you make it known to me.'[66] This is very similar to what God had said to Job in both speeches (38:3; 40:7). Job's response is that he had heard about God, but now he sees God. Job's deepest longing – to behold his Redeemer with his own eyes – has now come to pass (19:25-27).[67] The fact that Job sees God transforms his perspective (similar to Psalm 73:16-17). He despises himself and repents in dust and ashes.[68] Job's repentance while still

---

63. Hartley, *Job*, 536. He comments that the wording in 42:2a means that Job agrees with Yahweh's second speech and the wording of 42:3 that he accepts the argument of the first speech.

64. Newsom, 'Job,' 4:628.

65. Hartley, *Job*, 535-36.

66. Hartley (*Job*, 536) argues that v. 4 is Job's words to God to enjoin God to listen to his response. The view here is that these words are a quote of God's words to which Job will respond (Habel, *Job*, 576).

67. Hartley, *Job*, 537.

68. Some argue that the nifal (reflexive) of *nāḥam* followed by the preposition ʻal must carry the meaning 'concerning' for the preposition, leading to the idea

suffering shows that he is willing to fear God and submit to His purposes even if he is never publicly vindicated.[69]

Job acknowledges that his suffering in some way fits into the larger purposes of God. God has not treated him in an unjust way. Job repents of his ignorance of God's ways and his statements that called into question God's justice. Job does not withdraw his avowal of innocence (Job 31) in his confession.[70] It is important to keep in mind the original question argued by Job and the friends that Job has suffered because of sin he has committed. Job was correct on the point that he was not suffering because of sin. Thus, there was nothing of which he needed to repent in his avowal of innocence. But in his suffering Job spoke out of ignorance of God's ways in the world and called into question God's justice. Job must repent of the growing bitterness of his spirit and his accusations that God was unjust.[71] Those who do not make this distinction deny that Job repents or they argue that some sin must be discovered of which Job repents.[72] This distinction will also be important for understanding Job 42:7 where it is clear that the friends are wrong in their argument with Job.

Authentic, Plastic People

Do you ever try to mask your true self in order to impress those around you? Maybe it's only occasional, or maybe it's more frequent. For most of us, myself included, it's likely the latter. After all I was born and raised in the South – a culture known for parading its southern charm (or

---

that Job turns away from lamenting (dust and ashes). The meaning of this view is that Job is now ready to resume normal relations in society and no longer lament as an isolated sufferer. The preposition $'al$ can mean 'upon' and refers here to the humiliation of Job's suffering.

69. G. Wilson, *Job*, 468.

70. Hartley (*Job*, 537) argues that Job withdraws his avowal in innocence in renouncing his own self-righteousness, but this is not necessary because Job is not suffering because of his sin.

71. Longman, *Job*, 450. Thomas (*The Storm Breaks*, 306, 308) clearly recognizes this distinction and acknowledges that Job did not suffer because of sin, but he also makes the point that suffering can bring to the surface latent sins that are otherwise hidden from view. In other words, suffering is the crucible where our sinful tendencies are exposed.

72. G. Wilson (*Job*, 468).

fakeness?). So many days I pretend to be what others think I am, never revealing my true self. They say I'm strong, so I must act the part. Pull it together. Act strong, despite how weak I may feel. They say I'm a good wife/mom/friend, I must act that part as well. And while I will fail miserably at times in what I actually *do* while in those roles, I'll never admit it or let others know.

And so it goes, all this pretending. An endless cycle. And as I'm perfecting my acting skills, I am left feeling alone and isolated. 'No one gets this. No one could understand my struggle. She has her act together. She...she is strong.' I repeat things of this nature in my mind while forgetting that the 'she' I'm referring to is just another broken woman pretending to be things she simply is not. Maybe you do this too?

And perhaps you've walked into a church, the place where we should be our most broken, but instead of seeing other people's brokenness, you've just seen rows and rows of plastic people. People like us, who have put up their facades, afraid of letting the world know their secrets and hidden pains. What is our motivation for hiding our flaws? If it's to make ourselves look better then we should be reminded that Christians are called to make much of Him, and not ourselves.

Or it could be that our motivation for hiding comes from a sincere desire to protect our hearts from hurt and rejection. But this can't be how God created us to live in community. It just can't. Because what good is community if it's merely a counterfeit?

But the Gospel steps in, reminding us of what Christ has done for us despite our flaws and freeing us to bear those failures under that banner. The Gospel allows us to rejoice in a Savior who, despite our many sins, loves us deeply. He chooses to commune daily with our real self. Shouldn't that be enough for us to do the same with each other?

Every now and then, a genuine friend will come into your life. They'll gently help you to remove your mask. They'll let you know that they love you despite your flaws. They will be your token of grace. Maybe you'll have just one or maybe you'll have many. But you won't always need to be on the receiving end. In fact, for some of us, maybe our job right now is to be that token of grace in someone else's life? Perhaps it's your turn to show those around you your authentic self, flaws and all?

I know it's scary when you're vulnerable and real. You can get hurt when you let your guard down and I'm not promising that won't happen. But in dying to ourselves, we find that the only antidote for plastic people is authenticity. Be authentic. Show your struggles. And then point those who see your flaws to the only One who is flawless.

Lindsay Franks, www.lindsayfranks.com (3/7/16)

Study Questions

1) What is the focus of God's second speech? What is the false dilemma Job and the friends have been arguing?

2) God first challenges Job's knowledge. What does God challenge in this second speech? What is the purpose of that challenge?

3) What are the different views, and the evidence for each view, concerning the identification of Behemoth and Leviathan?

4) How are Behemoth and his habitat described? What is the point for Job?

5) How is the fierceness of Leviathan described? What is the point of the questions in 41:9-11? What evidence is there that Leviathan is more than a literal animal?

6) What is the focus of God's second speech? What are the different views of justice held by God and Job? What are the implications of God's view of justice for the issue of whether Job is being punished for his sin?

7) What does it mean that Job cannot control Leviathan?

8) What are the various views concerning Job's second response to God? What is the evidence for the view

that Job repented of what he had said about God in his speeches?

9) Why is it important to maintain the distinction between the original point of the debate of Job's innocence and the issue of how Job responds to his suffering?

31

The Renewal of God's Blessing
(Job 42:7-17)

The end of the book of Job, called the Epilogue, resolves the debate between Job and his friends and gives an account of the renewal of God's blessings in Job's life. Some struggle with the way the book of Job ends because it appears to substantiate the view of divine retribution argued by the friends. Do Job's blessings come as a reward for his repentance?

Several things argue against this view. Job submits to God after the second speech without any indication that he would be rewarded or that his suffering would end. Thus his response answers Satan's charge that humans will not fear God without the prospect of blessing. If the mechanical connection between deed and consequence has been shattered, so that suffering is not the consequence of sin, then it is also true that blessing is not the necessary result of obedience. It is within God's sovereign power to restore Job.[1] God is not angry with Job because of sin but He has allowed him to suffer for a higher purpose. Once that purpose has been fulfilled there is no reason for Job's suffering to continue.[2]

Job's Vindication (Job 42:7-9)

After the LORD addressed Job, He turned to address Eliphaz as the representative of the friends. God is angry at the

---

1. G, Wilson, *Job*, 469-70.
2. Smick, 'Job', 4:917-18.

friends, 'for you have not spoken of me what is right, as my servant Job has' (v. 7). This statement by God seems strange coming right after Job has repented for speaking words without knowledge. How has Job spoken what is right about God over against the wrong views of the friends? Some understand God's statement to refer to the fact that Job wins the debate with the friends because his words are more honest.[3] Job's bold assertions in the dialogue are free from blame because his response corresponds with reality more than the friends' conventional, unquestioning pronouncements.[4] This approach downplays the negative statements by Job about God in the speeches and could impact how one views Job's responses to God. Some argue that God's statement refers to the fact that Job confessed his sin of speaking arrogant words that were without knowledge. The friends also need to confess their sin.[5] This is true to a certain extent but it does not get at the heart of the debate that Job is right in the main argument with the friends that he is not suffering because of sin.

The best way to understand God's statement in 42:7 is in light of the distinction between the main point of the debate between Job and the friends and the inappropriate things Job said about God in the context of the debate. Job repented for his words spoken against God when he called into question God's justice. Job was right, however, on the main point of the debate with the three friends, that he was not suffering because of sin he had committed. It was made clear in Job 1–2 that Job was a blameless man who feared God and turned away from evil (1:1; 2:3). God even stated that Satan had incited Him against Job without cause (2:3). The prologue specifically states that in Job's initial response to his suffering he did not charge God with wrong (1:22) nor did he sin with his lips (2:10); that is, his words were true. The friends, however, tried to get Job to confess his sin as the cause of his suffering, even presenting to Job various sins that he might confess. Job was right on this point of the debate.

---

3. Andersen, *Job*, 293.

4. Habel, *Job*, 383.

5. Jones, *Job*, 293 and Talbert, *Beyond Suffering*, 232.

God was angry because the friends were wrong about the reason for Job's suffering and they made false statements about God. They must recognize their wrong by offering up burnt offerings and having Job intercede for them. Four times God calls Job 'my servant', a title of honor for one who serves God.[6] Job's honor is demonstrated when God states that He will accept Job's prayer for them and not deal with them according to their folly. Not only did they not comfort Job, but if Job would have followed their course of action it would not have led him out of his affliction.[7] If Job would have confessed sin he had not committed just to satisfy the friends or to get relief from his suffering, he would have lost his integrity.[8] God's response vindicates Job and confirms that he was not suffering because of sin he committed.[9] It is ironic that the one the friends had condemned as a sinner is the one they are dependent on for restoration.[10] In fact, Job is still suffering at the ash heap when he prays for the friends. God accepts Job's prayer while he is suffering, demonstrating that those who are suffering can be accepted even in their suffering.

Job's Restoration (Job 42:10-17)

When Job prayed for his friends God restored the fortunes of Job. God blessed Job abundantly by giving him twice as much as he had before. God restored Job to his family who now come to his house to show him sympathy for all the disaster the LORD had brought upon him. They also brought money and rings of gold.[11] God restored the fortunes of Job

---

6. Hartley, *Job*, 539. Job had also been called God's servant in 1:8 and 2:3.

7. Hartley, *Job*, 539. He comments that the friends' discourses coming after the wife's foolish counsel became Job's second temptation to curse God.

8. Carson, *How Long, O Lord?*, 167.

9. G. Wilson (*Job*, 472) denies that Job's claim to innocence is vindicated because he does not recognize the distinction between Job's situation of innocence before his suffering and the wrong things Job says after his suffering comes upon him.

10. G. Wilson, *Job*, 472-73.

11. Hartley (*Job*, 541) writes that the money could be used to rebuild Job's estate. He also asks why these family members and acquaintances of Job only came to console him at the end. It may be because human nature responds to trouble after it is over and the outcome is assured. Perhaps these acquaintances were operating with the same view of divine retribution as the friends and believed that Job was suffering because of his sin.

by giving him 14,000 sheep, 6,000 camels, 1,000 yoke of oxen, and 1,000 female donkeys. He also gave him seven sons and three daughters. The daughters of Job are highlighted. They are very beautiful, their names are given (Jemimah, Keziah, and Keren-happuch),[12] and they receive an inheritance along with their brothers. The great blessing of restoration at the end is not a divine blessing for righteousness but it shows that God provides for those who submit to Him.[13] The doubling of Job's fortunes shows God's full acceptance of Job.[14] It also proves that Yahweh is a life-giving God, not a capricious deity who takes pleasure in suffering.

The epitaph for Job is given in verses 16-17. His long life of 140 years is also evidence of God's blessing. He saw four generations of grandchildren and died an old man, full of days. The description of Job's death is very much like the description of other servants of God, like Abraham (Gen. 25:8), Isaac (Gen. 35:29), and David (1 Chron. 29:28). Although death is always an enemy in the Old Testament, a good death comes at the end of a long life. A bad death is to be cut off in the prime of life. Job is greatly blessed by God and ends his life well.

Living Beyond the Expectations of this Life

Last year at this time, life was moving right along rather nicely. And then our world was turned upside down. Our son, who looked beautiful and perfectly healthy in the ultrasound a few weeks' prior, had to be delivered four months early. He was two days' short of the age of viability. I remember praying that he would survive until Easter. I prayed that because I wanted to point to the fact that if he was still alive it was because Jesus Christ is alive. At four-days-old, the doctors told us that death

---

12. The names of the daughters mean the following: Jemimah means 'turtledove'; Keziah is the name of the aromatic plant *cassia*, a prized variety of cinnamon; and Keren-happuch refers to a horn of eye paint, black rouge to highlight the eyes (Hartley, *Job*, 543). Longman (*Job*, 461) writes that the daughters highlight the joy of Job's new condition.

13. Konkel, 'Job,' 6:241.

14. Hartley, *Job*, 540.

was certain for Pierce. His heart had stopped a couple of times and the doctors were sure that soon it would stop for good. Without hesitating, they gave Pierce a shot of calcium in order to keep his heart pounding long enough for us to hold him while he was still alive. Of course, today, by God's grace, Pierce is still here with us.

But what if Pierce didn't make it? Would I have still been able to proclaim that Pierce is alive because of Jesus Christ? Would I still think that Easter is that big of a deal? I hope so.

We live in a day and age where people think that all happiness is to be found in this life. To be certain, there is wonderful joy to be had in this life. But a life that places all its hope in finding satisfaction in the seventy or so years we are here is a sad life. By God's grace, Lindsay and I had the freedom to leave Pierce's fate in God's hands. We prayed for healing and knew very well that God could do it. But if God was to take Pierce, we knew that He could rightly do that as well. It was truly a bittersweet experience. To lose a child is heartbreaking, devastating. But to have absolute trust in God is utter joy.

We can have absolute trust in God because He is absolutely trustworthy. The deep, dark places of life are often the only things that shake us out of the slumber of mediocrity and selfishness. The pit is oftentimes the only place where we come to realize that we are terribly helpless and weak and where God is, well, God. And it is in that place where we can see beyond our expectations. We expect life to go on as usual and that everything will be dandy. We like to avoid death and thinking about death as much as possible. But when we are leveled with the fact that this life is messed up, death is real, and our only hope is God, we are on the road to a life that goes beyond our expectations. Jesus is the only one who causes this life to make sense. I have found that apart from Jesus, all is contradictory and shallow. Jesus says those who trust in Him will never see death (John 8:51).

Does Easter really matter when for many of us all we are expecting is heartache and pain in this life? Easter is everything if we are going to live beyond the expectations

that this world throws in our face. Death is dead. If Pierce
died last year, we could still say, without a doubt, that he
is still alive. When Christ rose on Easter morning, He
conquered sin and death. Everything that is wrong with
this world was dealt with on Easter morning. The sun has
been dawning for almost 2000 years now, with its rays of
light touching every aspect of human life. And one day,
perhaps soon, death and sin will be fully dealt when Jesus
appears. Until then, live beyond the expectations of this
world. Live beyond your current expectations. If the Lord
decided to take Pierce last year I could still trust God and
proclaim that my son was still alive. That is why I can live
with the expectation that this life, with all its heartache, is
preparing me for something beyond death.

In Christ,

Nik Franks (4/8/12)

Study Questions

1) Why does Job's restoration not support the mechanical
view of the deed-consequence relationship of the friends?
How does Job answer the original charge by Satan that
Job loves God only because God blesses him?

2) What is the best explanation of the statement by God that
the friends have not spoken of God what is right as Job
has?

3) What is significant about the fact that Job prays for the
restoration of his friends while he is still suffering?

32

Theological Issues in the Book of Job

The Sovereignty of God

It is clear in the book of Job that God is sovereign. God is the one who brings up the situation of Job with Satan and limits the activities of Satan when he acts against Job (Job 1–2). God has a plan for the world that He has created and nothing can hinder God from executing that plan (Isa. 45:7; Amos 3:6). God is a God of justice who can control evil for His own purposes. He should not be judged by appearances because the world is more complicated than human understanding can comprehend. Eventually, God's justice will prevail. Job's restoration came in this life, a picture of blessing that can give comfort and hope to God's people. The ultimate restoration and hope for the believer are not in this life but in the new heavens and earth where the original goodness of creation will once again be established for the benefit of God's people and for the glory of God.[1] This hope is much clearer to the believer today because of the work of Christ and the fullness of revelation in Him.

It is interesting that the reader of Job knows more about Job's situation than Job does because he or she gets a glimpse into the heavenly realities behind the suffering of Job in chapters 1–2. It is also significant that God never reveals to Job the reason for his suffering. He never tells him about

---

1. Carson, *How Long, O Lord?* 177.

Satan's challenge to his faith. Several conclusions can be drawn from this fact.

First, there may be many reasons for a person's suffering and part of the purpose may be to test people to see how they will respond. This idea goes back to Satan's first challenge that Job honors God because God has blessed him. In other words, Job only loves God because of the blessings He grants him, and if those blessings were taken away Job would curse God to His face. Job has passed the test even though God never told Job about the reasons for his suffering. This fact validates the value of Job's experience as a comfort to others who must suffer in ignorance of the reason behind the suffering.[2]

Second, God is not obligated to inform us why certain things are happening in our lives. This is part of the sovereignty of God and the mystery of His purposes. He is more concerned about how we respond to suffering. The major issue in the book of Job is not about the 'whys' of suffering. God does not explain all the reasons for suffering in the world or how they relate to His purposes. The book of Job is about wisdom. Where is wisdom to be found? How should one respond to the various situations of life, particularly, how should one respond to suffering? It is clear in the book of Job that wisdom is not found on this earth or among human beings. Job and the friends did not communicate wisdom. Elihu ultimately fell short of God's wisdom. Wisdom is found solely with God so that the fear of the Lord is the place where wisdom begins (Job 28). Wisdom is hidden until God speaks and sets things right with Job. The implication of this is that we should not get caught up in trying to figure out why someone is suffering, but should seek to respond in ways that would express the wisdom of God in our own suffering and in the suffering of others.

Suffering and Sin

The book of Job also clearly shows that suffering is not necessarily the result of sin. The relationship of sin and suffering is complex. There is a sense that all suffering is related to sin in a general way, because without the entrance of sin into the world, there would not be suffering. There are also situations

2. Smick, 'Job,' 4:912.

when suffering is a result of sin. On a national level, Israel lost her land, her temple, and her city because of her disobedience to the stipulations of the Mosaic covenant. God specifically told His people that obedience would bring blessing and disobedience would bring covenant judgment. On a personal level things are more complex. Sinful actions have consequences for human beings. If someone misuses their money and ends up with nothing, then their foolish actions result in their poverty. But not all poverty is due to the foolish actions of poor people. Some people are poor because of the unjust actions of others. If someone commits murder, or becomes addicted to drugs, such actions will result in negative consequences for both the person who commits these acts and for their families. The consequences of such actions are clearly seen.

There are many other situations, however, where there is not a clear connection between suffering and sin. Why does a godly wife and mother get cancer and die young? Why does a tornado hit one part of town and completely miss the other part of town? These questions cannot be answered but are a part of the mystery of God's sovereignty. There is no guaranteed connection between living a wise life and experiencing the blessings of life. The friends' view of retribution is false. Suffering is not proof that the sufferer has sinned, that the righteous do not always prosper, and that the wicked are not always quickly punished for their deeds.[3] People should not be judged on the quality of their life.[4] The rain falls on the just and the unjust. When the tower of Siloam fell on people and killed them, Jesus' response was not to blame this on the sin of the people who were killed, but to call everyone to repentance. Without repentance, we all face destruction that will come because of God's judgment. We normally do not know the 'why' of suffering, so instead of trying to answer that question we can seek to comfort people in their suffering.

Responses to Suffering

It is not easy for a person to endure suffering and it is not easy to know how to respond to suffering. There is a tendency

---

3. Hartley, *Job*, 544.
4. Longman, *Job*, 462.

to want to help someone by explaining the reasons for their suffering. This response is common because if we can explain why someone is suffering we feel a sense of control over the situation. Such a response can be disastrous because most of the time we do not know why someone is suffering, so it leads to unhelpful speculations.

Job's friends were caught in the dilemma of trying to explain why Job was suffering. Not only were they wrong and gave Job false information and false hope, but they did not comfort Job. They were more concerned about establishing their theological principle than about helping Job. They did not recognize that Job at times spoke rash words as he tried to come to grips with his suffering. They showed no compassion for Job.

It is easy to get caught up in the why of suffering, or in debating theological principles related to suffering, but such an approach will not always bring comfort to those who are suffering. Theology is extremely important because bad theology can lead to disastrous results,[5] but the first response to suffering should not necessarily be a theological response but a personal response of human presence and comfort. The first response of Job's friends was very good in this regard. They came to the place where Job was suffering, mourned with him, and sat in silence with him for seven days (Job 2:11-13).

Personal presence is an important response to suffering. It is at the heart of God's response. He sends His Son to take on human nature to experience suffering and death for our sins, and then the Holy Spirit is sent to be with us through the trials of life. God's presence is promised for all those who believe in Jesus. God is not a distant God who does not understand or is not concerned about our suffering, but He is a God who is near and will be with us in suffering.

How does God want the person who is suffering to respond? The answer to this question is straightforward, but the process of response is more complicated. The simple answer is that God wants us to respond with faith and trust in Him. When suffering strikes a person, many conflicting

---

5. For example, Harold S. Kushner, *Why Bad Things Happen to Good People* (New York: Avon Books, 1981).

thoughts can flood the mind that makes it difficult to acknowledge the goodness of God. Job's wife responds with 'Do you still hold fast your integrity? Curse God and die' (Job 2:9). This response arises out of pity because she sees her husband suffering, but she also seems to panic in not knowing what she should say. Job characterizes her words as foolish because he recognizes that both good things and bad things come from God. Job treats her with compassion by not condemning her but by redirecting her to a proper view.[6] Job can worship God by acknowledging that God does not owe us anything because we come into the world with nothing and we will leave the world with nothing. Job's initial response is worship, but worship is not the only response of Job.

There is also the protesting Job of chapter 3 who curses the day of his birth and wishes he had never been born. Job, at times, is full of despair with hopelessness overtaking his outlook, and at other times he expresses confident hope that God will bring him through this horrible ordeal. He expresses dark words that call into question God's justice, but he also expresses exuberant words of hope. One should not try to make Job consistent in these expressions because he is riding a roller-coaster of emotions. He will eventually come to a place where he will once again affirm the mystery of God's sovereignty and the goodness of God. This does not mean that every situation of suffering will end, for there are some situations that cannot be completely resolved in this life.[7] This does mean that a person can come to some acceptance of the situation even if there is little hope that the suffering will end. This acceptance does not mean the end of the struggle, but it does mean that a person has come to a place where they can affirm once again the principle in Romans 8:28.

It is important to realize, however, that it may take a process to arrive at this place, a process that could include many questions, much wrestling with God, and many sleepless nights. To help someone in such a situation is to give them the freedom to express their thoughts, feelings, and

6. Job does not call his wife foolish but calls her words foolish. He recognizes that her words were spoken out of desperation.

7. See the very helpful article by Michael R. Emlet, 'When It Won't Go Away: A Biblical Response to Chronic Pain', *JBC* 23 (Winter 2005): 21–28.

questions. This does not mean that everything a person says must be accepted, but it does mean that there is recognition that sometimes words spoken in the heat of suffering may be rash. Natural questions arise in the crucible of suffering. Although some of Job's questions and statements were not accurate, not all questions are inadmissible. The lament psalms are full of questions because God seems absent or his covenant promises are not being fulfilled in the psalmist's life. Personal presence can help someone through the confusion and questions that arise in the fog of suffering to come to a place of trust in God and acceptance of His will. In this way one of the major concerns of chapters 1–2 is answered. Are we willing to honor God only when it serves our self-interests? Do we only love God for the blessings He grants us? Is God worthy in-and-of Himself to be worshipped, regardless of our situation in life? Is He first in our life above all other things? To come to a place of joyful acceptance and a firm affirmation that all things work together for good for those who love God is to show that God is worthy of being worshiped above all other things in life. Job comes to such a position and Satan's accusations are seen to be false.

Job also consistently responds to God by praying to Him both in the good times of blessing and in the bad times of adversity. He intercedes for his children at the beginning of the book and for his friends at the end of the book. Even in the ups-and-downs of his suffering he never turned away from God but kept appealing to God concerning his situation. There were times of despair but his confidence also grew in the crucible of suffering. His first response to suffering was worship (1:21). The questions he raises in the midst of his struggle are addressed to God (3:11-23). Even when he is accusing God of the way he is being treated (7:11-21), he does not turn away from God. He keeps seeking ways to connect with God (9:33; 16:19; 19:23-27). And then in the midst of despair he will express a statement of confidence and hope (23:10). And when confronted with his limited knowledge and his finding fault with God, he repents (42:6). If one of the concerns of the book of Job is how we are to respond in suffering, then always seeking God in prayer, no matter what the circumstances, is a mark of wisdom.

The person who experiences suffering can also be a great blessing to others. It is a tremendous encouragement for God's people to watch someone wrestle through difficult situations and continue to express faith in God. This is especially so if someone perseveres through a situation that has no end in sight. Persevering faith strengthens the heart of the one suffering, but it also edifies the body of Christ. The individual who is suffering can become a conduit of God's grace by demonstrating perseverance. There are also ministry opportunities for people who are suffering. God used Job in his suffering as a mediator to help bring about reconciliation between God and the friends. God can use Christians who are suffering to draw people to Christ. Many use suffering as an excuse to blame God for their bad experiences in life. A believer in Christ can show a different response and testify to God's grace even in suffering.

The Repeated Grief of Special-Needs Parents

The sun was shining down as I pulled up to the Chick-fil-A drive thru line. We waited in line, because well, let's be honest, the line at Chick-fil-A always seems to wrap around the building regardless of the hour. My boy, happily playing in the backseat, quickly looked over to the play area. As I caught a glimpse of him studying the tall, exciting playset through the window, my heart sank. I knew with certainty what was coming next. Almost immediately, he asked to get out and go play with the other kids. And like so many times before, I had to tell him 'not this time', despite knowing there would likely never be another time. At 5 years old and 45 lbs., squeezing his body and mine into those tiny plastic tubes is virtually impossible and physically exhausting, much less any fun. And so we watched from our car as cute little kids popped in and out of the playset with ease, laughing and just being, well, kids.

Sadly, this isn't a rare occurrence for us (I won't start on how many things are not handicap accessible) and that's probably why I never heard a single protest from the backseat. He's used to his longings to play being answered with a 'no' and as his mama, that kills me.

If I'm honest, it can be challenging not to seethe with envy in moments like these. It's not that I wish the other kids *couldn't* do certain things, but that my kid *could* do them too. And so my heart grieves. And if you're a special-need parent, your heart grieves much the same way.

There's a unique type of grief that exists within the special-needs parenting community. It's a grief that is marked by repeated, recurring loss. It's elusive and hard to pinpoint. It can be coupled with trauma in the medically complex. It is often found in the desire to be normal while being profoundly aware of your less than normal circumstances. It catches you in the mundane, when you're shuffling from therapies or doctor's appointments.

The grief of a special-needs parent is paradoxical by nature because it marries the despair of lost dreams, the hardships of daily life, and the emotional pain of watching your child endure to the joy you have for your child's life, the love that you have for them just the way they are and the happiness that you were chosen to be their parent.

Some days you'll seem to have discovered all there is to mourn. You'll stand bold and confident, knowing you're a stronger person because you've made it through the losses and discovered the beauty beyond the pain. Other times, you'll stumble upon a lost dream or maybe a whole collection of lost dreams, and be completely overwhelmed with sadness and despair.

This type of grief requires a lot of time to process, but spare time is a luxury not afforded to special-needs parents. However, just as the many who've gone before us, we travel the dark tunnel despite not knowing what lies ahead. We advocate and fight for whatever our child needs despite our weariness. We connect with other families and draw from their experiences despite knowing that no two children are the same. And in spite of all our griefs, we somehow find our will to survive this beautifully complicated and bittersweet life that is special-needs parenting.

Lindsay Franks, www.lindsayfranks.com (4/4/16)

Suffering and Christ

Several times Job expresses the need for a mediator to help bring him and God together. Although Elihu seems to serve this function to some extent (Job 33:23, 31-33), he falls short of fully comprehending how God will respond to Job. The witness in heaven, the redeemer that Job longs for, turns out to be God Himself, who graciously confronts Job with his lack of understanding of how the world works and how God maintains justice. Many wrestle with how Job could conceive of God as his witness and redeemer because God seems to be Job's enemy. How could God witness for Job against Himself? Part of the answer is that suffering has affected the way Job views the world. At times, he is in despair because he thinks God is his enemy, but at other times he is hopeful, even confident, that God will vindicate him. In another sense, it becomes clear in the progress of redemptive history how God could intercede with God for afflicted human beings. Jesus Christ, God the Son incarnate, is the one mediator between sinful human beings and God the Father. Jesus is both fully God and fully man so that He can bring man and God together. He accomplishes this by offering Himself as the sacrifice for sin, thereby defeating sin, death, and Satan. In the cosmic battle against the forces of darkness, represented by Leviathan, Christ has won the victory (Col. 2:15). He can save completely those who come to Him because He now sits at the right hand of His Father interceding for His people (Heb. 7:25).

The work of Christ has implications for the role of Satan. He is still a powerful enemy who can do a lot of damage in the world and to God's people. Paul calls him the god of this world who has blinded the minds of unbelievers (2 Cor. 4:4) and Peter describes him as a prowling lion seeking someone to devour (1 Pet. 5:8). The picture of Satan as a prowling lion fits the description of him in Job 1–2 where his activities are described as 'going to and fro on the earth' (1:7). He appears to be aimlessly walking around seeking to do harm.

It is clear in Job 1–2 that he has access to the heavenly throne room and that he can accuse God's people of wrong. He accuses Job of loving God only because God has blessed him. In a later passage, he also brings accusations against the high priest Zechariah (Zech. 3:1). There is evidence in the

New Testament that, based on the work of Christ, Satan no longer has this same access to God. Certainly his accusations of God's people fall short because they are covered by the righteousness of Christ. Jesus Himself states, 'I saw Satan fall like lightning from heaven' (Luke 10:18). This comment comes as the disciples return from a mission and they report that even the demons are subject to them through the name of Jesus. In the book of Revelation, the child born to the woman is snatched to heaven with war in heaven breaking out (Rev. 12:1-12). Satan and his angels are defeated. There is no longer any place for him in heaven and he is thrown down to the earth. Satan is even identified as the one who accuses Christians day and night before God (Rev. 12:10) and his defeat by Christ means his access to God is greatly curtailed. Although Satan pursues the church to seek to do great harm to her in making war with her (Rev. 12:13-17), she is assured of victory because of Christ. Paul can even write that 'the God of peace will soon crush Satan under your feet' (Rom. 16:20).

Job's role as mediator for the friends prefigures the role of Jesus Christ. Job was innocent of any wrongdoing in his suffering, he was scorned and rejected by his peers, and he made intercession for others as he suffered. Job, called 'my servant' by God, prefigures the suffering servant. Jesus was the perfect Son of God who did not deserve the false accusations of the high priests against Him. Job's suffering was 'without cause' (Job 2:3) and Jesus was also hated 'without cause' (Ps. 69:4; John 15:25).[8] He also did not deserve the punishment inflicted upon Him on the cross for the sins of others (Isa. 53:5-6). He was 'stricken, smitten by God, and afflicted' (Isa. 53:4). He interceded for sinners in the humiliation of His suffering (Isa. 53:12) and then was given a portion among the great and divided the spoil with the strong (Isa. 53:11-12).[9] Jesus' vindication is demonstrated in His resurrection on the third day. He is the only one who is in a position to bring together God and man, who can lay His hand on both because He partakes of both the divine nature and the human nature (Job 9:33; 1 Tim. 2:5). He is the witness

---

8. Talbert, *Beyond Suffering*, 235-36.

9. Smick, 'Job,' 4:918.

in heaven who testifies for His people on high (Job 16:19). He is the only redeemer (Job 19:25), who may or may not vindicate His people in this life, but He will bring about for them the ultimate salvation in the resurrection of their bodies. God will vindicate His people, bring them to glory, and allow them into His glorious presence to be with Him forever. Such a prospect should cause hearts to faint within God's people (Job 19:27) because the glory of that day will overshadow the sufferings of this present time (1 Cor. 2:9; 2 Cor. 4:16-18).

Jesus shows us that the path of suffering leads to glory. The suffering of Jesus was meaningful in accomplishing God's purposes in the world. The suffering of His people, therefore, is not meaningless, but also has purposes which are many times beyond their understanding. What is clear is that the suffering of God's people will accomplish His purposes for their lives and for the advancement of His kingdom. This should give His people hope in the midst of horrible circumstances. The crucible of suffering leads to the sanctification of God's people so that they look more like Christ. Suffering also leads to glory where the trials of this life will be used to make of us trophies of God's grace, demonstrating the marvelous, matchless grace of God in the lives of His people. One day we will shine forth as marvels of His grace, not because of what we have done, but because of what God has done through us. We will one day be vindicated, we will one day receive perfect resurrected bodies, and on that day God will receive all the glory. Christ is our only hope, and Pierce's only hope, Hallelujah, Amen!

Study Questions

1) How does the book of Job present God as sovereign?

2) What conclusions can be drawn from the fact that God never tells Job about why he is suffering, that is, He never explains to him chapters 1–2 of the book? Does that bother you?

3) What do we learn from Job about the relationship between sin and suffering? Why is the view of the friends not correct?

4) Why do people seek to give reasons for suffering? What does someone in suffering really need?

5) Why is a process needed for a person to work through their suffering to be able to affirm the goodness of God? Are questions always wrong? How should this impact the way you respond to people are suffering?

6) Do you judge people based on the quality of their life? How can someone who is suffering be a blessing to others?

7) How is it that God can be a witness for Job against Himself? How does Job prefigure the work of Christ?

8) What does Jesus ultimately show us about suffering?

Selected Bibliography

Alden, Robert L. *Job.* Broadman & Holman, 1993.

Alter, Robert. *The Art of Biblical Poetry*. New York: Basic Books, 1985.

Andersen, Francis I. *Job: An Introduction and Commentary*. Downers Grove, IL: Inter-Varsity Press, 1974.

Ash, Christopher. *Job: The Wisdom of the Cross*. Wheaton, IL: Crossway, 2014.

Belcher, Jr., Richard P. *The Messiah and the Psalms*. Ross-shire: Christian Focus, 2006.

___. *Genesis: The Beginning of God's Plan of Salvation*. Ross-shire: Christian Focus, 2012.

___. 'Job,' in *A Biblical–Theological Introduction to the Old Testament*. Ed. Miles Van Pelt. Wheaton, IL: Crossway, 2016.

Brown, William P. *Wisdom's Wonder: Character, Creation, and Crisis in the Bible's Wisdom Literature*. Grand Rapids: Eerdmans, 2014.

Carson, D. A. *How Long, O Lord? Reflections on Evil and Suffering*. Grand Rapids: Baker, 1990.

Clines, David J. A. *Job 1–20*. Dallas, TX: Word Books, 1989.

Clines, David J. A. *Job 21–37*. Nashville, TN: Thomas Nelson, 2006.

Clines, David J. A. *Job 38–42*. Nashville, TN: Thomas Nelson, 2011.

Curtis, John B. 'On Job's Response to Yahweh' (*JBL* 98 [1979]: 497-511).

Day, John. *God's Conflict with the Dragon and the Sea.* Cambridge: Cambridge University Press, 1985.

Dick, Michael Brennan. 'The Legal Metaphor in Job 31' (*CBQ* 41 [January 1979]: 37–50).

Driver, S. R. and G. B. Gray. *A Critical and Exegetical Commentary on the Book of Job.* Edinburgh: T. & T. Clark, 1921.

Dumbrell, William J. 'The Purpose of the Book of Job' (Pages 91-105 in *The Way of Wisdom.* Ed. by J. I. Packer and Sven Soderlund. Grand Rapids: Zondervan, 2000).

Emlet, Michael R. 'When It Won't Go Away: A Biblical Response to Chronic Pain' (*JBC* 23 [Winter 2005]: 21–28).

Estes, Daniel J. *Handbook on the Wisdom Books and Psalms.* Grand Rapids: Baker, 2005.

Fox, Michael. 'Job the Pious' (*ZAW* 117 [2005]: 351-56).

___. 'Behemoth and Leviathan' (*Bib* 93 [2012]: 261-67).

___. 'God's Answer and Job's Response' (*Bib* 94.1 [2013]: 1–23).

Fyall, Robert S. *How Does God Treat His Friends?* Ross-shire: Christian Focus, 1995.

Fyall, Robert S. *Now My Eyes Have Seen You: Images of Creation and Evil in the Book of Job.* Downers Grove, IL: Inter-Varsity Press, 2002.

Gordis, Robert. *The Book of God and Man: A Study of Job.* Chicago: University of Chicago Press, 1965.

___. *The Book of Job.* New York: Jewish Theological Seminary of America, 1978.

Green, William Henry. *Conflict and Triumph: The Argument of the Book of Job Unfolded.* Carlisle, PA: The Banner of Truth Trust, 1999.

Habel, Norman C., *The Book of Job*. Philadelphia, PA: Westminster Press, 1985.

Hartley, John E., *The Book of Job*. Grand Rapids: Eerdmans, 1988.

Janzen, J. Gerald. *Job*. Atlanta: John Knox Press, 1985.

Johnston, P. *Shades of Sheol*. Downers Grove, IL: Inter-Varsity, 2002.

Jones, Hywel R. *Job*. Darlington: Evangelical Press, 2007.

Kline, Meredith G. 'Trial by Ordeal' (Pages 81-93 in *Through Christ's Word: A Festschrift for Dr. Philip E. Hughes*. Eds. W. Robert Godfrey and Jesse L. Boyd III. Phillipsburg, NJ: Presbyterian and Reformed, 1985).

Konkel, August H. 'Job'. (Pages 1-249 in *Cornerstone Biblical Commentary*. Vol. 6. Ed. Philip W. Comfort. Carol Stream, IL: Tyndale House Publishers, 2006).

Kynes, Will. *My Psalm Has Turned into Weeping: Job's Dialogue with the Psalms*. Berlin: Walter De Gruyter, 2012.

Lo, Alison. *Job 28: An Analysis of Job 28 in the Context of Job 22–31*. Atlanta: Society of Biblical Literature, 2003.

Longman III, Tremper and Raymond Dillard. *An Introduction to the Old Testament*. Grand Rapids: Zondervan, 2006.

Longman III, Tremper. *Job*. Grand Rapids: Baker, 2012.

Lucas, Ernest C. *A Guide to the Psalms and Wisdom Literature*. Downers Grove, IL: Inter-Varsity Press, 2003.

McCabe, Robert V. 'Elihu's Contribution to the Thought of the Book of Job' (*DBSJ* 2 [Fall 1997]: 47-80).

Newell, R. Lynne. 'Job: Repentant or Rebellious?' (Pages 441-56 in *Sitting with Job*. Ed. Roy B. Zuck. Grand Rapids: Eerdmans, 1992).

Newsom, Carol A. 'The Book of Job' (Pages 317-638 in *The New Interpreter's Bible, Volume IV*. Nashville, TN: Abingdon Press, 1996).

Newsom, Carol A. *The Book of Job: A Contest of Moral Imaginations*. Oxford: Oxford University Press, 2003.

Nicholson, E. W. 'The Limits of Theodicy as a Theme of the Book of Job' (Pages 71-82 in *Wisdom in Ancient Israel: Essays in Honour of J. A. Emerton*. Eds. John Day, Robert P. Gordon, and H. G. M. Williamson. Cambridge: Cambridge University Press, 1995).

Oblath, Michael. 'Job's Advocate: A Tempting Suggestion' (*BBR* 9 [1999]: 189-201).

Patrick, Dale. 'Job's Address of God' (*ZAW* 91 (1979): 268-82).

Perdue, Leo G. *Wisdom Literature: A Theological History*. Louisville: Westminster John Knox Press, 2007.

Reitman, James. *Unlocking Wisdom*. Springfield, MO: 21st Century Press, 2008.

Robertson, David A. 'The Book of Job: A Literary Study' (*Soundings* 56 [1973]: 446-69).

Rodd, C. S. *The Book of Job*. Philadelphia, PA: Trinity Press International, 1990.

Rowley, H. H. *The Book of Job*. rev. ed. Grand Rapids: Eerdmans, 1980.

Scholnick, Sylvia H. 'The Meaning of *mišpaṭ* in the Book of Job' (Pages 349-58 in *Sitting with Job*. Ed. Roy B. Zuck. Grand Rapids: Baker, 1992).

___. 'Poetry in the Courtroom: Job 38–41' (Pages 421-40 in *Sitting with Job*. Ed. Roy B. Zuck. Grand Rapids: Eerdmans, 1992).

Seow, C. L. *Job 1–21*. Grand Rapids: Eerdmans, 2013.

Smick, Elmer. 'Job' (Pages 675-921 in *The Expositor's Bible Commentary*. Vol. 4. Eds. Tremper Longman III and David Garland. Grand Rapids: Zondervan, 2010).

Steel, Allan. 'Could Behemoth Have Been a Dinosaur?' (*TJ* 15. 2 [2001]: 42-45).

Suriano, Matthew J. 'Death, Disinheritance, and Job's Kinsman-Redeemer' (*JBL* 129.1 [2010]: 49-66).

Talbert, Layton. *Beyond Suffering: Discovering the Message of Job*. Greenville, SC: Bob Jones University Press, 2007.

Thomas, Derek. *The Storm Breaks: Job Simply Explained*. Darlington: Evangelical Press, 1995.

Tsevat, Matitiahu. 'The Meaning of the Book of Job' (Pages 189-220 in *Sitting with Job*. Ed. Roy B. Zuck. Grand Rapids: Eerdmans, 1992).

Van Leeuwen, Raymond C. 'Psalm 8:5 and Job 7:17-18: A Mistaken Scholarly Commonplace?' in *The World of the Aramaeans I: Biblical Studies in Honour of Paul-Eugene Dion*. Eds. P. M. Michelle Daviau, John W. Wevers, and Michael Weigl. Sheffield: Sheffield Academic Press, 2001.

Walton, John H. and Tremper Longman, III. *How To Read Job*. Downers Grove, IL: InterVarsity Press, 2015.

Walton, John H. *Job*. Grand Rapids: Zondervan, 2012.

Whitekettle, Richard. 'When More Leads to Less: Over-statement, *Incrementum*, and the Question in Job 4:17a'. (*JBL* 129 [2010]: 445-48).

Whybray, Norman. *Job*. Sheffield: Sheffield Academic Press, 1998.

Wilson, Gerald H. *Job*. Peabody, MA: Hendriksen, 2007.

Wilson, Lindsay. *Job*. Grand Rapids: Eerdmans, 2015.

Subject Index

Scripture Index

Other books in the Focus on the Bible commentary series

Other books in the Focus on the Bible commentary series

Christian Focus Publications

Our mission statement –

STAYING FAITHFUL
In dependence upon God we seek to impact the world through literature faithful to His infallible Word, the Bible. Our aim is to ensure that the Lord Jesus Christ is presented as the only hope to obtain forgiveness of sin, live a useful life and look forward to heaven with Him.

Our books are published in four imprints:

CHRISTIAN
FOCUS

Popular works including biographies, commentaries, basic doctrine and Christian living.

CHRISTIAN
HERITAGE

Books representing some of the best material from the rich heritage of the church.

MENTOR

Books written at a level suitable for Bible College and seminary students, pastors, and other serious readers. The imprint includes commentaries, doctrinal studies, examination of current issues and church history.

CF4•K

Children's books for quality Bible teaching and for all age groups: Sunday school curriculum, puzzle and activity books; personal and family devotional titles, biographies and inspirational stories – because you are never too young to know Jesus!

Christian Focus Publications Ltd,
Geanies House, Fearn, Ross-shire,
IV20 1TW, Scotland, United Kingdom.
www.christianfocus.com